CAPITALISM
AT THE
CROSSROADS

NEXT GENERATION BUSINESS STRATEGIES
FOR A POST-CRISIS WORLD

THIRD EDITION

STUART L. HART
JOHNSON GRADUATE SCHOOL OF MANAGEMENT
CORNELL UNIVERSITY

HD
60
H388
2010

Wharton School Publishing

Vice President, Publisher: Tim Moore
Associate Publisher and Director of Marketing: Amy Neidlinger
Wharton Editor: Steve Kobrin
Executive Editor: Jim Boyd
Editorial Assistant: Pamela Boland
Development Editor: Russ Hall
Operations Manager: Gina Kanouse
Senior Marketing Manager: Julie Phifer
Publicity Manager: Laura Czaja
Assistant Marketing Manager: Megan Colvin
Cover Designer: Chuti Prasertsith
Managing Editor: Kristy Hart
Project Editor: Anne Goebel
Copy Editor: Language Logistics, LLC
Proofreader: Water Crest Publishing, Inc.
Indexer: Lisa Stumpf
Senior Compositor: Gloria Schurick
Manufacturing Buyer: Dan Uhrig

© 2010 by Pearson Education, Inc.
Publishing as Wharton School Publishing
Upper Saddle River, New Jersey 07458

This book is sold with the understanding that neither the author nor the publisher is engaged in rendering legal, accounting, or other professional services or advice by publishing this book. Each individual situation is unique. Thus, if legal or financial advice or other expert assistance is required in a specific situation, the services of a competent professional should be sought to ensure that the situation has been evaluated carefully and appropriately. The author and the publisher disclaim any liability, loss, or risk resulting directly or indirectly, from the use or application of any of the contents of this book.

Wharton School Publishing offers excellent discounts on this book when ordered in quantity for bulk purchases or special sales. For more information, please contact U.S. Corporate and Government Sales, 1-800-382-3419, corpsales@pearsontechgroup.com. For sales outside the U.S., please contact International Sales at international@pearson.com.

Company and product names mentioned herein are the trademarks or registered trademarks of their respective owners.

Printed in the United States of America

Second Printing September 2010
ISBN-10: 0-13-704232-9
ISBN-13: 978-0-13-704232-6

Pearson Education LTD.
Pearson Education Australia PTY, Limited.
Pearson Education Singapore, Pte. Ltd.
Pearson Education North Asia, Ltd.
Pearson Education Canada, Ltd.
Pearson Educación de Mexico, S.A. de C.V.
Pearson Education—Japan
Pearson Education Malaysia, Pte. Ltd.

Library of Congress Cataloging-in-Publication Data:
Hart, Stuart L.
Capitalism at the crossroads : next generation business strategies for a post-crisis world / Stuart L. Hart. — 3rd ed.
p. cm.
Includes bibliographical references and index.
ISBN 978-0-13-704232-6 (pbk. : alk. paper) 1. Social responsibility of business. 2. Capitalism. I. Title.
HD60.H388 2010
658.4'08—dc22
2010010594

To all the children, yet unborn.

Contents

About the Author

Stuart L. Hart is one of the world's top authorities on the implications of sustainable development and environment for business strategy. He is currently the Samuel C. Johnson Chair in Sustainable Global Enterprise and Professor of Management at Cornell's Johnson Graduate School of Management. He also serves as Distinguished Fellow at the William Davidson Institute (University of Michigan) and President of Enterprise for a Sustainable World.

Previously, he taught strategic management and founded both the Center for Sustainable Enterprise (CSE) at the University of North Carolina's Kenan-Flagler Business School and the Corporate Environmental Management Program (now the Erb Institute Dual Master's Program) at the University of Michigan. His consulting clients range from DuPont and SC Johnson to Unilever and General Electric. He is an internationally recognized speaker and has delivered hundreds of keynote addresses on the topic of sustainable business around the world.

He wrote the seminal article "Beyond Greening: Strategies for a Sustainable World," which won the McKinsey Award for Best Article in *Harvard Business Review* in 1997, and helped launch the movement for corporate sustainability. With C.K. Prahalad, Hart also wrote the path-breaking 2002 article "The Fortune at the Bottom of the Pyramid," which provided the first articulation of how business could profitably serve the needs of the four billion poor in the developing world. He invites his readers to email him at slh55@cornell.edu and to visit his website at www.stuartlhart.com.

Acknowledgments

This book pulls together and extends work I have been doing in the area of sustainability and business over the past 20 years, but it has actually been 40 years in the making. Indeed, there is no doubt that this work was influenced, shaped, and determined to a large extent by my prior experiences in college, graduate school, and the real world. I owe a great debt, therefore, to a number of people—mentors, professors, benefactors, colleagues, associates, and students—as well as friends and family.

As an undergraduate student at the University of Rochester, I would have never embarked on the path of environmental studies and management were it not for the inspiration of professors Larry Lundgren and Christian Kling. These two professors were the ones who awakened my interest and stirred my passion for this domain and set me on a course that has continued to this day. I am living proof that college professors really do have an enormously important, shaping influence on their students. To them I owe a huge debt of gratitude.

At Yale, during my time at the School of Forestry and Environmental Studies, I am very thankful to have had the honor to work with the late Professor Joe Miller, as well as Professors Lloyd Irland and Garth Voight. These three in particular helped to shape my interest and deepen my knowledge in environmental policy and management. They also enabled me to develop a much broader intellectual grasp of the history of the environmental movement and how it fit into the larger pattern of societal evolution toward greater inclusiveness.[1]

My first encounter with the "real world" (in the form of an actual job) came at the Institute on Man and Science in upstate New York in the late 1970s. As a research associate in economic and environmental studies, I worked with Dr. Gordon Enk—my first boss. This job resulted in a professional and personal relationship that continues to this day. In fact, if I had to name the one person who has had the biggest impact on me, it would have to be Gordon Enk. With his background and deep commitment both to the environment and to the economic system (Gordon holds a Ph.D. from Yale in natural resource economics), he was the first person to show me that we need not accept trade-offs when it comes to societal and economic performance. Gordon was also way ahead of his time when it came to stakeholder involvement in strategic decision making. Under his guidance, we embarked on a series of projects that sought to involve diverse voices in important social and strategic decisions. We wrote about learning from these experiences in a range of publications that stand the test of time to this day.[2]

Since that time in the late 1970s, Gordon and I have continued to work together: He served on my dissertation committee at Michigan;[3] I served as a consultant to him during his years as an executive at International Paper Company. More recently, he has been an active participant in the advisory boards for the Corporate Environmental Management Program at the University of Michigan, the Center for Sustainable Enterprise at UNC, and now the Center for Sustainable Global Enterprise at Cornell. He is also a key figure in the development of my new nonprofit organization, Enterprise for a Sustainable World. In reading the pages of this manuscript, Gordon will no doubt see the shaping effect he has had on my point of view. He should take satisfaction in knowing that he has taught me well.

During my time in the doctoral program at the University of Michigan, I was mentored and influenced by several key faculty members. Professors Pete Andrews (now at UNC), Rachel Kaplan, Jim Crowfoot, Kan Chen, Paul Nowak, and (the late) Bill Drake were of particular influence and importance. Rachel Kaplan deserves special mention for her encouragement and support of my dissertation work. After completing my doctoral work in 1983, I was appointed post-doctoral fellow and research scientist at the Institute for Social

Research in Ann Arbor. During this time, I worked closely with Dr. Mark Berg, Dr. Don Michael, and professors Donald Pelz and Nate Kaplan. This was also the time that I met and established life-long personal and professional relationships with two other highly influential people: Professor Dan Denison (now at IMD in Switzerland) and Professor Jac Geurts (at Tilburg University in the Netherlands). They had an enormous influence on my intellectual development, especially when it came to combining interests in strategy and organizational change with a concern for social impact and environmental management. I continue to work with both of them to this day.[4]

My career as a professor of strategic management began in the mid-1980s at the University of Michigan Business School. There, I was greatly helped by relationships with professors Jane Dutton, Bob Quinn, and Noel Tichy. Professor Jim Walsh has also been a particularly helpful and special friend, confidant, and advisor over the years. Without him, it would have been much more difficult to work up the courage to take the career risks that I have taken. Most recently, my work with Bob Kennedy, Director of the Davidson Institute at Michigan, and Professor Michael Gordon has been especially productive.

However, there is one faculty mentor, in particular, who deserves special mention: the late Professor C.K. Prahalad. By the late 1980s, I was becoming frustrated with my career: I was increasingly spending time on research and teaching that did not reflect my real interests or passions. My performance in both research and teaching was, as a result, mediocre. Where most senior faculty advised me to forget about my background and interest in environment and sustainable development, C.K. was one of the few supportive voices. I still remember how he urged me to pursue my passion and leverage my unique background in this area. Were it not for C.K., I never would have made the conscious decision (which I did in 1990) to devote the rest of my professional career to the connections between business and sustainability. C.K.'s unique perspective on strategy as innovation has also had a huge impact on how I have formulated my ideas about sustainable enterprise. For this, and much more, I owe C.K. a huge debt of gratitude. He will be sorely missed.

Other early contributors who had important influence on my thinking included Paul Hawken, particularly his work *The Ecology of*

Commerce; Ed Freeman, with his important book *Strategic Management: A Stakeholder View*; John Elkington, with his concept of the "triple bottom line," first published in *Cannibals With Forks*, and professors Dick Vietor and Forest Reinhardt at the Harvard Business School, who produced most of the early teaching cases on environmental management and business in the early 1990s.

Two other faculty members also deserve special mention for inspiring me to pursue this path: Professor Paul Shrivastava, now at Concordia University, and Professor Tom Gladwin, now at the University of Michigan.[5] In my view, Paul and Tom were the academic pioneers in this area. They were both working this space before most others in business schools even gave it a second look. Like C.K. Prahalad, Paul and Tom provided both the example and encouragement that led me to take the bold step of dedicating my professional life to this topic. It was the best decision I ever made, and I am tremendously thankful to both of them.

Were it not for two other people, it would have never been possible to successfully develop the Corporate Environmental Management Program (CEMP) at Michigan, a dual-degree program between two previously disconnected entities (now the Erb Institute's Dual Masters Program). Garry Brewer, who came to Michigan from Yale as the Dean of the School of Natural Resources and Environment in 1990, and Joe White, who became the new Dean of the Business School at the same time. Garry Brewer, in particular, was instrumental in forging the relationship between the two schools and helping to secure the early support for the program. Without the commitment of Garry and Joe, the CEMP Program would have never happened. Both also helped me to better understand the challenges and opportunities in attempting to bring these two worlds together.

At the University of North Carolina, I am indebted to professors Hugh O'Neill, Rich Bettis, and Ben Rosen, and, later, Dean Robert Sullivan for giving me the opportunity to develop the Center for Sustainable Enterprise. However, it was really Professor Anne York who deserves the most credit for attracting me to UNC in the first place. It was her passion, vision, and persistence that helped to make it a reality. With regard to the center itself, however, my professional and personal relationship with Professor Jim Johnson has been especially fruitful. In his role as faculty codirector of the center with me, Jim has taught me a great deal about the social aspects of sustainability, particularly those relating to minorities and the economically disadvantaged. I also owe Jim a debt of thanks for helping to create the title for this book: For several years, the two of us discussed (but never completed) an article together entitled (tentatively) "Capitalism at the Crossroads." For Jim's unswerving support as both a friend and a close colleague, I am very grateful.

As with the creation of CEMP at Michigan, the Center for Sustainable Enterprise at UNC would have never been possible if it were not for the visionary support of two people: Professor Jack Kasarda (Director of the Kenan Institute for Private Enterprise) and Professor Bill Glaze (former Director of the Carolina Environmental Program). Both showed the willingness to financially support the fledgling concept for a new Center before anyone else at either the business school or the university would pay any attention. Without them, the body of new work generated over the past decade would not have been possible—nor would the establishment of an MBA concentration at Kenan-Flagler Business School that, by the early 2000s, attracted nearly one-third of the admitted students each year to the school. For this accomplishment, I should also thank Jim Dean, now the Dean of the School but who was Dean of the MBA program during the creation of the concentration.

For the opportunity at Cornell, I am indebted to several people: Dean Robert Swieringa; Senior Associate Dean Joe Thomas; and professors Alan McAdams, Norm Scott, Bob Libby, Beta Mannix, and Bob Frank, to name but a few. Over the past two years, Cornell President David Skorton has also become an important supporter; he was instrumental in helping us launch the Cornell Global Forum on Sustainable Enterprise in 2009. The opportunity to work with Cornell Trustee Kevin McGovern and the start-up team at The Water Initiative (TWI) over these past two years has also been an invaluable experience. However, the ultimate acknowledgment must be made to the late Sam Johnson, Chairman Emeritus of S. C. Johnson & Son, Inc. It was Sam and the Johnson family who had the vision to endow both the S. C. Johnson Chair in Sustainable Global Enterprise and the new Center for Sustainable Global Enterprise. Other pioneering benefactors also deserve recognition: Dr. Hans Zulliger, Swiss scientist and businessperson, for endowing the Chair in Sustainable Enterprise at UNC; and Fred Erb and the Max McGraw Foundation for endowing the Erb Institute for Global Sustainable Enterprise and the Max McGraw Chair, respectively, at Michigan. It is important to recognize the crucial contribution that such gifts make to the legitimacy and institutionalization of this work at major universities and business schools.

There are also a number of people from the corporate and not-for-profit sector who deserve recognition for both their support and influence over the years. Paul Tebo at DuPont, in particular, deserves special recognition. Like Gordon Enk, Paul and DuPont have been involved with the initiatives at Michigan, UNC, and now Cornell. DuPont has also financially supported the initiatives at all three institutions. Dawn Rittenhouse, John Lott, John Hodgson, Eduardo Wanick, and Tony Arnold, all of DuPont, have also been key supporters of our work, as has former CEO Chad Holliday. Matt Arnold, originally of the Management Institute for Environment and Business (MEB) and later the World Resources Institute (WRI), has been enormously influential over the years. We began together on this adventure in the early 1990s, as he was forming MEB and I was developing the CEMP Program at Michigan. Matt has since gone on to found a practice in Sustainable Finance at PWC.

Like DuPont, WRI has been a long-term partner for more than a decade, with people like Jonathan Lash, Rick Bunch, Jennifer Layke, Rob Day, Meghan Chapple, Al Hammond, and Liz Cook providing key support. Dow Chemical Company, in general, and Dave Buzzelli and Scott Noesen, in particular, also deserve special mention. Dow was among the early supporters of the CEMP Program at Michigan and has since endowed a chair jointly between the Business School and the School of Natural Resources and Environment. Jane Pratt and Jed Schilling of the World Bank and (later) the Mountain Institute have also been key long-term collaborators and partners. Both have been indispensable champions of the content area and the programs over the years.

For their business leadership and program involvement, I am also indebted to Lee Schilling and Mac Bridger, then senior executives at Tandus Group (Collins & Aikman Floorcoverings), as well as Sam Moore of Burlington Chemical Company, Dan Vermeer from Coca

Cola (now at Duke University), and Debbie Zemke, then at Ford. Jim Sheats, Barbara Waugh, and Gary Herman from Hewlett-Packard also deserve acknowledgment, as do Greg Allgood, Chuck Gagel, Keith Zook, and George Carpenter at Procter & Gamble. Over the past five years, Fisk Johnson, Scott Johnson, and Jane Hutterly, all of SC Johnson, deserve special mention as key supporters and collaborators in moving the sustainable global enterprise agenda forward—both at Cornell and within the company.

While this list of acknowledgments has grown long, I would be terribly remiss if I did not directly recognize the crucial contributions of coauthors and colleagues in influencing and shaping both my thought and, in some instances, the actual words written in this book. Although the conceptual foundation for this book was clearly laid in several single-authored articles during the 1990s, later collaborations were of critical importance.[6] I would like to recognize Professor C.K. Prahalad (University of Michigan Business School) for his important influence in our joint work that developed the original idea of the bottom of the pyramid as a business opportunity.[7] This work can be found in parts of Chapters 5, 6, and 8. Professor Clayton Christensen (Harvard Business School) also deserves special note. He and I have coauthored two articles that join his theory of disruptive innovation with my work on sustainable development and the base of the pyramid.[8] This joint work can be found in Chapter 5. I have also worked closely with Professor Sanjay Sharma (now Dean of the Molson School of Business at Concordia University) in recent years. Our joint work on engaging fringe stakeholders and radical transactiveness can be found in the pages of Chapter 7.[9]

Two former doctoral students at the University of North Carolina have also been important colleagues and collaborators over the past ten years. I have known Mark Milstein for over 15 years, beginning at Michigan, where he was a student in the CEMP Program. Since he began as a doctoral student at UNC, he and I have coauthored three articles.[10] Our joint work on creative destruction and sustainability can be found in the pages of Chapters 2 and 4; portions of Chapter 3 are also directly attributable to our collaboration on creating sustainable value. I am proud to say that our work together continues—Mark is currently Director of the Center for Sustainable Global Enterprise at Cornell. Collaboration with Ted London, given his extensive international experience, has also been extremely valuable. Joint work with Ted during his doctoral student days at North Carolina examining emerging market strategies for the base of the pyramid business entry can be found in parts of Chapters 6 and 8.[11] Ted, who is now a Senior Fellow at the Davidson Institute at Michigan, heading up their program on the Base of the Pyramid, has already made several important written contributions to this emerging field. Ted and I are also in the final stages of editing a new book on the Base of the Pyramid, to be published by Wharton School Publishing later this year.

Two current doctoral students at Cornell also deserve special mention: Erik Simanis and Duncan Duke. My collaboration with Erik began in Chapel Hill where he worked with me to help launch the Base of the Pyramid Protocol project. Erik led the field teams for both the SC Johnson and DuPont/Solae BoP Protocol Projects and has led the development of the BoP field cocreation process. Since then, he and I have written three pieces together, and he has had a significant influence on my thinking over the past few years.[12] The mark of his work, which brings anthropology and action research into the business strategy field, can be found in parts of Chapters 7, 8, and 9. In fact, significant portions of Chapter 9 are adapted from our recent article in *Sloan Management Review*. Duncan Duke has also become a key contributor to the development of the BoP Protocol process. Duncan led the field team in the cocreation process for The Water Initiative (TWI), which is described in Chapter 9. Along with Erik, Duncan and I have written an additional piece together, which has greatly influenced my thinking.[13]

All four of these current and former students made tremendous contributions to both the Center for Sustainable Enterprise at UNC and most recently the Center for Sustainable Global Enterprise at Cornell: Mark Milstein served as research director for the center at UNC and, with Monica Touesnard, essentially ran the Center before joining me at Cornell in 2005. Erik Simanis helped me to conceive the original idea for the Base of the Pyramid Learning Laboratory at UNC in 2000 as a recently minted MBA, prior to starting the doctoral program. And Ted London served with great effectiveness as the Director of the BoP Learning Lab from 2001–2004 and has been a close collaborator in our international work in Asia, Africa, and Latin

America. Duncan Duke has been especially important in developing the BoP protocol work at Cornell. Look for these four to make important independent contributions in the near future.

My participation as a core faculty member in the Sustainable Enterprise Academy (SEA) has also provided a wonderful venue for trying out new ideas—and learning in the process. In this regard, I would like to recognize and thank my faculty colleagues in SEA, particularly Brian Kelly, David Wheeler, Bryan Smith, John Ehrenfeld, David Bell, and Nigel Roome, for their honest feedback and support in helping me develop and present my ideas in such a way to achieve maximum impact.

Finally, I would like to acknowledge the patience, support, and editorial skills of my publisher, Wharton School Publishing—in particular, my editor, Jim Boyd (fellow University of Rochester classmate); developmental editor, Elisa Adams; project editors, Kristy Hart and Anne Goebel; copy editors, Krista Hansing and Chrissy White; and Wharton representative Professor Paul Kleindorfer. The book has been vastly improved as a direct result of their skilled eyes—and pens. My colleagues Gordon Enk, Jac Geurts, Ted London, Erik Simanis, Paul Tebo, Bob Frank, Alan McAdams, and Mark Milstein also provided invaluable feedback on the many drafts of the manuscript. My long-time colleagues Jac Geurts and Gordon Enk were especially helpful in commenting on the revisions for the third edition. Charlie Hargroves of the Natural Edge Project also provided valuable feedback during the revision process. Thanks also to Peter Knight for facilitating the Preface by Al Gore.

Clearly, the writing of a book like this "takes a village," as Hillary Clinton would say. While I have done my best to recognize as many of the important contributors to my professional life as space allows, there are many more who could have been included. For my friends and colleagues in this group, please forgive me! However, no acknowledgment would be complete without recognizing my parents, Lloyd and Katherine Hart, for their support of my education, and, I'm sure what seemed to be aimless wanderings, for the better part of a decade during the 1970s and 80s. I'm just sorry that my father did not live to see this book finally come to fruition. I'd also like to recognize my brother, Paul, who set the example for me in pursuing the academic route long before I ever imagined doing doctoral work.

Finally, my wife Patricia has been nothing short of an inspiration over the years. She has been the ultimate enabler of my work for over 35 years. Without her love and support, none of this would have been possible. She is also a very talented editor and confidante. I shudder to think how much time she has spent reading and commenting on my work. My older daughter Jaren also deserves special recognition. For the past two years, she has worked with me as part of both Enterprise for a Sustainable World and The Water Initiative (TWI). In the process, she has made important material contributions to this third edition, both as an editor and research assistant. Much of the updating of cases was done by her, and she helped to write the section on TWI in Chapter 9. It has been an honor to work with her over these past two years, and I look forward to continuing the collaboration in the future.

I dedicate this book to my two daughters, Jaren and Jane, in the hopes that it is of some use to them in navigating the troubled waters ahead. For better or worse, it will be their generation that will ultimately have to ensure our transition toward a sustainable world. I wish them both Godspeed and hope it is not too late.

Stuart L. Hart
Ithaca, New York
April 2010

Notes

1. See, for example, Stuart Hart, "The Environmental Movement: Fulfillment of the Renaissance Prophesy?" *Natural Resources Journal* 20 (1980): 501–522.

2. A few of these publications include the following: Gordon Enk and Stuart Hart, "An Eight-Step Approach to Strategic Problem Solving," *Human Systems Management*, 5 (1985): 245–258; Stuart Hart, Mark Boroush, Gordon Enk, and William Hornick, "Managing Complexity Through Consensus Mapping: Technology for the Structuring of Group Decisions," *Academy of Management Review*, 10 (1985): 587–600; Stuart Hart, Gordon Enk, and William Hornick, (eds.), *Improving Impact Assessment* (Boulder, CO: Westview Press, 1984); and Stuart Hart and Gordon Enk, *Green Goals and Greenbacks* (Boulder: Westview Press, 1980).

3. Stuart Hart, *Strategic Problem Solving in Turbulent Environments* (Ann Arbor, MI: University of Michigan, 1983).

4. A couple of sample publications include Jac Geurts, Stuart Hart, and Nate Caplan, "Decision Techniques and Social Research: A Contingency Framework for Problem Solving," *Human Systems Management*, 5 (1985): 333–347; and Daniel Denison and Stuart Hart, *Revival in the Rust Belt* (Ann Arbor, MI: Institute for Social Research, 1987).

5. Some of my earliest published work in the area was done with Paul Shrivastava. See, for example, his (and Stuart Hart's) Greening Organizations, *Academy of Management Best Paper Proceedings*, 52 (1992): 185–189.

6. Two of my most important single-authored articles were "A Natural Resource-Based View of the Firm," *Academy of Management Review*, 20 (1995): 986–1014; and "Beyond Greening: Strategies for a Sustainable World," *Harvard Business Review* (January–February 1997): 66–76.

7. C.K. Prahalad and Stuart Hart, "The Fortune at the Bottom of the Pyramid," *Strategy+Business*, 26 (2002): 54–67.

8. Christensen, Clayton, Thomas Craig, and Stuart Hart, "The Great Disruption," *Foreign Affairs*, 80(2) (2001): 80–95; and Stuart Hart and Clayton Christensen, "The Great Leap: Driving Innovation from the Base of the Pyramid," *Sloan Management Review*, 44(1) (2002): 51–56.

9. Stuart Hart and Sanjay Sharma, "Engaging Fringe Stakeholders for Competitive Imagination," *Academy of Management Executive*, 18(1) (2004): 7–18.

10. Stuart Hart and Mark Milstein, "Global Sustainability and the Creative Destruction of Industries," *Sloan Management Review*, 41(1) (1999): 23-33; "Creating Sustainable Value," *Academy of Management Executive*, 17(2) (2003): 56-69; and "In Search of Sustainable Enterprise: The Case of GE's Ecomagination Initiative," *Value*, 1(1) (2006): 36-43.

11. Ted London and Stuart Hart, "Reinventing Strategies for Emerging Markets: Beyond the Transnational Model," *Journal of International Business Studies*, 35 (2004): 350-370; and Stuart Hart and Ted London, "Developing Native Capability: What Multinational Corporations Can Learn from the Base of the Pyramid," *Stanford Social Innovation Review*, Summer (2005): 28-33.

12. Erik Simanis and Stuart Hart, "Expanding the Possibilities at the Base of the Pyramid," *Innovations*, Winter (2006): 43-51; Erik Simanis and Stuart Hart, "The Base of the Pyramid Protocol: Toward Next Generation BoP Strategy," *Cornell Center for Sustainable Global Enterprise*, 2008; and Erik Simanis and Stuart Hart, "Innovation from the Inside Out," *Sloan Management Review*, Summer (2009): 77-86.

13. Erik Simanis, Duncan Duke, and Stuart Hart, "The Base of the Pyramid Protocol: Beyond 'Basic Needs' Business Strategies: *Innovations*, Winter (2008): 57–83.

Preface:
Al Gore, Former Vice President
of the United States

The global context for business continues to change at an unprecedented rate, and Stuart Hart has effectively captured important insights into the nature of this contextual shift in this third edition of *Capitalism at the Crossroads*. I agree. In fact, my partners and I at Generation Investment Management believe that sustainability will be a key driver of global economic change over the next 50 years. And we think companies face an unprecedented opportunity to create shareholder value by helping to chart the way forward, and by contributing to sustainable development.

Now, more than ever, factors beyond the scope of economist John Maynard Keynes' "national accounts" (the backbone of today's gross domestic product) are directly affecting a company's ability to generate revenues, manage risks, and sustain competitive advantage. While our current system is precise in its ability to account for capital goods, it is imprecise in its ability to account for natural, social, and human capital. Natural resources, for example, are still—in some ways—assumed to be limitless. This, in part, explains why our current model of economic development is hardwired to externalize as many costs as possible, therefore imposing environmental and social costs on society at large.

The interests of shareholders, both public and private, over time, will be best served by companies that maximize their financial performance by strategically managing their economic, social, environmental, and ethical performance. This is increasingly true as we confront the limits of our ecological system and its ability to hold up under current patterns of use. "License to operate" can no longer be taken for granted by business when challenges such as the climate crisis, HIV/AIDS, and other pandemics, water scarcity, and poverty reach a point where civil society and consumers demand a response from business and government. Leading companies understand this and are already moving ahead of legislators and regulators and, in so doing, securing competitive advantage.

The global climate crisis is the perfect example of a challenge that pushes our companies and our policymakers beyond their traditional comfort zone. The risks and opportunities presented by global warming are clearly material to the long-term health of our economic system. Companies that are part of the climate change solution will be able to enhance revenues, attract the best talent, and develop brand benefits—all of which will translate into optimized shareholder value over the long run. Today, action on the climate crisis makes sense not only for reputation and risk management, but for revenue generation and competitive positioning. Investors and companies that fully integrate climate considerations into their strategies, cultures, and operations will be best positioned to create shareholder value.

Business, as Hart points out, is a powerful agent of change and is well equipped to forge the way to a more sustainable future in conjunction with government and a strong civil society. However, he points out the inherent short- and long-term tensions within companies, which still have to balance forward-looking sustainability initiatives with legacy investments and old (and often unsustainable) habits.

There are, of course, limits to the ability of traditional business to deal with sustainability challenges by themselves. Now, more than ever, our societies need new models to address systemic, long-term challenges like the climate crisis, poverty, pandemics, water scarcity, and demographic shifts. This will involve more business and government innovation, social entrepreneurship, public-private partnerships, and more effective civil society participation.

The age of sustainability has arrived, but now we must drive it fully through our economic system. To do so, markets will have to continue to evolve to take into account the full environmental and social externalities of business in order to enable the efficient allocation of capital to its highest and best use. The regulated carbon markets in Europe, worth $25 billion in 2006, are a good example of how capitalism can powerfully address environmental challenges when a price signal exists—in this case, the price of a ton of carbon dioxide.

Only as markets improve their ability to price externalities, will we see capital allocated more effectively to sustainable development. This shift will require nothing less than a complete change in mind-set—one that views our planet as a long-term investment, rather than a business in liquidation.

Al Gore
Cofounder and Chairman, Generation Investment Management, and
Former Vice President of the United States

Foreword:
Fisk Johnson, Chairman and
CEO, S. C. Johnson & Son, Inc.

The release of the third edition of Stuart L. Hart's book underscores a time when it is becoming increasingly crucial that business leaders grasp their roles and responsibilities in building a sustainable future. Hart's book gives voice to an inescapable reality: that the corporate sector can be the catalyst for a truly sustainable force of global development for all on the planet.

As the chairman and CEO of a consumer products company with global operations, I see every day the value that business can bring. I see that its products can improve the health and safety of people around the world. I see that its jobs enable parents to support their children and allow children to achieve dreams not even imagined by their parents.

I also recognize that business has provided fuel for those who oppose globalization. But despite what some see as the inevitable stain of "progress," I know there are many business leaders who share my belief that you cannot purely pursue greater profitability every quarter and have that be an acceptable mission statement. Or that improving the lives of workers in one country while degrading the environment in another is an acceptable demonstration of civic responsibility. Short-term quarterly profits cannot trump long-term sustainability.

As the author makes clear in *Capitalism at the Crossroads*, there is no inherent conflict between making the world a better place and achieving economic prosperity for all. Maintaining a principled commitment to global sustainability is not a soft approach to business—it is, in fact, the only pragmatic approach for long-term growth.

Capitalism at the Crossroads presents a scenario in which business can generate growth and satisfy social and environmental stakeholders. By focusing on the four billion people currently at the "Base of the Pyramid," Hart contends that companies can reap incredible growth while sowing tremendous improvement in people's lives and at the same time preserving the other species that live on this planet.

The early stages of our company's own work at the Base of the Pyramid gives further credence to Hart's argument. As Hart describes, in testing the Base of the Pyramid Protocol and developing more holistic relationships in Nairobi, Kenya, we have cocreated a mutually valuable business model. Moving beyond charity to create a sustainable business partnership in the slums of Kenya where many businesses may never venture is not without challenges. While too premature to call this project a success, we remain committed to building a viable business at the Base of the Pyramid.

Business driving sustainability is not a new concept to me. The seed was planted and then cultivated throughout a lifetime of conversations with my father, Samuel C. Johnson. He shared stories about my grandfather, who traveled to Brazil in the 1930s in search of a sustainable source of wax for our products. He described his own 1975 decision to voluntarily and unilaterally ban CFCs from our products despite fervent opposition from colleagues and competitors alike.

My father's pioneering social and environmental efforts led to his selection as an original member of the President's Council on Sustainable Development and as a founding member of the World Business Council on Sustainable Development. He led our family company, SC Johnson, to new heights of corporate environmental and social achievement.

Perhaps most important, my father ensured that the dialogue on sustainability would continue. In 2000, he endowed the Samuel C. Johnson Chair in Sustainable Global Enterprise, and it is this Chair that Hart now so ably and deservedly occupies. He also endowed the new Center for Sustainable Global Enterprise of the Johnson School at Cornell University. By doing so, he was fulfilling a vital obligation that Hart sets forth for business in this book: being optimistic about the future and the opportunities inherent in the global challenges we face.

I share that optimism. That is why in 2001 our company unilaterally developed the Greenlist environmental classification system to institutionalize the selection of environmentally preferred raw materials and packaging components, far exceeding government regulation and driving our business with better products. It is why in 2003 we launched programs to attack the menace of malaria in sub-Saharan Africa and the misery of asthma among Hispanic children in Miami, and we are working to significantly expand these programs. It is why in 2004 we joined with Conservation International's Carbon Conservation Program to help save one of the world's most critically threatened hotspots of biodiversity. It is why we have a comprehensive program to reduce greenhouse gas emissions and have implemented innovative systems like cogeneration to fuel our largest global manufacturing facility with natural gas and waste methane from a public landfill. This program has reduced emissions for our top global factories by 42 percent from our 2000 baseline year.

Although Hart calls for "drastic changes" to "avert catastrophe," optimism underlies all the arguments in *Capitalism at the Crossroads*, and the author presents us with a call to optimistic action. He asks us to involve the full range of stakeholders in crafting solutions to the issues of sustainability. He demands that we embrace a new business paradigm built not on incremental change, but on creative destruction and reinvention. He challenges us to base our policies and businesses on the unassailable truth that shareholder value can be created while solving social and environmental problems.

Some might say linking "global business" and "sustainable development" is an oxymoron, but they would be sorely mistaken. All of us are tied together: the radical environmentalist and the corporate CEO, the Sudanese refugee and the British socialite, the U.S. factory worker and the Argentine farmer. We all share a stake in the future of our global environment and economy. That is the undeniable truth of *Capitalism at the Crossroads*: We are all fundamentally linked, dependent on the same finite resources and driven by the same hopes for ourselves and our children.

I steadfastly believe there is honor and value in business. In *Capitalism at the Crossroads*, Stuart Hart demands that we embrace that truth. I'm convinced this may well be the best opportunity global businesses have to ensure their long-term sustainability. And I am tremendously optimistic about the future.

Dr. H. Fisk Johnson
Chairman and CEO
S. C. Johnson & Son, Inc.

Part One

Mapping the Terrain

Prologue: Reinventing Capitalism for the Post-Crisis World

Each human generation believes that it is endowed with special importance, that it faces a particularly important challenge (for example, the "greatest" generation and World War II), that it has a special quality or character (for example, the baby boomers), or that it lives at a particularly important time (for example, the age of enlightenment). The term for this is *chronocentrism*. Although each generation earnestly believes in its own significance, there is objective evidence that those of us alive today actually are witnessing the most important time in human history. We truly stand at a crossroads.

From the dawn of our species two million years ago until roughly 12,000 years ago, there were never more than some tens of millions of our brethren walking the planet at any one time. With the advent of agriculture and surplus food production, however, our species embarked on a path of population expansion that continues to this day. By the time of the American Revolution, the human family had grown to approximately one billion. Propelled further by the expansion to the New World and the industrial revolution, the population continued to grow so that by the close of World War II, there were two billion people on the planet.[1]

As a baby boomer born in 1952, I entered a world of about two billion people. In less than half a century, that population had ballooned to more than six billion. If I live to a ripe old age, I could easily see eight billion or more people on the planet. Thus, in a single lifetime, the human population will have grown from two billion to more than eight billion. This growth is truly unprecedented. Never before in human history has a single generation witnessed such explosive change. It seems self-evident, therefore, that the policies we adopt, the decisions we make, and the strategies we pursue over the next decade or two will determine the future of our species and the trajectory of the planet for the foreseeable future. That is an awesome responsibility, to say the least. It is also a huge opportunity.

The Great Disruption

When the first edition of *Capitalism at the Crossroads* appeared in 2005, some readers commented that the title of the book seemed a bit "over the top." After all, with the collapse of communism in the early 1990s, capitalism appeared to be the only game in town. Certainly there were challenges to be addressed—witness the dot-com bust, the Enron debacle, and the 9/11 terrorist attacks in the early 2000s—but by and large, most countries in the world seemed to have been persuaded that "free-market" capitalism was the wave of the future. Today—a scant five years later—many people are no longer so sure.

Indeed, as I revise this prologue in early 2010, few people question the title of the book. The landscape has changed substantially even since the publication of the second edition of the book in 2007. In fact, I believe the year 2008 will come to be recognized as the turning point. Beginning that year, a series of crises gripped the planet— the oil price spike, the world food shortage, the subprime debacle, the global financial crisis, and finally, the Great Recession. Add these crises to the already long list of ongoing mega-problems—melting glaciers, climate change, loss of biodiversity, deep poverty, growing inequity, hopelessness, terrorism—and it finally became clear to most that something fundamental was wrong.

The world—and global capitalism—now clearly do stand at a crossroads. At the World Economic Forum (WEF) in January 2009, Klaus Schwab, Founder of the WEF, proclaimed that "the financial crisis is a wake-up call to reformulate the world's institutions and corporations for the twenty-first century." Jeff Immelt, CEO of GE, declared that there would be no "recovery" given that the world would never return to where it had been before. Rather, we should be thinking in terms of "reset."

New York Times columnist Tom Friedman recently observed that we have perhaps reached the global "inflection point"—that the growth model we created over the last 50 years is simply unsustainable economically and ecologically, and 2008 is when it finally imploded. Australian sustainability commentator Paul Gilding even had a name for this moment: "The Great Disruption"—when both Mother Nature and Father Greed hit the wall at the same time.[2] The significance of the transformation we are experiencing cannot be overstated, and organizations ill-prepared for this new world will simply not survive.

The Best of Times, The Worst of Times

We are truly poised at the threshold of an historic moment. Globalization critic David Korten suggests that one hundred years from now, our progeny will look back on this time as either the Great Unraveling or the Great Turning.[3] Indeed, ours is a deliciously paradoxical time: Two hundred years ago, virtually everyone alive was "poor" by today's standard, and famines and disease were commonplace. In the first half of the twentieth century, great wars erupted, killing millions and destroying entire countries in the process. Clearly, humanity has made astounding progress in a relatively short amount of time.

During the past two decades, for example, we have witnessed the fall of communism and the birth of a planetary economy and civilization. The United States emerged in the 1990s as the world's only superpower, championing a message of liberty and democracy rather than conquest and subjugation. China and India experienced unprecedented rates of growth and became significant players on the world stage. Multinational corporations, international institutions, and global civil society have exploded onto the scene, bringing with them state-of-the-art technology, advanced business practices, and a new accountability. Life expectancy and literacy are on the rise throughout the world.[4]

A revolution in information and communication technologies (ICT) has unfolded before our eyes, changing the way we live and speeding the spread of information and ideas. It took 20 years for wireless IT to reach the first billion people, largely through high-end commercial experiments in the United States, Western Europe, and Japan. But once the need and business model for wireless IT was demonstrated in the developing world's underserved urban and rural areas, it took off like wildfire: It took only two years to reach the second billion and less than one year to reach the third billion people. Today over half of humanity has access to wireless telecommunications, with the low-income market serving as the innovation driver—for cost reduction and technological innovation in hand-held and solar recharging devices.

The new information-based economy has greatly increased transparency, fostered local self-help, and facilitated the spread of democracy throughout the world. Along with life science and nanoscience, ICT will revolutionize the way we live in the coming century. Technological innovation has already led to dramatic reductions in the material and energy intensity of the economy. Consider, for example, that the U.S. economy "weighed" about the same (in terms of material intensity) at the end of the twentieth century as it did at the beginning of the century, despite being approximately 20 times larger in real terms.[5] As the Iron Age gives way to the Information Age, there is no question that we have much to be thankful for.

Yet, as noted earlier, fault lines and fissures are readily visible. Although U.S. consumers did a yeoman's job of driving the world economy during much of the 1990s and early 2000s, it is now clear that there are limits even to Americans' ability to consume goods and services. Indeed, China's rapid economic growth has depended primarily upon growing consumer spending in the United States. This co-dependency was a vicious circle destined to collapse. Sure enough, when the American real estate bubble burst with the sub-prime debacle in 2008, "Chimerica" came tumbling down, with both the U.S. and Chinese economies taking a beating. After the bubble burst in 2008, thousands of Chinese export factories closed, and tens of millions of unemployed migrant workers returned home to the rural areas in search of work, where 700 million plus peasants still struggle to earn a livelihood.

As with China, the recent global economic slowdown also had a profound effect on India: The information technology and business services sectors in large cities like Mumbai, Bangalore, and Hyderabad took a beating. The "flat world" described in Tom Friedman's well-known book was literally flattened.[6] The Indian stock market was down by more than 50%, and real estate prices in the cities collapsed. And even though Indian banks were not impacted by the subprime meltdown, investment capital in India decreased by half. Fully two-thirds of India's population—in excess of 700 million rural villagers—had yet to see the benefits of economic globalization, leading to an explosion of squatter communities, tent cities, shantytowns, and urban slums. And while the new government has made rural development a focus, without opportunity creation on a massive scale in India's 600,000 villages, it will be difficult to achieve a sustainable form of development—one that avoids dividing the country into 200–300 million "haves" and 700–800 million "have-nots."

In short, nearly two decades of economic globalization, privatization, and free trade have produced mixed results at best. Whereas the wealthy in developed countries have grown richer, and a new middle class has emerged in China and India, the vast majority of nations and people in the world have yet to benefit from the apparent triumph of capitalism and liberal democracy. Even the United States, famous for its economic opportunity, has become increasingly divided into a wealthy elite class and a burgeoning number of unemployed, under-employed, and working poor. America's vaunted "middle class" has now become the "missing class."[7] Indeed, the $40 trillion–plus world economy is simply not growing fast enough to provide jobs for the tens of millions of young people from around the world joining the labor force each year. Contrary to popular belief, the so-called "roaring '90s" was actually the slowest-growing decade in the world economy in the past 40 years.[8] In fact, the poorest countries in the world have had zero or negative economic growth since the early 1980s.[9]

Environmental Meltdown?

While developed countries' economies have indeed become more information- and service-intensive, globally, the unsustainable use of raw materials and fossil energy has exploded during the past 50 years, with dire consequences for the world environment. There is a "clash" all right—not a clash of civilizations as some would have us believe, but a clash of humankind with the Earth's natural systems. The 2005 publication of the *Millennium Ecosystem Assessment* provided sobering evidence that we are headed for a global train wreck: Well over a thousand of the world's leading biologists and ecologists agreed that the majority of the natural systems supporting life on the planet—soils, watersheds, oceans, frontier forests, coastal coral reefs, and the climate system—are in serious jeopardy.[10] The scientists warn that ongoing degradation of natural systems is increasing the likelihood of potentially abrupt changes that will seriously affect human well-being, including the collapse of fisheries, dead zones along the coasts, and the emergence of new diseases. Indeed, the proliferation of new viruses such as AIDS, Ebola, and SARS reminds us that the potential for a global scourge is only one plane ride away. Already our cows are mad and the birds are sick with the flu.

The scientific evidence for climate change is now overwhelming, and Al Gore's award-winning 2006 film, *An Inconvenient Truth*, provided a much-needed wake-up call that global action is overdue. With the Greenland and West Antarctic ice sheets now melting much faster than predicted, the potential for abrupt, even catastrophic climate change can no longer be ruled out, and a significant rise in ocean levels is now a virtual certainty. Indeed, with the 2006 publication of the Stern Report, it is now clear that inaction on climate change could create the risk of major economic and social disruptions by mid-century, on a scale similar to those associated with the Great Wars and the economic depression in the first half of the twentieth century.[11] Even the recent "Climategate" debacle at the University of East Anglia's Climate Research Unit, while a public relations disaster, does not alter the accumulating weight of the scientific evidence.

The failure of the world community in 2009 to reach consensus in Copenhagen on a unified set of actions to combat climate change serves only to underscore the difficulty of achieving political solutions to such daunting and complex global challenges: Sadly, expecting 192 countries of every shape and size to agree on meaningful actions may simply be a bridge too far.[12] Mark Halle at the International Institute for Sustainable Development (IISD) recently observed that the entire UN effort to address climate change is like the beaching of whales: Nobody really understands why presumably healthy creatures head for the beach where they will certainly die and efforts to haul them back to sea are always unsuccessful. As Halle notes, the UN process is like those brave volunteers who pour buckets of water over the whales to keep them hydrated a bit longer.

The Demise of Development

Recent events have also called into question the whole paradigm of international development that has evolved over the past several decades: The Russian fiasco, the Asian financial crisis, and most recently the Argentinean crisis have made it clear that the so-called Washington Consensus, which focuses on "structural adjustment" as its strategy for international development, is coming apart at the seams: The International Monetary Fund, the World Bank, and the World Trade Organization are all under increasing fire, even from insiders such as Jeffery Sachs, Joseph Stiglitz, William Easterly, and George Soros.[13] Indeed, the Bretton Woods Institutions, designed after the Second World War to manage the international financial system, no longer appear to be up to the task. Lack of an international standard of value, currency instability, and wild swings in the business cycle have contributed to simultaneous recession in the three major world economies and a lack of investment in the developing world, as well as an ongoing conflict between the short-term financial demands of shareholders and long-term sustainability. Across the developing world, there is less enthusiasm for globalization's potential to bring prosperity to the masses.[14]

The 2008 *Human Development Report* makes it clear that while extreme income poverty (that is, the proportion of those in the world earning less than one dollar per day) might be declining, inequity continues to grow throughout most of the world, and ecosystem destruction makes life increasingly precarious for most of the world's poor—particularly those in rural areas. Mass migration to cities now appears inevitable unless decline in the rural areas—still home to nearly four billion people—can be reversed. If present trends continue, we could witness over a billion people flooding the already overcrowded squatter communities, urban slums, and shantytowns of the world's megacities in the coming decade. Migration on this scale has never happened before in the history of our species. And despite the important recent campaign to "Make Poverty History," it is unlikely that more aid, medicine, bed nets, and fertilizer alone will do the job.

A rising tide of anti-globalization has emerged that combines concerns about environmental degradation, inequity, human rights, cultural imperialism, and loss of local autonomy. Wealthy protesters organize massive demonstrations against multinational corporations and the institutions of global capitalism, such as the WTO and the World Economic Forum. The disenfranchised become increasingly organized—and militant—in their desire to assert their autonomy. Indian-led movements in Bolivia, for example, succeeded in toppling the Western-friendly government in that country and have joined a continent-wide backlash against free-market reforms. Over the past decade, the number of riots and protests in rural China has risen almost exponentially to nearly 100,000 annually, as tens of millions are driven off the land as part of the country's rapid urbanization policy.[15] Many, in fact, assert that the whole concept of "development" must be abandoned in favor of a new concept that gives a greater voice to the views and aspirations of local people.[16]

In a very real sense, the 2009 global financial crisis was the straw that broke the camel's back; it served to further erode the already negative image that most people hold about corporations, capitalism, and the profit motive. People from all walks of life began to question the kind of economy that makes sense for their businesses, communities, and families. And while anger was initially directed at the bankers who received hundreds of billions of taxpayer "bailout" money—only to invest it for their own personal gain—the distaste for this brand of greed has caused many to ask deeper questions about the financial system and capitalism in general: Is it the public's duty to "prop up" unsuccessful companies when capitalism dictates that they should simply fail and be replaced by more innovative, adaptive, or creative players? Why should corporations get "bailed out" when ordinary people are forced to sink or swim on their own? Should any bank or corporation be allowed to become "too big to fail?" What form of economic governance is needed to prevent similar abuses from occurring again in the post-crisis world?

In short, the world today is on a collision course with the future. Drastic changes will be required in the coming decade or two to avert catastrophe. Unfortunately, global responses thus far have been woefully insufficient. Ten years ago, for example, the Millennium Development Goals (MDGs) were adopted by the world's governments as a blueprint for building a better world for the twenty-first century. The MDGs consist of eight goals to be achieved by 2015 that respond to the world's main development challenges outlined here. These important goals include: eradicating extreme poverty and hunger, achieving universal primary education, ensuring environmental sustainability, and promoting a global partnership for development.[17] Unfortunately, like most international policy documents, the mechanisms for implementation and accountability are unclear.

To make matters worse, the quantifiable targets associated with the MDGs do not go nearly far enough. For example, using 1990 as the baseline, the poverty target for 2015 is to "reduce by half the proportion of people living on less than a dollar a day." Unfortunately, with population growth, even if the world meets this target, there could still be more people (in absolute numbers) living on less than a dollar a day in 2015 than there were in 1990. The MDGs also aim to "achieve significant improvement in the lives of at least 100 million slum dwellers, by 2020." Yet, if current trends continue, there may well be over two billion slum dwellers by that time.

The Kyoto Protocol, the international agreement to address climate change, has a similar shortcoming: Its target to reduce greenhouse gas emissions by anywhere from 6–8 percent by 2010 (off a 1990 base) is a great start but does not get us anywhere close to the 70–80 percent real reductions needed to actually stabilize the climate system. To make matters worse, the incremental greenhouse gas reductions resulting from the Copenhagen negotiations in 2009 still fall far short of what most scientists now believe will be necessary to avert catastrophe.

One year after the global financial meltdown, there have been precious few actions taken to re-regulate or change the rules of the game for the global financial system to make it less speculative and more sustainable. Despite widespread calls for "reset" and "reinvention" in the throes of the crisis, now that "stability" has been restored, the more likely scenario is modest reform and a return to "business as usual"—at least until the next crisis hits.

Implications for Corporations

The global dynamics just described have significant implications for large multinational corporations (MNCs), given their centrality to the global economy. There are now more than 60,000 MNCs (defined as any corporation with operations in more than one country) with more than a quarter of a million affiliates around the world. MNCs account for more than 25 percent of world economic output. During the 1990s, foreign direct investment (FDI) by MNCs overtook official development assistance (ODA); by 2000, it exceeded ODA by more than a factor of five. Indeed, MNCs have become the primary instruments of economic globalization, facilitating the diffusion of more efficient and competitive business practices throughout the world.[18]

However, a growing chorus of voices points out that the process of economic globalization driven by MNCs over the past decades has also had a dark side.[19] For example, the 10 largest MNCs have annual sales of more than the GNPs of the 100 smallest, poorest countries in the world, raising concerns about sovereignty and the ability of governments to determine their own fates.[20] Given the ability of MNCs to shift resources and production across borders, many have also suggested that they encourage a global "race to the bottom" by chasing subsidies, incentives, and lower costs wherever they might lead, at the expense of national and community interests.[21]

Of the top 200 MNCs in the world, the vast majority have their origins in the most affluent, developed countries of the world—the United States, European countries, and Japan. A growing number of critics have voiced concern that such corporate dominance is leading to a worldwide commercial monoculture based on the values of Western consumerism and bringing with it the decline of local cultures, products, and traditions.[22] Others decry the environmental consequences associated with spreading the energy- and material-intensive industries associated with global capitalism to the rest of the developing world.[23]

And although MNCs account for a quarter of global economic activity, they employ less than 1 percent of the world's labor force, while one-third of the world's willing-to-work population is either unemployed or underemployed.[24] Furthermore, while a substantial number of Americans now hold shares in companies either directly or through pension accounts, less than 1 percent of the world's population participates in the financial markets as shareholders. As a consequence, the wealth created by MNCs accrues almost exclusively to a relatively small number of wealthy people in the world—corporate executives, employees, and Western shareholders.[25]

We can also discern a similar trend on the corporate investment side, where the vast majority of foreign direct investment (FDI) occurs within the richest countries.[26] Investment in emerging markets has been limited largely to the wealthiest of the poor countries or those with the largest potential markets, such as China, India, and Brazil. Even there, most MNC products are aimed at the wealthy, elite customers or those in the rising middle-class segments of the market.[27] Virtually no commercial attention has been paid to serving the needs of those at the base of the economic pyramid.[28]

The result is that during the past 50 years, the gap between the richest and the poorest in the world has continued to widen. In 1960, for example, the richest 20 percent accounted for 70.2 percent of global GDP, while the poorest 20 percent accounted for 2.3 percent (a ratio of 30:1). By 2000, however, this gap had widened considerably: The richest quintile controlled 85 percent of global GDP, while the poorest accounted for only 1.1 percent (a ratio of 80:1).[29]

Clearly, MNCs alone are not responsible for all these problems: Banks and international financial institutions such as the International Monetary Fund and the World Bank have played a central role. Corrupt and repressive regimes in the poorest countries have also been major contributors to the problem. Still, these dynamics are increasingly being viewed as unacceptable. MNCs, for better or worse, are on the "front line" of globalization. If current trends continue, they can only become more frequent targets of antiglobalization protests, sabotage, and terrorism.

The Fork in the Road

Global capitalism stands at a crossroads: Without a significant change of course, the future for economic globalization, free trade, and multinational corporations appears increasingly bleak. It might be argued, in fact, that global capitalism stands at a juncture similar to the one faced nearly a century ago, at the end of the first era of globalization. Urban squalor, pallid air, labor strife, and rising inequity, along with growing militarism, anarchism, assassination, and terrorism were the order of the day. The outbreak of World War I in August of 1914 literally ended the British-led nineteenth-century global capitalist economy. Between 1914 and 1945, two World Wars, revolution, depression, and fascism almost succeeded in eliminating liberal democracy and capitalism from the face of the Earth. In her classic book, *The Proud Tower*, Barbara Tuchman made the following observations about the period leading up to the First World War:

> Industrial society gave man new powers and new scope while at the same time building up new pressures in prosperity and poverty, in growth of population and crowding of cities, in antagonisms of classes and groups, in separation from nature and from satisfaction in individual work. Science gave man new welfare and new horizons while it took away belief in God and certainly in a scheme of things he knew. By the time he left the Nineteenth Century he had as much new unease as ease.[30]

Tuchman's observations are eerily applicable today. Failure to address the challenges we face—from global-scale environmental change, to mass poverty, to international terrorism, to financial collapse—could produce catastrophe on an even grander scale than that experienced in the first half of the twentieth century: Constructively engaging these challenges thus holds the key to ensuring that capitalism continues to thrive in the coming century—to everyone's benefit. We are faced with nothing less than the challenge of reinventing capitalism for the twenty-first century.

The Brundtland Commission defined sustainable development as that which "meets the needs of the present without compromising the ability of future generations to meet their own needs."[31] It has become increasingly clear that one-size-fits-all solutions for poverty or environmental degradation dictated from the top must give way to local investment and bottom-up entrepreneurial development. The challenge of our time is to transform the millions of towns, small cities, and villages of the world from declining poverty traps into dynamic, opportunity-rich communities—the incubators for the sustainable ways of living of tomorrow. By creating a new, more inclusive brand of capitalism, one that incorporates previously excluded voices, concerns, and interests, the business sector could become the catalyst for a truly sustainable form of global development—and prosper in the process. To succeed, however, corporations must learn how to open up to the world: Strategies need to take into account the entire human community of 6.7 billion, as well as the host of other species with which we share the planet.

Sustainable enterprise thus represents the potential for a new private sector–based approach to development that creates profitable businesses that simultaneously raise the quality of life for the world's poor, respect cultural diversity, inspire employees, build communities, and conserve the ecological integrity of the planet for future generations. Making such a societal contribution while simultaneously creating shareholder value will take real imagination and a fresh approach to business strategy. These exciting and uplifting challenges are the focus of the pages that follow.

Notes

1. For a fascinating account of the human species' emergence, see Jared Diamond, *Guns, Germs, and Steel* (New York: W.W. Norton, 1999).

2. Paul Gilding, "Scream, Crash, Boom II: The Great Disruption," Unpublished White Paper, 2008.

3. David Korten, *The Great Turning* (San Francisco: Berrett-Koehler, 2008).

4. Allen Hammond, *Which World?* (Washington, D.C.: Island Press, 1998).

5. Diane Coyle, *Paradoxes of Prosperity* (New York: Textere, 2001).

6. See Tom Friedman, *The World Is Flat* (New York: Farrar, Straus, and Giroux, 2005).

7. Katherine Newman and Victor Tan Chen, *The Missing Class* (Boston: Beacon Press, 2007).

8. Thomas Palley, "A New Development Paradigm: Domestic Demand-Led Growth," Foreign Policy in Focus (September, 1999), www.fpif.org/papers/development_body.html.

9. William Easterly, *The Elusive Quest for Growth* (Cambridge, MA: MIT Press, 2002).

10. The Millennium Ecosystem Assessment, Ecosystem and Human Wellbeing (Washington D.C.: World Resources Institute, 2005).

11. Stern Review, *The Economics of Climate Change* (Cambridge: Cambridge University Press, 2006).

12. Paul Gilding and Jurgen Randers, "The One Degree War," Unpublished White Paper, 2009.

13. See, for example, Jeff Sachs, "Helping the World's Poorest." *The Economist* (14 August 2000): 17–20; Joseph Stiglitz, *Globalization and its Discontents* (New York: W.W. Norton, 2002); and George Soros, *George Soros on Globalization* (New York: Perseus Books, 2002) and William Easterly, *The White Man's Burden* (New York: Penguin Press, 2006).

14. This point is made convincingly by Hernando DeSoto, *The Mystery of Capital* (New York: Perseus Books, 2000).

15. Peter Navarro, *The Coming China Wars* (Upper Saddle River: Prentice Hall, 2006).

16. See, for example, Wolfgang Sachs, *Planet Dialectics* (London: Zed Books, 1999).

17. Millennium Development Goals, www.undp.org/mdg.

18. Rajan Raghuram and Luigi Zingales, *Saving Capitalism from the Capitalists* (New York: Crown Business, 2003).

19. Perhaps the best articulation of this point of view can be found in David Korten, *When Corporations Rule the World* (San Francisco: Berrett-Koehler, 1995).

20. As Jagdish Bhagwati points out in his book *In Defense of Globalization* (New York: Oxford University Press, 2004), this comparison, while appealing, is conceptually flawed. When we compare sales volumes, which are gross values, with GDP, which includes only value-added figures for the goods and services, we are comparing apples and oranges. In other words, corporate sales figures across an entire economy will add up to numbers that vastly exceed the GDPs of the countries where these sales occur.

21. David Korten, *When Corporations Rule the World*.

22. See Colin Hines, *Localization: A Global Manifesto* (London: Earthscan, 2000).

23. Allen Hammond, *Which World?*

24. The World Bank, *World Development Report* (New York: Oxford University Press, 2000).

25. David Korten, *When Corporations Rule the World*.

26. Jeff Sachs, "Helping the World's Poorest."

27. C.K. Prahalad and Ken Lieberthal, "The End of Corporate Imperialism," *Harvard Business Review* 76(4) (1998): 68–79.

28. C.K. Prahalad and S. Hart, "The Fortune at the Bottom of the Pyramid," *Strategy+Business*, 26 (2002): 2–14.

29. The World Bank, *World Development Report*.

30. Barbara Tuchman, *The Proud Tower: A Portrait of the World Before the World* (New York: Ballantine Books, 1962).

31. Brundtland Commission, *Our Common Future* (New York: Oxford University Press, 1997).

1

From Obligation to Opportunity

This book takes the contrarian's view that business—more than either government or civil society—is uniquely equipped at this point in history to lead us toward a sustainable world in the years ahead. I argue that corporations are the only entities in the world today with the technology, resources, capacity, and global reach required. Properly focused, the profit motive can accelerate (not inhibit) the transformation toward global sustainability, with nonprofits, governments, and multilateral agencies all playing crucial roles as collaborators and watchdogs. The book is written with a practical focus and should be of direct use to executives, entrepreneurs, and technologists, as well as business school faculty and students. The contents are equally appropriate, however, for those from the nonprofit world, the public sector, and society at large, especially those interested—and inclined—to collaborate with the private sector.

The book carries an optimistic message. Despite the gathering storm of environmental degradation, poverty, financial crisis, and terrorism, it envisions a central and expanding role for commerce in fostering global sustainability. It foresees massive opportunities for companies both to make money and to make the world a better place, particularly among the four billion poor at the base of the economic pyramid. This book is the result of an intellectual journey that began for me nearly four decades ago. My own personal evolution is reflected in its structure and flow. Allow me to explain.

Having grown up in western New York in the 1950s and '60s, I have memories of family vacations spent at destinations like Niagara Falls. Although the Falls themselves were indeed magnificent, equally memorable for a 10-year-old was the soot from nearby factories that accumulated on the porch furniture, requiring that we cleaned the furniture daily, lest we ruin our clothes. The accompanying stench was also something to experience. I still remember asking why, in a place of such natural beauty and splendor, did it have to be so polluted? The answer, accepted wisdom in those days, was that this was "the smell of money." If we were going to have economic prosperity, then we would have to put up with some minor inconveniences, such as soot, stench, rivers that catch fire, and mountains of waste. It was the cost of progress. I remember being singularly unsatisfied by this response.

Fast-forward to 1974. As a freshly minted college graduate headed to Yale for graduate work in the School of Forestry and Environmental Studies, I was convinced that corporations were the "enemy" and that the only way to deal effectively with environmental problems was to "make them pay" through regulation—to internalize their externalities, in the jargon of economics. This was probably a correct perception at that point in history: Large corporations, by and large, had been unresponsive to environmental issues, and it appeared that the only way to deal with the problem was to force them to clean up the messes they were making. The Environmental Protection Agency and scores of other regulatory agencies were created precisely for this purpose. A mountain of command-and-control regulation was passed during the decade of the 1970s, aimed at forcing companies to mitigate their negative impacts.

Regulators and citizen activists, buoyed by their newfound power, increased the pressure on companies through fines, penalties, campaigns, and consent decrees. The courts became clogged with lawsuits aimed at halting projects that were deemed unacceptable due to their environmental or social impacts. Economists of the "environmental" variety wrote books about externalities and the public policies that would be required for them to be "internalized" most efficiently by companies.[1] In the process, companies became convinced that social and environmental issues were necessarily costly problems, usually involving lawyers and litigation. For better or worse, the message was that environmental and social issues were "responsibilities" that companies were required to deal with—and it was going to be expensive.

The Great Trade-Off Illusion

There can be no question that command-and-control regulation was of enormous importance; it required, perhaps for the first time, that business address directly its negative societal impacts. Since the time of the industrial revolution, enterprises had relied upon the extraction of cheap raw materials, exploitation of factory labor, and production of mass quantities of waste and pollution (think of those "dark, satanic mills"). Indeed, pollution was assumed to be part of the industrialization process. When economists conceived the concept of externalities, in other words, it seemed virtually impossible that firms could behave in any other manner. For the better part of 200 years, industrial firms engaged in what might be described as "take, make, waste" as an organizing paradigm.[2] Command-and-control regulation seemed a necessary and appropriate counter to the prevailing industrial mindset.

Paradoxically, this mindset also resulted in what I call the "Great Trade-Off Illusion"—the belief that firms must sacrifice financial performance to meet societal obligations.[3] A massive wall of environmental and social regulation has been spawned over the past 30 years, most of which has been written in a way that makes the Great Trade-Off Illusion a self-fulfilling prophecy. Just track the thickness (and lack of flexibility) of the Code of Federal Regulations in the United States for confirmation.[4] Too often, command-and-control regulations prescribed specific treatment technologies without regard to their efficiency or cost-effectiveness.

A generation of businesspeople was shaped by this framing of the situation. Not surprisingly, the managers and executives who rose to prominence during the postwar years were predisposed to think of environmental and social issues as negatives for business. A socially minded executive or company might "give back" to the community through philanthropy or volunteering, but such concerns would certainly never be part of the company's core activities! The social responsibility of business was to maximize profits, as Milton Friedman advocated, and it seemed clear that social or environmental concerns could only serve to reduce them.[5]

Even today, this mindset lingers. Try the following thought experiment: Imagine that you are a general manager in a business or company of your choosing. Your assistant calls saying that the environment, health, and safety (EHS) manager and the public affairs director are in your outer office, and they say the matter is urgent. What is your first reaction? If you are honest with yourself, you will have to admit that the first thoughts that come to mind are something like: problem, crisis, spill, incident, accident, boycott, protest, lawsuit, fine, or jail time. Your first instinct was probably to head for the back door of your office to escape.

But now try a second thought experiment: Your assistant calls saying that the heads of marketing and new product development are in your outer office, and they are anxious to meet with you. Now, what is your first reaction? What thoughts or issues come to mind? In all likelihood, your mind probably flashes to images like: breakthrough, opportunity, blockbuster, innovation, or growth. Your first instinct is to run to the front door of the office to let them in.[6]

The Great Trade-Off Illusion trained a generation of corporate, business, and facility-level managers to assume that societal concerns could only be drags on their business. As a consequence, their attitude tended to be reactive—they would do only the bare minimum necessary to avoid legal sanction. Unfortunately, when lawmakers and activists unfamiliar with operations or market dynamics write the rules for compliance, it is a virtual certainty that the rules will not integrate well with company strategy or operations. Taking a reactive posture thus doomed companies to a decade or more of onerous regulations that treated the symptoms rather than the underlying problems. These regulations targeted specific wastes, emissions, pollutants, and exposure levels through command-and-control-style rules that forced companies to deal with problems "at the end of the pipe" rather than addressing them as part of their core strategy or operations. Unfortunately, pollution-control devices can never improve efficiency or produce revenue; they can only add cost.

The Greening Revolution

The decade of the 1980s brought with it a growing sense of unease with command-and-control regulation. Despite enormous expenditures, it was not at all clear that the end-of-the-pipe approach to pollution control and regulation was working.[7] Alternatives such as market-based incentives and tradable emission permits demonstrated that pollution levels could be reduced in a dramatically more efficient and cost-effective manner. In Europe, a more collaborative and goal-oriented approach to regulation was the norm; the focus was on actual environmental and social improvement rather than the specification of particular treatment technologies or pollution control devices.

I, too, was undergoing a transformation of sorts. In 1986, I joined the faculty at the University of Michigan Business School, having completed my doctoral work in strategy and planning in 1983. My transition from a regulatory to a business strategy orientation reflected my own growing disenchantment with the command-and-control approach to dealing with environmental and societal problems. Rather than simply trying to halt polluting projects or mitigate damage, I became increasingly interested in understanding why such seemingly bad projects were being proposed in the first place.

This change proved fortuitous: By the late 1980s, there was a growing receptivity to environmental and social issues within companies—and business schools. As luck would have it, this openness developed through innovation in another arena: quality management. As you might recall, in the late 1970s and early 1980s, Japanese companies were literally overrunning their American and European competitors with higher-quality and lower-cost goods. From steel makers to automobile firms, to consumer electronics manufacturers, companies were scrambling to match the Japanese quality advantage. Because of widespread plant closures and downsizing, there was palpable concern that the West would lose to "Japan, Inc."[8]

After three glorious postwar decades of high-volume, standardized mass production with quality inspected in (after the fact) rather than built in (as part of the design and production process), Western companies were being out-competed by a new and better way. Instead of countering with their own unique strategies, American and European companies became obsessed with learning and copying the ways of Japanese quality management.[9] Among other things, they built the capacity for "continuous improvement" (kaizen) into the management system by empowering workers to improve their work processes rather than blindly following prescribed procedures. Managers' mindsets changed from a fixation on centralized control and a "results" orientation (detecting defects and fixing them) to a preoccupation on decentralization and a "process" orientation (improving the management system so that employees could prevent quality problems from occurring in the first place).[10]

Shattering the Trade-Off Myth

The confluence of the quality and environmental movements was a marriage made in heaven: By the late 1980s, it had become clear that preventing pollution and other negative impacts was usually a much cheaper and more effective approach than trying to clean up the mess after it had already been made. The emergence of market-based incentives such as tradable emission permits made prevention even more appealing. Furthermore, the discipline of quality management could be easily expanded to incorporate social and environmental issues. In the early 1990s, this confluence produced a flurry of so-called environmental management system (EMS) approaches and "total quality environmental management" protocols, culminating in the advent of the International Standards Organization (ISO) 14001, the environmental equivalent of ISO 9000 for quality.

Community advisory panels and stakeholder dialogue intended to involve affected parties in company affairs instead of doing battle in court proved to be a much more effective way to maintain legitimacy and the "right to operate." Indeed, in designing its self-regulation program called Responsible Care, the chemical industry enshrined the principles of pollution prevention and community engagement as part of its product stewardship process. In short, the quality revolution taught us that *muda* (waste) was the enemy of good management. Pollution and litigation were the ultimate forms of muda.

As social and environmental issues became more deeply embedded in the ongoing operations of enterprises, managers began to see that corporate and societal performance need not be separated. Whereas companies previously sought to first make money through their business operations and then give back to society through philanthropy, now these two agendas could be merged. What had been a virtual firewall separating business from philanthropy was now transforming into a host of new and creative approaches to combining the two through corporate partnerships with nongovernmental organizations, strategic philanthropy, and other forms of social innovation.[11]

Furthermore, in certain situations, preventing pollution through process or product redesign could actually save money, reduce risk, and even improve products for the firm. An extensive body of research began to document the situations and contexts in which pollution prevention and product stewardship resulted in superior financial performance.[12] Not surprisingly, parlaying environmental and social performance into improved business performance required a set of supporting or complementary capabilities, such as employee empowerment, quality management, cross-functional cooperation, and stakeholder engagement. This meant that the greening revolution had not only succeeded in elevating the significance of social and environmental issues, but it also had converted them from expensive problems into strategic opportunities for certain firms with the necessary skills, capabilities, and leadership vision.[13]

Breaking Free of Command-and-Control

Accompanying the greening revolution in the corporate sector was the emergence of a new philosophy in regulation and public policy that recognized the limitations (and expense) of conventional regulation and the end-of-the-pipe mentality. In response, a slew of new voluntary initiatives were introduced that recognized the power of information disclosure and transparency.[14] The pioneering initiative was the Toxic Release Inventory (TRI) in the U.S. Passed in 1988 as a rider on the Superfund Reauthorization (the law establishing strict liability for toxic waste sites), the TRI received relatively little attention in its early days. This seemingly innocuous provision required only that manufacturers disclose their use, storage, transport, and disposal of more than 300 toxic chemicals (all of which were perfectly legal at the time). Much to everyone's surprise, this data, maintained by the U.S. Environmental Protection Agency, became an important new source of information for activist groups, the media, and third-party analysts to track corporate environmental performance. Top 10 lists of corporate polluters became *de rigeur*.

The TRI also provided, for the first time, a metric for corporate and facility managers to track their own firms' performance and benchmark it against competitors. What gets measured gets done. Ten years later, toxic emissions in the United States had been reduced by more than 60 percent, even though the U.S. economy boomed during the 1990s. Indeed, many companies actually saved tens of millions of dollars in the process of reducing or eliminating their toxic emissions.[15] We could argue that the TRI was one of the most important and effective pieces of social legislation ever passed. And it required nary a lawsuit, court battle, or inspector to make it happen. Since then, many developing countries have adopted a similar philosophy of transparency and information disclosure as the basis for their environmental policies, given that these can be implemented at a fraction of the cost of command-and-control regulations.

Equally important was the advent of "extended producer responsibility" laws, primarily in Europe.[16] Quite simply, these laws stipulate that manufacturers are responsible for the products they create all the way to the end of their useful lives. Beginning with regulations on packaging waste in Germany in the late 1980s, these laws now extend to several industrial sectors, including automobiles, consumer electronics, and computers. Requiring that producers take back their products after they have reached the end of their lives has obvious effects on the way companies go about designing products in the first place. This simple requirement has fomented a revolution in product stewardship and "green design" protocols, using life-cycle management as its core principle. Rather than focusing only on the phase of the product's life cycle that the company controls (manufacture or assembly), product stewardship means designing products to take account of their entire life cycle, from the sourcing of raw materials and energy from the Earth to the reuse, remanufacture, or return of the materials to the Earth. Rather than thinking linearly, in terms of "cradle to grave," increasingly, designers think cyclically, in terms of "cradle to cradle."[17]

In the process, companies have discovered that life-cycle design principles can yield competitively superior products. During the early 1990s, for example, Xerox pioneered take-back, remanufacturing and design-for-environment strategies in the photocopier business and reaped significant competitive benefits. Given the company's extensive field presence for servicing commercial copiers, it was relatively easy to take back used machines, refurbish parts and components, and produce a line of remanufactured machines. However, it was not until the mid-1990s that Xerox actually began to *design* copiers with an eye toward taking them back. This program, dubbed Asset Recycle Management, was founded on the notion that by reusing assets as many times as possible (recall that most Xerox commercial copiers were leased, not owned by customers), the company would not only reduce its environmental footprint, but also lower its costs and increase its return on assets. It set the goal of producing "waste-free products from waste-free factories."[18] By the late 1990s, Xerox was saving close to $500 million per year through this program, a figure approaching 2.5 percent of company sales. In fact, it can be argued that, given Xerox's failure to shift its strategy toward printers (considering documents were increasingly being stored electronically and printed rather than duplicated), the Asset Recycle Management Program kept the company afloat for much of the 1990s.

As the green revolution progressed, leading companies began to shift their energy and attention more toward proactive strategies that reduced waste, emissions, and impacts while simultaneously reducing costs and risks. Paying real money for raw materials and inputs only to dump substantial amounts of these into the environment in the form of waste made little economic sense. In fact, Dow Chemical estimated in the early 1990s that reactive efforts such as regulatory compliance, cleanup, and remediation result in returns in the range of -60 percent while proactive initiatives typically produce positive returns in excess of 20 percent.[19] The problem was that most corporate activity (perhaps as much as 90 percent) was still of the reactive variety. The challenge was to transform the portfolio so that more was of the proactive sort. Ultimately, the goal is to get out of the regulatory compliance business entirely.

It was becoming clear that under the right circumstances, firms could actually improve their own competitive position by creating societal value. They could, for example, lower costs by internalizing externalities through pollution prevention. Furthermore, through product stewardship, it was sometimes possible to supply public goods and achieve superior performance. Witness Volvo's new radiator that actually cleans the air as it cools the engine or BP's climate-change policy that reduces its greenhouse gas emissions while reducing its costs. We should emphasize, however, the caveat "under the right circumstances:" Only through creativity, imagination, and the persistent development of particular skills and capabilities can firms simultaneously optimize financial, social, and environmental performance.

By the early 1990s, the greening revolution had led to the creation of a new dual-degree program at the University of Michigan involving both the Business School and the School of Natural Resources and Environment: the Corporate Environmental Management Program (CEMP), now the Erb Institute's dual masters program. Integrating pollution prevention and product stewardship into the management curriculum was the backbone for this program. As the founding director of CEMP, I had completed a virtual turnabout:

It was now clear to me that the corporate sector itself was the key leverage point for achieving substantial and lasting change in societal performance and that financial performance need not suffer in the process. I could finally put aside the demons from the past associated with "the smell of money." I came to realize instead that pollution was the smell of waste and poor management.

Beyond Greening

Yet this personal reconciliation was by no means the end of the road. The corporate "greening" initiatives of the late 1980s and early 1990s—pollution prevention and product stewardship—were important first steps. They shattered the myth that business should treat societal issues as expensive obligations. Instead, seen through the prism of quality and stakeholder management, these issues could become important opportunities for the company to improve its societal and operating performance simultaneously. A growing body of research pointed to the potential for enhanced financial performance through well-executed pollution prevention and product stewardship strategies. Pioneers such as 3M, Dow, and Dupont realized significant cost reductions and enhanced reputations as a result of their activities. The World Business Council for Sustainable Development, with its mantra of "eco-efficiency," helped to erase the false dichotomy between business and environmental performance.

However, greening alone fell well short of what was possible—and needed: Incremental improvements to current product systems and production processes only slowed the rate of environmental damage. Sustainability means inventing a new form of "natural capitalism."[20] As University of Virginia architect Bill McDonough points out, greening is akin to heading in the wrong direction, but at a slower rate of speed—being less bad. Sustainability, however, means actually turning around and heading in the right direction—being more good. It is, as McDonough and his colleague Michael Braun-gart point out, the difference between being eco-efficient and being eco-effective.[21]

Furthermore, most corporations continued to serve the needs of the wealthy exclusively while exploiting the developing world prima-rily for its abundant resources and cheap labor pool. A sustainable form of global enterprise would instead seek to create corporate and competitive strategies that simultaneously deliver economic, social, and environmental benefits for the entire world.[22] By the mid-1990s, it was clear that the corporate agenda was much bigger than just greening—and that the business opportunity was much more sub-stantial as well. This was the key message of my 1997 McKinsey award-winning article in the *Harvard Business Review*, "Beyond Greening: Strategies for a Sustainable World." It was also my primary motivation for moving to the University of North Carolina at Chapel Hill in 1998 to become the founding director of the Center for Sus-tainable Enterprise at the Kenan-Flagler Business School.

Corporations were being challenged to move beyond greening, first by pursuing new technologies that had the potential to be inher-ently clean (renewable energy, biomaterials, wireless IT), and second by reaching out to bring the benefits of capitalism to the entire human community of 6.7 billion people (rather than just the one billion at the top of the economic pyramid). In recognition of this challenge, my colleagues at UNC and I launched in 2000 The Base of the Pyramid Learning Laboratory, a consortium of large corporations, new ven-tures, and nongovernmental organizations (NGOs) all focused on how best to serve the needs of the four billion people at the base of the economic pyramid (BoP) in a way that is culturally appropriate, environmentally sustainable, and economically profitable.

By moving beyond greening, companies hope not only to address mounting social and environmental concerns, but also to build the foundation for innovation and growth in the coming decades. In so doing, they would outperform their competitors in today's businesses and, even more importantly, outrun them to tomorrow's technologies and markets. In short, sustainable global enterprises would create competitively superior strategies that simultaneously move us more rapidly toward a sustainable world.

In fact, over the past decade, there has been an explosion of clean technology investment—a veritable "revolution."[23] Venture capitalists have pumped in excess of $20 billion into clean tech companies since 2005. The Obama administration has pledged more than $100 billion for clean technologies, and China plans to invest $200 billion.[24] There are now literally thousands of new "clean tech" startups flush with investment capital, particularly in the strategically significant arenas of biofuels, renewable energy, and biomaterials.

Alongside the "clean tech" revolution, commercial strategies for serving the bottom (or base) of the income pyramid have also emerged over the past decade. Dozens of global corporations and hundreds of smaller social enterprises around the world have now initiated or deepened commercial experiments to serve the four billion poor who have been largely bypassed by economic globalization to date. These early initiatives may hold the keys to a new, more inclusive form of capitalism.[25]

Exhibit 1.1 summarizes the evolutionary path that corporations have followed over the past 50 years. Crossing the chasm from seeing societal performance as a trade-off or obligation (the left side of the figure) to a possible win-win opportunity (the lower-right side) was the major breakthrough of the 1980s. By 2000, many large corporations had internalized the capabilities and disciplines associated with greening, although some still had a long way to go. As a result, the competitive front migrated to the "beyond greening" domain (the upper-right portion).

Exhibit 1.1
The Long and Winding Road

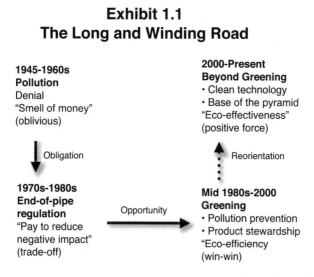

1945-1960s
Pollution
Denial
"Smell of money"
(oblivious)

2000-Present
Beyond Greening
• Clean technology
• Base of the pyramid
"Eco-effectiveness"
(positive force)

Obligation

Reorientation

1970s-1980s
End-of-pipe
regulation   Opportunity
"Pay to reduce
negative impact"
(trade-off)

Mid 1980s-2000
Greening
• Pollution prevention
• Product stewardship
"Eco-efficiency
(win-win)

Rather than seeking incremental improvements to what already exists, moving beyond greening often means pursuing innovations that may make obsolete what currently constitutes the company's core business—it is an inherently disruptive act. Thus, given its focus on new technologies and markets, the "beyond greening" space is blessed with much greater opportunities, but also fraught with bigger risks. One case in particular—Monsanto's controversial entry into genetically modified seeds—illustrates the potential opportunities and pitfalls of pursuing such strategies.[26]

Raging Against the Machine

In the mid-1990s, new CEO Robert Shapiro sought to revolutionize Monsanto. Through the power of his vision, he hoped to convert the firm from a chemicals manufacturer to a life-sciences company focused on "Food, Health, and Hope." Consistent with this vision, Shapiro spun off several strategic business units (SBUs) associated with the organization's chemicals business heritage, retaining only those closely tied to its life sciences focus. Simultaneously, he took the company on an acquisition binge, aggressively buying up biotech and seed companies, and accumulating huge debt in the process. The more focused—and leveraged—company then set out on a rapid growth strategy to make agricultural biotechnology a practical reality.

Shapiro also articulated how Monsanto's genetically engineered seeds gave the firm an advantage in the drive toward sustainability because they could increase farmers' yields, reduce pesticide use, and help to deliver nutrients to the world's chronically undernourished poor. In the space of a few years, Monsanto convinced farmers to plant nearly 60 million acres in the U.S. in genetically modified crops. In 1997, Shapiro also launched a new Sustainable Development Sector, empowering dozens of internal champions to identify and grow the new businesses of the future that would address global social and environmental concerns in an economically profitable manner. Between 1995 and 1997, Monsanto's stock price soared amid rosy projections of blockbuster products and rapidly expanding markets for agricultural biotechnology.

As a result of these developments, Monsanto was thrust into the public eye in a way that few companies had ever been in the past. Shapiro's portrayal of biotechnology's role in the future of agriculture generated unprecedented levels of public attention and scrutiny. This scrutiny resulted in problems for Monsanto as critics cast bright lights on incidents in which company actions did not match the spirit of Shapiro's vision.

For example, when Monsanto attempted to launch its genetically modified seeds in Europe, it met intense resistance from organic farmers and environmentalists, despite the fact that all the necessary regulatory approvals had been secured. Some Monsanto managers hired private investigators to ensure that customers (farmers) were not illegally saving Monsanto's genetically modified seed for replanting the following year. These actions and others alienated many who called into question Monsanto's true dedication to sustainable development and environmental stewardship. Shapiro's vision, in other words, did not always align with the actions taken by people in the company.

Other stakeholder groups included the millions of small farmers in developing countries such as India. These farmers protested against Monsanto in the streets, fearing that the company would enforce patents on essential grains and make them pay international prices for the seed they planted. Moreover, the farmers were concerned that Monsanto's patent ownership (via acquisition) of the "terminator" gene (seed-sterilization technology) would not allow them to practice the age-old tradition of propagating seeds from their own crops.

Regrettably, Monsanto did not enable these voices to reach business decision makers. The firm consulted with its immediate customers (large-scale farmers), regulators, and consumer groups in the United States. Despite efforts by the company's Sustainable Development Sector to access other voices, the business decision makers did not consider consumer groups in Europe or small farmers in developing countries to be legitimate or persuasive, even if their claims seemed urgent.

Instead of becoming a more open, innovative culture, the firm became more defensive and had to back away publicly from several of its biotechnology initiatives under pressure from growing protest. Indeed, in October 1999, Monsanto publicly apologized for its behavior: "Our confidence in this technology (genetic engineering) and our enthusiasm for it has, I think, been widely seen, and understandably so, as condescension and indeed arrogance."[27] External support for the firm's strategy had eroded, and in late 1999, the company followed through on merger talks with pharmaceutical maker Pharmacia & Upjohn. This move effectively ended the Shapiro era of sustainability-driven corporate strategy at Monsanto.

Smart Mobs Versus Smart Globalization

How do we account for the rapid rise—and even more precipitous fall—of a major corporation such as Monsanto, which had done nothing wrong according to society's legal and regulatory institutions and had, in fact, transformed its business model to add value to its customers while reducing environmental impact?[28] Certainly, the emergent nature of biotechnology had something to do with the problems that Monsanto experienced. Indeed, an accelerating pace of technological change appears to be generating ever-faster cycles of creative destruction.[29]

Yet there is even something more fundamental at work here. The power of governments has eroded in the wake of globalization and the growth of transnational corporations with global supply chains that span several continents. NGOs and civil society groups have stepped into the breach, assuming the role of monitor and, in some cases, enforcer of social and environmental standards.[30] Today, for example, there are more than 50,000 international NGOs, compared to fewer than 20,000 only a decade ago.[31]

At the same time, the spread of the Internet and other information technologies has enabled not only these groups, but also millions of individuals, to communicate with each other in ways that were unimaginable even a decade ago.[32] Indeed, Internet-connected coalitions of NGOs and individuals—smart mobs—are now making it impossible for governments, corporations, or any large institution to operate in secrecy.[33] The varied claims of these smart mobs have created a dynamically complex business environment in which organizations find it difficult to determine what knowledge is relevant for managing strategic change; just ask senior managers at Shell, Nike, the World Trade Organization, or the World Economic Forum.

As might be expected, the past decade has been a combination of good news and bad news for Monsanto. In 2000, it merged with Pharmacia and Upjohn and was incorporated as a subsidiary called "Monsanto Ag Company." Later that year, its name was changed to "Monsanto Company" when a Separation Agreement transferred the operations, assets, and liabilities from Pharmacia to the subsidiary. But name and legal changes haven't deterred the company's critics.

Abroad, the company has been under fire in India (where a number of farmer suicides have been linked to Monsanto's high Bt cotton seed price), in South Africa (where farmers have experienced reduced maize yields due to variations in pollination), and in Europe (where labeling laws were passed in 2004 to appease anxiety over the possible risks of GM foods).

At home, legal battles haven't helped the company's image: Since the late 1990's, Monsanto has filed some 140 lawsuits against U.S. farmers for claims of seed patent infringement.[34] However, despite this continued public scrutiny, the company *has* created economic value with its GMOs. In 2009, it sold $7.3 billion in GMO products (versus competitor DuPont's $4 billion) and has seen sales increase at an annualized 18% rate over the past five years. And as a testament to its economic success, Monsanto was named Forbes' Company of the Year for 2009.[35] The question is: Has Monsanto really found its groove, or is it just a matter of time until the next stakeholder swarm takes the company down again?

As the Monsanto case illustrates, most companies still tend to focus management attention only on known, powerful, or "salient" stakeholders—those who can directly impact the firm.[36] Even recent efforts at "radical transparency," the complete and truthful disclosure of an organization's plans and activities, appear inadequate because they entail reporting only what has already been decided or, in fact, accomplished. Yet in a world of smart mobs, firms cannot manage stakeholders. Instead, swarms of stakeholders self-organize on the Internet in chaotic and unpredictable ways.

Groups at the "fringe" of a firm's stakeholder network can acquire an important voice in such swarms. To avoid the wrath of the smart mob, it has now become essential to proactively seek out the voices from the fringe that had previously been ignored. To survive and compete for the future, firms must harness these voices to identify creative new business models and opportunities. The tyranny of the smart mob can yield to a new form of what might be called "smart globalization:" growth via disruptive business models that address the social and environmental concerns of fringe stakeholders.[37]

Becoming Indigenous

The Monsanto experience holds an important lesson: If corporate sustainability strategies are narrowly construed, they will fall seriously short. It is not enough to develop revolutionary technology with the potential to leapfrog currently unsustainable methods. Antiglobalization demonstrators have made it apparent that if corporate expansion is seen to endanger local autonomy, it will encounter vigorous resistance. Multinationals seeking new growth strategies to satisfy shareholders increasingly hear concerns from many quarters about consumer monoculture, labor rights, and cultural hegemony. As long as multinational corporations persist in being outsiders—alien to both the cultures and the ecosystems within which they do business—it will be difficult for them to realize their full commercial, let alone social, potential.

Today corporations are being challenged to rethink global strategies in which one-size-fits-all products are produced for the global market using world-scale production facilities and supply chains. Even so-called locally responsive strategies are often little more than pre-existing corporate solutions tailored to "fit" local markets: Technologies are frequently transferred from the corporate lab and applied in unfamiliar cultural and environmental settings; unmet needs in new markets are identified through demographic (secondary) data. The result is stillborn products and inappropriate business models that fail to effectively address real needs. As GE CEO Jeff Immelt recently noted, existing large corporations will be pre-empted by more nimble local players from the developing world unless they learn how to innovate from the ground up—what he calls "reverse innovation."[38]

Indeed, in response to the failure of traditional development assistance and large corporations' inability to effectively address the needs of the poor, "social entrepreneurship" has burst onto the scene.[39] Rather than innovating from within existing institutions, this new breed of change agent seeks to launch new enterprises that address directly the problems of poverty, inequity, and unsustainability. Led by organizations such as Ashoka and Grameen Bank, there are now thousands of such fledgling enterprises around the world, each seeking to develop the new strategies and business models needed to catalyze social change.

The past decade has also seen the emergence of a new brand of financier—the "patient capitalist." Patient capitalists are not aid agencies or large corporations, but rather groups of investors and intermediaries focused on supporting small, high-impact entrepreneurs on the ground. This emerging sector includes groups such as the Acumen Fund, E+Co, Root Capital, Grassroots Business Fund, Intellicap, Microvest, New Ventures, and Technoserve. Taken together with the rapidly growing social investing, clean tech investing, and microfinance sectors, we are witnessing the birth of an entirely new industry—*impact investing.* Indeed, at the 2009 Clinton Global Initiative, the Global Impact Investing Network (GIIN) was announced as a vehicle for accelerating the development of this new financial sector.

Clearly then, the next challenge for large corporations will be learning how to become "indigenous" to the places in which they operate (see Exhibit 1.2). Doing so will require that they first widen the corporate bandwidth by admitting voices that have, up to now, been excluded; this means becoming radically *transactive* rather than just radically transparent. It will also entail the development of new "native" capabilities that enable a company to develop fully contextualized solutions to real problems in ways that respect local culture and natural diversity. When combined with multinational corporation's (MNC) ability to provide technical resources, investment, and global learning, native capability can enable companies to become truly embedded in the local context. It was with this realization that I embarked on a new professional challenge in 2003, having accepted the Samuel C. Johnson Chair in Sustainable Global Enterprise at Cornell University's Johnson School of Management. Our initiative at Cornell has spawned a new effort, the Base of the Pyramid Protocol, which seeks to develop a practical approach for becoming indigenous.

Exhibit 1.2
Indigenous Enterprise:
The Next Sustainability Challenge

Beyond Greening ⟶ Becoming Indigenous

Base of the Pyramid

• "Target" the unmet needs at the base of the ··········▶ pyramid

Radical Transactiveness

• Broaden the corporate bandwidth by engaging fringe stakeholders

Clean Technology

• "Deploy" the disruptive sustainable technologies ··········▶ of the future

Native Capability

• Coinvent contextualized solutions that leverage local knowledge

"Alien" ⟶ "Native"

Unilever's Indian subsidiary, Hindustan Lever Limited (recently changed to Hindustan Unilever Limited), provides an interesting glimpse of the development of native capabilities in its efforts to pioneer new markets among the rural poor.[40] Hindustan Lever Limited (HLL) requires all employees in India to spend six weeks living in rural villages, actively seeks local consumer insights and preferences as it develops new products, and sources raw materials almost exclusively from local producers. The company also created an R&D center in rural India focused specifically on technology and product development to serve the needs of the poor. HLL uses a wide variety of local partners to distribute its products and also supports the efforts of these partners to build local capabilities. In addition, HLL provides opportunities and training to local entrepreneurs and actively experiments with new types of distribution, such as selling via local product demonstrations and village street theaters.

By developing local understanding, building local capacity, and encouraging a creative and flexible market development process, HLL has been able to generate substantial revenue and profits from operating in low-income markets. Today more than half of HLL's revenue comes from customers at the base of the economic pyramid. Using the approach to product development, marketing, and distribution pioneered in rural India, Unilever has also been able to leverage a rapidly growing and profitable business focused on low-income markets in other parts of the developing world. Not surprisingly, Unilever has encountered challenges and bumps in the road in its journey to reach the base of the pyramid; these are discussed in later chapters. Importantly, however, through its strategy, the company has created tens of thousands of jobs, improved hygiene and quality of life for millions, and become a partner in development with the poor themselves.

The Road Ahead

To summarize, the greening initiatives of the late 1980s and early 1990s were revolutionary, if insufficient, steps: They repositioned social and environmental issues as profit-making opportunities rather than profit-spending obligations. More recent "beyond greening" strategies are even more significant: They hold the potential to reorient corporate portfolios around inherently clean technologies and create a more inclusive form of global capitalism that embraces the four billion poor at the base of the economic pyramid. If narrowly construed, however, such strategies still position MNCs as outsiders, alien to both the cultures and the ecosystems within which they do business. The challenge is for multinationals to move beyond "alien" strategies imposed from the outside to become truly indigenous to the places in which they operate. To do so will require companies to widen their corporate bandwidths and develop entirely new "native" capabilities that emphasize deep dialogue and local codevelopment. A more inclusive commerce thus requires innovation not just in technology, but also in business models, business processes, and mental frames.

Indeed, over the past ten years, "Clean Technology" and "Base of the Pyramid" strategies have exploded onto the scene, and social entrepreneurship has emerged as a new force for innovation. Each strategy provides important pieces to the sustainable enterprise puzzle: The former contributes "next generation" technologies with dramatically lower environmental impacts, and the latter creates innovative new ways to reach and include all of humanity in the capitalist dream. Yet each also comes with its own baggage and blind spots. Therefore, a crucial next step is to converge these strategies into what I call the "Green Leap." Such a strategic convergence recognizes that clean technologies are almost always "disruptive" in character. (That is, they threaten incumbents in current served markets at the top of the pyramid.) As a result, the base of the pyramid might be the best place to focus initial commercialization attention. At the same time, the Green Leap approach also recognizes that successful strategies must be cocreated with communities and local partners so as to ensure cultural embeddedness, rather than imposing technological solutions from the top down.[41]

Given the urgency of both the need and opportunity described here, Cornell's Center for Sustainable Global Enterprise launched the Cornell Global Forum on Sustainable Enterprise—an initiative to accelerate the rate of change toward this Great Convergence in the world. Indeed, nearly 100 of the world's leading practitioners on the forefront of the "Green Leap" participated as delegates to explore entrepreneurial strategies for the growth and scaling of ventures in the "convergence zone." The inaugural Global Forum was held in New York City, June 1–3, 2009, and the plan is to build this initiative into a growing global social network and an ongoing business movement.

Thus, as we enter the second decade of the new millennium, capitalism truly does stand at a crossroads. The old strategies of the industrial age are no longer viable. The time is now for the birth of a new, more inclusive form of commerce, one that lifts the entire human family while at the same time replenishing and restoring nature. The path to a sustainable world, however, will be anything but smooth. It will be a bumpy ride strewn with the remains of companies that variously dragged their feet, made promises they could not keep, bet on the wrong technology, collaborated with the wrong partners, and separated their social and business agendas. Only those companies with the right combination of vision, strategy, structure, capability, and audacity will succeed in what could be the most important transition period in the history of capitalism.

Overview of the Book

This chapter has provided a guided tour of the argument contained in this book. The book itself is divided into three parts. Part One, "Mapping the Terrain," provides the background and context for the chapters that follow; it describes the global situation and establishes the business case for pursuing strategies that aim to solve social and environmental problems. It also outlines the challenges and opportunities that remain to be addressed, particularly those that involve the development of new, more sustainable technologies and the needs of the four billion people who have been largely bypassed thus far by globalization. Part Two, "Beyond Greening," then develops the logic and content of these "beyond greening" strategies in more depth. Finally, in Part Three, "Becoming Indigenous," I suggest how corporations might begin to move beyond even these strategies for sustainability by learning to become more embedded in the local context. Learning to become indigenous, I argue, is the next strategic challenge on the road to building a sustainable global enterprise.

Chapter 2, "Worlds in Collision," places the global challenges associated with sustainability in the larger context. It seeks to cut through the complexity by providing a readily digestible framework for thinking about the current global situation, characterizing it as the collision of three economies or worlds—the money economy, the traditional economy, and nature's economy. Ultimately, the challenge is to develop a sustainable global economy: an economy that the planet is capable of supporting indefinitely, while simultaneously providing for the entire human community in a way that respects cultural, religious, and ethnic diversity. This chapter seeks to put this challenge into perspective and offers some thoughts about appropriate roles for companies.

Chapter 3, "The Sustainable Value Portfolio," closes out the first section of the book by developing a detailed framework for connecting the agendas of sustainability and value creation. Just as companies must succeed on many fronts in order to create shareholder value, so, too, must they master economic, social, and environmental challenges to achieve sustainability. These challenges affect virtually every aspect of a firm's strategy. There need not be a trade-off between stakeholder satisfaction and value creation. The chapter makes clear that although the biggest opportunity for the future lies in moving beyond greening, most companies still focus virtually all their attention on greening or (worse) mere compliance.

Part Two of this book develops the strategies that move beyond greening in greater depth. Chapter 4, "Clean Technology and Creative Destruction," articulates the strategic logic for pursuing leapfrog strategies to clean technology in ways that open exciting new growth markets but also often make the firms' existing technologies and products obsolete. The chapter also shows how the lens of whole-systems thinking can help to prioritize investment in the new technologies and capabilities that will be important to the future competitiveness of the enterprise.

Chapter 5, "Innovation from the Bottom-Up," demonstrates why the four billion people at the base of the world economic pyramid represent the most attractive early market for many of the most exciting new clean technologies. Because most such technologies are disruptive and will, therefore, be resisted by established markets, the vast underserved populations in shantytowns and rural villages offer the most promising places to incubate and grow the technologies of tomorrow. In the process, they also provide platforms for new growth industries that hold the potential to revolutionize markets at the top of the pyramid—and move us much more rapidly toward a sustainable world.

Chapter 6, "Raising the Base of the Pyramid," articulates some basic principles for successfully tapping into these emerging markets and shows how effective strategies will generate not only corporate growth and profits, but also local jobs, livelihoods, and solutions to social and environmental problems. By removing the constraints imposed on the poor, increasing their earning power, and creating new potential in poor communities, companies can identify and pursue previously invisible opportunities. To be successful in these new markets, therefore, companies must seek to actually *raise* the BoP through their commercial models, making the measurement and tracking of "triple bottom line" impacts increasingly important.

Finally, Part Three of this book critically evaluates early "beyond greening" experiences and offers some prescriptions for how to move toward a more indigenous and embedded form of commerce. Chapter 7, "Broadening the Corporate Bandwidth," first describes how the existing conceptions of "development" and "modernization" reflect a Western cultural bias and a preoccupation with simply raising income and GDP per capita. Together, these shortcomings significantly hinder efforts to imagine and build communities and markets at the base of the pyramid. To successfully serve the needs of the entire human community, therefore, corporations must broaden their bandwidth and expand their conception of the global economy to include the myriad other forms of economic activity beyond the formal economy. Radical transactiveness is the tool proposed to enable companies to hear the true voices of those who have been marginalized or ignored by globalization.

Chapter 8, "Developing Native Capability," then shows how to avoid the trap of simply "selling to the poor." Development at the base of the economic pyramid does not follow traditional patterns found in the developed world. Indeed, the chapter shows that success in this space means engaging in deep dialogue, coinventing solutions, starting small, building trust, and developing an ecosystem of local partners on the ground. To be successful, therefore, companies must consciously develop "next generation" skills needed to create mutual value in the BoP. Native capability thus enables global firms to move beyond the existing multinational model, with its emphasis on global supply chains, world scale, and centrally developed—and often alien—solutions.

Chapter 9, "Re-Embedding Innovation Strategy," builds on the previous chapter by first demonstrating why, at this point in history, it is so important that capitalism become reintegrated into society. Many BoP strategies that appear on the surface to be embedded can actually remain disconnected unless explicit attention is paid to the *process* by which they are created in the first place. The chapter thus focuses on a specific business process methodology for becoming embedded—the Base of the Pyramid Protocol. Through an analysis of selected applications of this approach over the past five years, the chapter lays out the key challenges to and important lessons for cocreating sustainable, locally embedded enterprises that also have the potential to scale.

The final chapter suggests how to go about actually "Building the Sustainable Global Enterprise." Most of the book focuses on *what* companies might do to pursue the sustainability path—the strategies, practices, and capabilities that are required. What is less clear is *how* to pursue this path, particularly within the context of large, incumbent, multinational corporations. This chapter therefore closes with some thoughts on what it will take for leaders and change agents to make this happen in the real world of budgets, bosses, quarterly earnings reports, discounted cash flow analysis, and the discipline of the investor community. Specifically, this chapter lays out a framework for building the organizational infrastructure for sustainability.

Notes

1. For example, Allen Kneese and Charles Schultze, *Pollution, Prices, and Public Policy* (Washington, D.C.: Brookings, 1975); and Robert Dorfman and Nancy Dorfman, *Economics of the Environment* (New York: W.W. Norton, 1972).

2. Ray Anderson, *Mid-Course Correction* (White River Junction, VT: Chelsea Green, 1998).

3. It is not my intention here to suggest that trade-offs do not exist between corporate economic and societal performance. Clearly, in some situations, command-and-control regulation is the only viable solution. In others, however, it is possible to internalize externalities or even supply public goods in a way that facilitates economic performance. The problem has been blind adherence to the belief that such "win-win" situations are generally not possible.

4. Again, my intention here is not to suggest that command-and-control regulation does not serve an important purpose. For laggards and criminals, there is no option. However, for those firms seeking to move beyond compliance, such regulation can sometimes limit degrees of freedom and slow the rate of innovation.

5. Milton Friedman, "The Social Responsibility of Business Is to Increase Its Profits," *The New York Times Magazine*, 13 September (1970): 32–33, 122–126.

6. My thanks to Paul Tebo at DuPont for this wonderful illustration.

7. Indeed, the Reagan administration in the United States was bent on reforming—or, better yet eliminating—these regulations.

8. Clyde Prestowitz, *Trading Places* (New York: Basic Books, 1988); Barry Bluestone and Bennett Harrison, *The Deindustrialization of America* (New York: Basic Books, 1982); and Ira Magaziner and Robert Reich, *Minding America's Business* (New York: Vintage Books, 1982).

9. Ironically, quality management was an American invention in the first place, but it was rejected in the 1950s by U.S. companies who were making too much money through high-volume, standardized mass production. Proponents such as Deming and Crosby found willing adopters, however, in the struggling companies of postwar Japan.

10. See, for example, Masaki Imai, *Kaizen: The Key to Japan's Competitive Success* (New York: Random House, 1986).

11. Excellent examples include Bill Shore, *The Cathedral Within* (New York: Random House, 1999); and Mark Albion, *Making a Life, Making a Living* (New York: Warner Books, 2000).

12. Michael Porter and Claas van der Linde, "Green and Competitive: Ending the Stalemate." *Harvard Business Review* (September/October 1995): 120–134; Stuart Hart and Gautam Ahuja, "Does It Pay to Be Green? An Empirical Examination of the Relationship Between Emission Reduction and Firm Performance," *Business Strategy and the Environment*, 5 (1996): 30–37; Michael Russo and Peter Fouts, "A Resource-Based Perspective on Corporate Environmental Performance and Profitability," *Academy of Management Journal*, 40(3) (1997): 534–559; Petra Christmann, "Effects of 'Best Practices' of Environmental Management on Cost Advantage: The Role of Complementary Assets," *Academy of Management Journal*, 43(4) (1998): 663–680; and Sanjay Sharma and Harrie Vredenburg, "Proactive Corporate Environmental Strategy and the Development of Competitively Valuable Organizational Capabilities." *Strategic Management Journal*, 19 (1998): 729–753.

13. For an excellent and in-depth treatment of greening as business opportunity and strategy, see Forest Reinhardt, *Down to Earth* (Cambridge, MA: Harvard Business School Press, 2000).

14. A. Marcus, D. Geffen, and K. Sexton, *Reinventing Environmental Regulation: Lessons from Project XL* (Washington, D.C.: Resources for the Future/Johns Hopkins University Press, 2002).

15. Andy King and Michael Lenox, "Exploring the Locus of Profitable Pollution Reduction," *Management Science*, 47(2) (2002): 289–299.

16. See Nigel Roome and Michael Hinnells, "Environmental Factors in the Management of New Product Development," *Business Strategy and the Environment*, 2(1) (1993): 12–27; and Ulrich Steger, "Managerial Issues in Closing the Loop," *Business Strategy and the Environment*, 5(4) (1996): 252–268.

17. William McDonough and Michael Braungart, *Cradle to Cradle* (New York: North Point Press, 2002).

18. Fiona Murray and Richard Vietor, *Xerox: Design for Environment*, (Boston: Harvard Business School Publishing, 1993).

19. Personal communication with Dave Buzzelli, Dow Chemical Company, 1996.

20. Paul Hawken, Amory Lovins, and Hunter Lovins, *Natural Capitalism* (New York: Little, Brown, and Company, 1999).

21. William McDonough and Michael Braungart, *Cradle to Cradle*.

22. This is referred to as the "triple bottom line." See John Elkington, *Cannibals with Forks* (Gabriola Island, B.C.: New Society Publishing, 1998).

23. Ron Pernick and Clint Wilder, *The Clean Tech Revolution* (New York: Collins, 2007).

24. Mark Johnson and Josh Suskewicz, "How to Jump-Start the Clean Tech Economy," *Harvard Business Review*, November 2009: 53–60.

25. C.K. Prahalad and Stuart Hart, "The Fortune at the Bottom of the Pyramid," *Strategy+Business*, 26 (2002): 54–67.

26. Erik Simanis and Stuart Hart, *Monsanto Company (A) and (B): Quest for Sustainability* (Washington, D.C.: World Resources Institute, 2000).

27. Robert Shapiro, *Address to Greenpeace's Annual Conference*, 1999.

28. This section is excerpted from Stuart Hart and Sanjay Sharma, "Engaging Fringe Stakeholders for Competitive Imagination," *Academy of Management Executive*, 18(1) (2004): 7–18.

29. Robert Foster and Sarah Kaplan, *Creative Destruction* (New York: Currency Books, 2001).

30. David Korten, *When Corporations Rule the World* (West Hartford, CT: Kumarian Press, 1995).

31. Christopher Gunn, *Third-Sector Development* (Ithaca, NY: Cornell University Press, 2004).

32. Ann Florini, ed., *The Third Force: The Rise of Transnational Civil Society* (Washington, D.C.: Carnegie Endowment for International Peace, 2000).

33. Howard Reingold, *Smart Mobs: The Next Social Revolution* (Cambridge, MA: Perseus Publishing, 2002).

34. www.Monsanto.com.

35. Robert Langreth and Matthew Herper, "The Planet versus Monsanto." *Forbes Magazine*, January 18, 2010.

36. R. K. Mitchell, B. R. Agle, and D. J. Wood, "Toward a Theory of Stakeholder Identification and Salience: Defining the Principle of Who and What Really Counts," *Academy of Management Review*, 22 (1997): 853–886.

37. See, for example, Anil Gupta and Eleanor Westney, eds., *Smart Globalization* (San Francisco: Jossey-Bass, 2003).

38. Jeffrey Immelt, Vijay Govindarajan, and Chris Trimble, "How GE Is Disrupting Itself," *Harvard Business Review*, October 2009.

39. See John Elkington and Pamela Hartigan, *The Power of Unreasonable People*, (Boston, MA: Harvard Business Press, 2008).

40. Brian Ellison, Dasha Moller, and Miguel Angel Rodriguez, *Hindustan Lever: Reinventing the Wheel* (Barcelona, Spain: IESE Business School, 2003).

41. Stuart Hart, "Taking the Green Leap," Cornell University, Working Paper, 2009.

2

Worlds in Collision

Nearly three decades ago, environmentalists made this simple but powerful observation. The total environmental impact (I) created by human activity on the planet is a function of three factors: population (P); affluence (A), which is a proxy for consumption; and technology (T), which is how wealth is created. The total environmental impact of human activity can thus be expressed as a formula: $I = P \times A \times T$.[1]

Achieving sustainability will require stabilizing and ultimately reducing the human impact on the planet. We can do that by drastically decreasing the human population, lowering the level of affluence (consumption), or fundamentally changing the technology used to create wealth—effectively moving technology (T) into the *denominator* of the formula. The first option, decreasing population, is not feasible short of draconian political measures unless we experience a major public health crisis that causes mass mortality (such as a global pandemic created by a new disease). Indeed, while the rate of population growth is slowing, it is not expected to stabilize until mid-century, at somewhere between eight billion and ten billion.

The second option, decreasing the level of affluence, is also not viable; it would only make sustainability harder to achieve because poverty and population growth go hand in hand. Demographers have long known that birth rates are inversely correlated with the standard of living and level of education. Thus, stabilizing the human population will require improving the education and economic standing of the world's four billion poor, particularly women of childbearing age.

Many believe that the problems of poverty can be addressed through the redistribution of existing wealth. Closer examination, however, reveals the impracticality of this approach: Even if all the assets of the world's seven million millionaires (totaling about $25 trillion), were divided among the world's four billion poorest, that would still give only about $6,000 to each in the form of a one-time payment—clearly not a viable solution to the problem.[2] In the end, elevating the standing of the poorest can be accomplished only by building capability and creating new wealth on a massive scale. Indeed, it might be necessary to increase world economic activity tenfold to support a population of eight billion to ten billion.

That leaves the third option: changing the technology used to create the goods and services that constitute the world's wealth. Although population and consumption are societal issues, technology is the business of business. If economic activity must increase tenfold over what it is today to support a population nearly double its current size, then technology will have to reduce its impact *twenty-fold* merely to keep the planet at its current levels of environmental impact. For example, to stabilize the climate we may have to reduce real carbon emissions by as much as 80 percent, while simultaneously growing the world economy by an order of magnitude. For those who believe that ecological disaster will somehow be averted, it must also be clear that, over the next decade or so, sustainable development will constitute one of the biggest opportunities in the history of commerce. And innovation will be the name of the game.

For example, bio- and nanotechnology create products and services at the molecular level, holding the potential to completely eliminate waste and pollution.[3] Biomimicry emulates nature's processes to create novel products and services without relying on brute force to hammer out goods from large stocks of virgin raw materials.[4] Wireless information technology and point of use water treatment are distributed in character, meaning that they can be applied in the most remote and small-scale settings imaginable, eliminating the need for centralized infrastructure and wireline distribution, both of which are environmentally destructive. Renewable energy and distributed generation are key to confronting carbon emissions and stabilizing the climate. Such technologies thus hold the potential to meet the needs of the billions of rural poor (who have thus far been largely ignored by global business) in a way that dramatically reduces or even reverses environmental impact.[5]

The Three Economies

It should be clear from this that transformation toward global sustainability will mean the creation of trillions of dollars in products, services, and technologies that barely exist today. Whereas yesterday's businesses were often oblivious to their negative impacts and today's responsible businesses strive to reduce their impact, tomorrow's businesses will learn to make a *positive* contribution. Increasingly, companies will be selling solutions to the world's social and environmental problems and doing so in a way that respects diversity and cultural differences. Envisioning tomorrow's businesses, therefore, requires that we gain a fuller appreciation of a complex set of global interdependencies.[6] In fact, the global economy is really composed of three different, overlapping economies: the money economy, the traditional economy, and nature's economy.

The Money Economy

The money economy is the familiar world of industry and commerce comprising both the *developed economies* and the so-called *emerging economies*. Roughly three billion people participate in the money economy, with less than a third of those living in the wealthy countries of the developed world. Those affluent people, however, account for more than 75 percent of the world's energy and resource consumption and also create the bulk of its industrial, toxic, and consumer waste.

Although industrialization has produced tremendous economic benefits, it has also generated significant pollution burdens and continues to consume virgin materials, resources, and fossil fuels at an increasing rate.[7] In fact, with its rapid growth in emerging economies such as China and India, industrial activity has reached the point that it might now be having irreversible effects on the global environment, including impact on climate, biodiversity, and ecosystem function.[8] The money economy thus leaves a large ecological footprint, defined as the amount of land and resources required to meet a typical consumer's needs. For example, with only about 4 percent of the world's population, the United States, the largest money economy, consumes in excess of one-quarter of the world's energy and materials and generates in excess of 25 percent of the world's greenhouse gas emissions.[9]

Despite such intense use of energy and materials, levels of conventional industrial pollutants have declined in the developed economies over the past 30 years. Three factors account for this seeming paradox: stringent environmental regulation, the greening of industry, and the relocation of the most polluting activities (such as commodity processing and heavy manufacturing) to the emerging market economies. Thus to some extent, the greening of the developed world has come at the expense of the environments in emerging economies. Given the much larger population base in those countries, their rapid industrialization could easily offset the environmental gains made in developed countries. Consider, for example, that China has now become the largest emitter of greenhouse gasses in the world.

With industrialization in emerging economies comes urbanization—people leaving the countryside in search of wage employment. Today, about one of every two people in the world lives in a city. By 2025, if trends continue, it will be two out of three.[10] Demographers predict that by that year, there will be more than 30 megacities with populations exceeding eight million and more than 500 cities with populations exceeding one million. Urbanization on this scale presents enormous infrastructural challenges because the major portion of such growth is in the form of urban slums, shantytowns, and squatter communities. Consider, for example, that over the next 10 years, given current trends, more than 300 million people in China alone will relocate from rural areas to cities. This is the equivalent of the entire current population of the United States moving to cities in the next decade.[11] Indeed, providing water, sanitation, power, and mobility to a billion new city dwellers in the coming decade could be the greatest infrastructure challenge humanity has ever faced.

Because industrialization has focused initially on commodities and heavy manufacturing, cities in many emerging economies suffer from oppressive levels of pollution. Acid rain is a growing problem, especially in places where coal combustion is unregulated. The World Bank estimates that by the end of 2010, there will be more than one billion motor vehicles in the world. Concentrated in cities, they will double current levels of energy use, smog precursors, and emissions of greenhouse gas. The result is that, although environmental conditions have improved on some dimensions in the developed world, rapid industrialization in emerging economies is a mounting problem, with an associated explosion of urban slums and shantytowns in the developing world. Another part of the price to be paid for a cleaner environment in the developed world has been large-scale outsourcing of manufacturing industries, with associated job loss and dislocation. Indeed, in the United States, only the wealthiest quintile has seen real income increase over the past two decades. For the vast majority of Americans, real income has actually decreased during this time.[12]

The Traditional Economy

The second economy is the *traditional economy*: the village-based way of life found in the rural parts of most developing countries. It is made up of nearly four billion people—more than half of humanity—mainly Indians, Chinese, and Africans who are subsistence-oriented and meet their basic needs directly from nature, while participating only sparingly in the cash or money economy. Demographers generally agree that the world's population, currently growing by about 100 million people per year, will continue to increase until it levels off at somewhere between eight billion and ten billion after midcentury. Developing countries will account for 90 percent of that growth, and most of it will occur in the traditional economy.[13]

Owing in part to the rapid expansion of the money economy, existence in the traditional economy is becoming increasingly precarious. Indigenous cultures, once able to live in a self-sufficient manner based upon the principles of community, frugality, and sufficiency, have been irreversibly changed by the introduction of cash and wage employment.[14] Structural adjustment, privatization, and free trade have accelerated this trend over the past two decades. Indeed, massive poverty appeared only when the spread of the money economy eroded community ties and traditional cultures. Extractive industries and the development of infrastructure have also, in many cases, degraded the ecosystems upon which the traditional economy depends.

Rural populations are driven further into poverty as they compete for natural resources often made scarce through expansion of the money economy. Women and children in rural areas spend most of their time searching for fuel wood and drawing and carrying water. Ironically, these conditions encourage high fertility rates because, in the short run, children help the family to garner needed resources. But in the long run, population growth in the traditional economy only reinforces a vicious cycle of resource depletion and poverty.

Indeed, survival pressures often force these rapidly growing rural populations into practices that cause damage to forests, soil, and water. When wood becomes scarce, people burn dung for fuel, one of the greatest—and least known—environmental hazards in the world today. Contaminated drinking water is an equally grave problem. The World Health Organization estimates that burning dung and drinking contaminated water together cause eight million deaths per year.

As it becomes more difficult to live off the land, millions of people migrate to already overcrowded cities in search of wage employment, often splitting up families and fracturing village communities. Increasingly, the young are migrating to foreign countries in search of wage jobs. It is estimated, for example, that repatriation of income by migrant Mexicans working in the United States has now approached $30 billion per year.[15]

Although some find employment in the formal sector, others fall prey to the vicissitudes of the criminal sector: prostitution, drug trafficking, and child labor. Most never find full-time wage employment and instead join the burgeoning informal or extralegal sector of the economy, working in literally millions of small, unregistered enterprises. In fact, Hernando de Soto, the well-known Peruvian economist, estimates that the informal sector accounts for 40–70 percent of total economic activity in developing countries. Because corrupt governments and bureaucratic red tape make official registration of small businesses by the poor prohibitively expensive, the informal economy has become the fastest-growing sector in much of the developing world.[16]

A growing number in the traditional economy have simply become permanent refugees. In China, for example, an estimated 120 million people roam from city to city, landless and jobless, driven from their villages by deforestation, soil erosion, droughts, and floods. Worldwide, the number of such environmental refugees from the traditional economy could be as high as 500 million people, and the figure is growing.[17]

The result is that, although humanity as a whole is clearly better off than it was a hundred years ago (even the poorest of the poor have better access to education, health care, and food than they did back then), inequity has grown, and the poor—particularly those in the traditional economy—generally face a bleak future. Either they can leave their families in search of potential wage employment in the cities, or they can remain to face an increasingly difficult economic and environmental situation at home. This combination of factors is particularly conducive to the rise of religious extremism. As we have seen, in the Muslim world, when a growing sense of humiliation is combined with widespread joblessness and hopelessness, the result can be terrorism.

Nature's Economy

The third economy is *nature's economy*, which consists of the natural systems and resources that support the money and the traditional economies. In fact, the money and traditional economies are actually *embedded* in nature's economy because the former could not exist without the latter. Nonrenewable resources such as oil, metals, and other minerals are finite. Renewable resources such as soils, fisheries, and forests will replenish themselves—as long as their use does not exceed critical thresholds.

Technological innovations have created substitutes for many commonly used nonrenewable resources; for example, optical fiber now replaces copper wire. And in the developed economies, demand for some nonrenewable materials might actually diminish in the decades ahead because of reuse and recycling. Ironically, the greatest threat to sustainable development today is depletion of the world's *renewable* resources.

Indeed, as we begin the second decade of the twenty-first century, the money and traditional economies are slowly destroying their own support system.[18] Increasing demands of the two economies are surpassing the sustainable yields of the ecosystems that underpin them. For example, one-third of the world's cropland is losing topsoil at a rate that is undermining its long-term productivity, fully half of the world's rangeland is overgrazed and deteriorating into desert, and the world's frontier forests have shrunk by about half since the dawn of agriculture and are continuing to shrink.

Water tables are falling under large expanses of the three leading food-producing countries—China, India, and the U.S. In China, for example, the combination of land clearing, overplowing, and over-grazing to satisfy rapidly expanding food demand is creating a dust bowl like the U.S. Dust Bowl of the 1930s, but on a much larger scale. Insufficient fresh water may prove to be the most vexing problem in the developing world over the next decade, as agricultural, commercial, and residential uses increase.[19]

Existing crop varieties are no longer responding to increased use of pesticides and fertilizer. As a consequence, per capita world production of both grain and meat peaked and began to decline during the 1980s.[20] Meanwhile, the world's 18 major oceanic fisheries have reached or exceeded their maximum sustainable yields. Some even believe that the great North Atlantic Cod fishery could go extinct within the decade.

There is now international scientific consensus that human activity, driven primarily by carbon emissions from fossil fuel use, is having a direct effect on the Earth's climate system.[21] The world has already warmed by more than a half a degree Celsius. For the past two decades, weather-related natural disasters have been on the increase, with property damage worldwide rising roughly 10 percent per year. In the year 2000, open water was discovered at the North Pole, stunning many in the scientific community.[22]

Even if we capped carbon emissions at today's rate, the stock of greenhouse gases in the atmosphere would still reach double the pre-industrial level by 2050—about 550 ppm CO_2. Unfortunately, emissions are accelerating, as fast-growing economies like China and

India demand more and more fossil energy. Without a serious global response, a 2-3 degree Celsius rise in global average temperature is a virtual certainty, bringing with it falling crop yields in many developing regions, rising sea levels threatening major world cities, irreversible damage to coral reefs and rainforests, rising intensity of storms, and an increasing risk of abrupt, large-scale shifts in the climate system.

By some estimates, humankind now uses more than 40 percent of the planet's net primary productivity, the total amount of the sun's energy fixed by green plants. As a result, loss of biodiversity is already a significant problem, especially in the tropics where the vast majority of life forms exist.[23] This biological impoverishment is the result of habitat destruction, pollution, climate alteration, and hunting. If, as projected, the human population increases from 6.7 billion to perhaps 8–9 billion over the next 30 years, we may ultimately drive the majority of remaining species into extinction, with potentially disastrous consequences. In short, nature's economy is under assault on a global scale.

Collision Course

The interdependence of the three economic spheres is plain. In fact, the three economies have become worlds in collision, creating the major social and environmental challenges facing the planet, but also opening up business opportunities of vast proportions (see Exhibit 2.1). Consider, for example, that the average American today consumes 17 times more than his or her Mexican counterpart and hundreds of times more than the average Ethiopian.[24] The levels of material and energy used in the United States require massive quantities of raw materials and commodities, sourced increasingly from the traditional economy and produced in emerging economies.

Exhibit 2.1
Worlds in Collision: The Business Opportunity

Source: Adapted from Hart, S. 1997. "Beyond greening: Strategies for a sustainable world." *Harvard Business Review*, January-February: 66-76.

In the traditional economy, massive infrastructure development projects (dams, irrigation projects, mining operations, highways, and power stations), often aided by agencies, banks, and corporations in the developed countries, have provided access to raw materials. Unfortunately, such development has often had devastating consequences for nature's economy and has tended to strengthen existing, often corrupt, political and economic elites, with little benefit to those in the traditional economy. At the same time, such development projects have contributed to a global glut of raw materials and, hence, to a long-term fall in commodity prices.

And as commodity prices have fallen relative to the prices of manufactured goods, the currencies of developing countries have weakened, and their terms of trade have become less favorable. Their purchasing power declines while their already substantial debt load becomes even larger. The net effect of this dynamic has been the transfer of vast amounts of wealth (an estimated $40 billion per year

since 1985) from developing to developed countries, producing a
vicious cycle of resource exploitation and pollution to service mounting debt.[25] Some commodities, however, such as oil are coming into
increasingly short supply due to the growing energy demands of
emerging economies (like China and India) and the continued consumption of oil by the United States. Unfortunately, the long-term
trend of rising oil prices, combined with the oil price spike in 2008
have had the tragic side-effect of bolstering some of the world's worst
dictatorships and enriching the very countries that foment religious
extremism and intolerance.[26]

In the past, ignorance and isolation meant that those in the traditional and emerging economies were largely unaware of their plight.
Today, however, the digital revolution is bringing information—and
ideas—to growing numbers of the world's poor. Such knowledge is
potentially empowering, as we will see, creating the potential to
reform corrupt regimes, solve environmental problems, and spur
more equitable forms of development.[27] However, the global information economy also possesses a dark side: It facilitates the efforts of
nihilists, anarchists, terrorists, and others bent on derailing the evolution of a planetary civilization.

New Lenses on the Global Market

The growing interdependence among the three economies has
defined the major social and environmental challenges of our time.
But as Exhibit 2.1 also makes clear, the worlds in collision have also
created new opportunities for those companies with the capacity to
understand and address these challenges. Indeed, there are business
opportunities in each of the three economies, as well as at the inter-
section points. In the money economy, there is significant need for
lower material and energy consumption and the development of

clean products and technologies. In the traditional economy, the ability to foster village-based businesses to understand and serve the needs of those at the base of the economic pyramid is of paramount importance. In nature's economy, ensuring sustainable use of natural capital offers significant opportunities for the future. The collision points are also pregnant with opportunity: Reducing waste and pollution, replenishing depleted resources, and building the skills of the poor and the dispossessed are all crucial for achieving a more sustainable world. They also represent significant business opportunities.

As my colleague Mark Milstein and I have argued, however, managers, particularly in multinational corporations, are more accustomed to viewing the global market as a single monolithic entity.[28] They focus almost exclusively on the money economy and customers who have achieved a certain level of affluence. They consider markets to be of value only to the extent that consumers have purchasing power comparable to that found in the United States, Western Europe, or Japan. Throughout human history, however, wherever there have been people, there have been markets. Indeed, markets are ubiquitous—they are not unique to the wealthy.[29] Thus, within any country or region, even the United States, there are *three* types of markets: developed, emerging, and traditional. The developed and emerging markets make up the money economy; traditional markets correspond to the traditional economy. All three are embedded in nature's economy. Not surprisingly, the sustainability challenges— and business opportunities—associated with each are dramatically different (see Exhibit 2.2).

In the developed, or consumer, market, about one billion global customers have the purchasing power to afford virtually anything they want. A global supply chain and well-developed infrastructure allow for the rapid production and distribution of products and services, and consumption occurs at high levels. In the emerging market (about two billion people), rapid industrialization and urban migration are increasing demand for basic products and services.

However, inadequate infrastructure and distribution hamper the ability of companies to effectively serve this rapidly growing, largely urban market. Finally, in the traditional market, consisting of more than half of humanity, nearly four billion people have been adversely affected by globalization, ignored by the world of commerce, and victimized by corruption. In most rural areas, there is virtually no infrastructure, credit and collateral are lacking, and legal protections are nonexistent; few companies, as a result, have dared to invest in what they perceive as a risky and potentially dangerous long-term proposition.

Exhibit 2.2
Major Challenges to Sustainability

	Pollution	Depletion	Poverty
Developed Markets	• greenhouse gases • use of toxic materials • contaminated sites	• scarcity of materials • insufficient reuse and recycling	• urban and minority unemployment
Emerging Markets	• industrial emissions • contaminated water • lack of sewage treatment	• overexploitation of renewable resources • overuse of water for irrigation	• migration to cities • lack of skilled workers • income inequality
Traditional Markets	• dung and wood burning • lack of sanitation • ecosystem destruction due to development	• deforestation • overgrazing • soil loss	• population growth • low status of women • dislocation

Source: Adapted from Hart, S. 1997. "Beyond greening: Strategies for a sustainable world." *Harvard Business Review*, January-February: 66-76.

Given their distinctive characters, each market requires a different strategy to achieve a more sustainable form of development. To succeed in the developed (consumer) market, managers must focus on reducing the ecological footprint of their firms by reinventing products and processes. To meet the long-term needs of the emerging market, managers must avoid the collision between rapidly growing demand for products and the physical basis for supply or waste disposal. Finally, in the traditional market, managers must recognize the opportunity presented by a massive group of potential customers whose real needs remain poorly served. Each of these is addressed in more detail in the rest of the chapter.

Developed Markets: Reducing Corporate Footprint

In the consumer economy, many of the resource- and energy-intensive industries—chemicals, automobiles, energy, and mining, to name a few—leave very large corporate footprints. Product systems with large footprints are usually based on mature technologies. As technologies mature, they reach a point at which even large additional investments in technical development yield only small gains in performance. The combination of large footprint and technological maturity creates openings for innovation. To identify sustainability-related opportunities in the developed (consumer) economy, managers should therefore ask these questions:

- Are most of our technological advances incremental instead of breakthrough?
- Does our core technology hold us back from making significant reductions in footprint?
- Where can we remove material content from our products?
- How can our service content be dramatically increased?
- Can our waste be utilized productively in other processes?

Former DuPont CEO Chad Holliday once commented: "The objective for our industry ought to be sustainable growth. In the [twenty-first] century, we are going to have to find ways to create value while decreasing our environmental footprint."[30] In the late 1990s, I worked with DuPont Vice President Paul Tebo and others to create a tool for analyzing the corporate footprint by comparing the total pounds of materials consumed per annum in each business with shareholder value added (SVA) per pound. The analysis highlighted three distinct groups of businesses for DuPont (see Exhibit 2.3).

Exhibit 2.3
Reducing the Corporate Footprint at DuPont

Source: Hart, S. and Milstein, M. 1999. "Global sustainability and the creative destruction of industries." *Sloan Management Review*, 41(1): 23-33.

Small-footprint businesses, those using fewer materials and having a high SVA per pound, were seen as "differentiated" businesses; these included photopolymers, electronic materials, agricultural biotech, Lycra™, Tyvek™, Corian™, and auto finishes. Businesses with medium footprints and medium SVA per pound—Nylon and Polyester—were seen as "foundation" enterprises because they represented the traditional core of the company's business. Businesses with large footprints and low SVA per pound, such as the petroleum subsidiary Conoco, represented the company's least desired enterprises. DuPont sees the high earnings, cash flow, and intellectual content (R&D/capital) of the differentiated businesses as the models for the future. As a result, over the past few years, large-footprint businesses such as Conoco and even foundation (core) enterprises such as

Nylon and Polyester have been divested or spun off in an effort to fuel future growth in the differentiated businesses and to reduce corporate footprint.

Collins & Aikman Floorcovering (now part of the Tandus Group) is another company that has premised its entire competitive strategy on footprint reduction. In the mid-1990s, the company became the first commercial carpet manufacturer in the world to convert old carpet and post-industrial PVC waste into carpet backing for a new product line.[31] Called ER3 (which stands for Environmentally Redesigned, Restructured, and Reused), this product actually possesses superior functionality (it is more stable and "cushy" than conventional backing made from virgin material) and is cheaper to produce (at least in part because much of the raw material is available in the form of "waste" from customer sites). The combination of lower cost and higher functionality fueled the company's double-digit growth in both revenue and profit in an industry that was growing at only about 4 percent per year during the late 1990s and early 2000s. Today the company no longer sells a virgin product in the carpet tile segment. Tandus is also seeking to move beyond PVC with its new PVB-based carpet product (dubbed "ethos") made from recycled safety glass polymer. Appropriately, the company's motto is "Mining buildings rather than resources."

Finally, Wisconsin-based SC Johnson Company, makers of Raid™, Glade™, and Windex™, among other household brands, has dramatically reduced its footprint—and realized substantial savings in the process.[32] As part of its campaign to reduce fossil fuel use and greenhouse gas emissions, the company partnered with a nearby landfill operator to access its methane potential. The company invested in a gas turbine unit and piped the methane gas from the nearby landfill to help power its Waxdale manufacturing facility, one of the company's major production sites. The 3200-kilowatt turbine with cogeneration capability (which utilizes the waste heat to make process steam) cut fossil fuel use in half at the facility while simultaneously saving the company more than $2 million per year. A second turbine (which uses a mixture of landfill and natural gas), combined with the first now supplies 100 percent of the average daily power needs at Waxdale. These two landfill gas projects alone have enabled the company to more than meet its aggressive goals for reduction in greenhouse gas emissions worldwide through 2005, a total of more than 50,000 tons of carbon dioxide per year.

Emerging Markets: Avoiding the Collision

Rapid urbanization and industrialization, together with increasing demand for products and services, are placing intense pressure on ecological and social systems in the emerging economies of the developing world. Technologies that previously fueled the development of the consumer market will be inadequate for meeting those future demands without exceeding nature's capacity for replenishment. Avoiding a collision between rapidly growing demand and a diminishing stock of material supply will, therefore, be the biggest challenge in emerging markets. To identify sustainability-related opportunities in emerging markets, managers should ask these questions:

- Is it environmentally feasible to triple or quadruple the size of our industry?
- What factors prevent our industry from achieving such growth?
- Can we meet growing consumer needs without depleting the natural systems on which we depend?
- Can we use emerging markets to develop "leapfrog" technologies?
- How can we meet growing needs without exacerbating urban problems?

More than two billion people have joined the ranks of the emerging market during the past 30 years—part of the emerging "flat world" phenomenon described by Tom Friedman in his book, *The*

World Is Flat (Farrar, Straus, and Giroux, 2005). Paradoxically, this rapid "development" has resulted in burgeoning shantytowns, mountains of garbage, dead rivers, noxious air, and cesspools of toxic waste. These problems seriously jeopardize the public health and future growth prospects in many developing countries. Nonetheless, demand for products and services continues to rise.

In meeting growing demand, firms have replicated the strategies, products, and processes that were successful in the developed, consumer market. Given the scale and speed of development in the emerging market, however, a repeat performance of the consumer market is almost certain to lead to environmental and social meltdown. For example, if China came to consume oil at the current U.S. rate, it would need more than 80 million barrels per day—nearly as much as the *world* now consumes.[33] Sustainable development in the emerging market will, therefore, depend on firms' ability to meet rapidly growing demands without repeating the wasteful, outdated practices used in the consumer economy.

Because of the high rate of manufacturing growth in the emerging market, the capital stock in manufacturing is being rapidly replaced. In Asia, for example, the equipment stock of manufacturing plants doubles every six years.[34] Thus, firms can leapfrog to clean (closed-loop, zero-discharge) manufacturing technologies much more easily in the emerging market than in the developed market, where growth in demand is much slower. Technological leapfrogging will be essential if economic development is to occur at the rates required to lift people out of poverty. Indeed, as Tom Friedman has astutely observed, there is good reason that "Red" China is rapidly transforming into "Green" China.[35]

Achieving sustainability in the emerging market is particularly challenging for industries that depend on renewable resources. For example, the global forest products industry must meet worldwide demand that is forecasted to grow 1 to 2 percent per year for the next several decades, even as the overall global supply of available timber declines. The industry, built primarily on the rapid harvesting of standing native forests, must find an alternative approach. Recognizing the collision course they are on, some companies have embarked on intensive agroforestry practices to ensure increased fiber supplies. Through high-yield practices, which rely on selective breeding, cloning, and careful site management, companies such as Aracruz Celulose have realized high returns while minimizing and containing environmental impact by producing high-quality wood and fiber on fewer continuously regenerated acres.

The Chinese textile company, Redbud, has also devised a strategy to avoid the collision course in sourcing fiber.[36] Rather than continuing to produce fabrics and other materials exclusively from cotton, which requires massive amounts of pesticides and water to grow, the company has developed a line of new materials made from jute, a rugged plant that can be grown on depleted soils and requires very little water and virtually no chemicals to grow. The company works with poor farmers to reclaim wastelands by planting specially developed varieties of jute, which they then purchase for use in textile production. After a few years of growing jute, depleted soils are replenished, and farmers can then also begin to plant other crops like rice, significantly increasing their income, supplementing the food supply, and ensuring a sustainable source of fiber for the company as well.

Indeed, the agricultural industry must supply the world's burgeoning population with food while water resources become more scarce, croplands less arable, climate less stable, and crops more homogenized and susceptible to mass failure. The existing model of commercial agriculture, heavily dependent on the intensive use of water, chemical pesticides, and fertilizers, is experiencing diminishing returns. Despite its controversial nature, the use of biotechnology to design crops that are resistant to pests, require less water and fertilizer, and are more nutritious may hold one of the keys to sustainable agriculture in the emerging markets.[37]

Fingerlakes Aquaculture, a start-up company in Upstate New York, has based its entire strategy on avoiding the collision course.[38] Overfishing, combined with pressures from development and pollution, has strained wild fish stocks, leading to irregular supply, higher prices, and decreasing quality. As the limits of rangelands and fisheries are reached, there are only three options for increasing the supply of protein in the world: improve the efficiency of grain conversion into animal protein; shift from the less efficient forms of conversion, such as beef or pork, to more efficient ones, such as farmed fish; or rely on ruminants to convert more roughage into either meat or milk.[39]

Fingerlakes Aquaculture incorporates the first two of these options directly into its strategy. The company has perfected a proprietary water filtration and recirculation technology that enables it to cost-effectively grow fish in a controlled indoor setting, which avoids the pollution problems associated with pond-based fish-farming operations. The company has focused its attention on the production of tilapia, a fish species from the tropics with a firm, mild-tasting white meat reminiscent of cod, haddock, flounder, and other species that are under stress in the wild. Given their omnivorous nature, tilapia can be raised on an inexpensive grain-fed diet (soymeal). Tilapia are also highly efficient converters of grain to protein: 1.2 pounds of feed produce a pound of fish (compare this to beef, which requires 6 pounds of feed for every pound of meat). Furthermore, the company believes that it can produce tilapia on a cost per pound basis competitive with the cost of Central and South American producers. If successful, this approach could revolutionize the industry—and help to reinvent the protein economy in the process.

Traditional Markets: Serving Real Needs

Unlike either the developed or the emerging markets, the traditional market is dominated by the poverty and isolation found in the rural villages of the developing world, particularly those ravaged by resource extraction, cultural disruption, and attendant population growth. As we have seen, nearly four billion people at the base of the economic pyramid are subsistence-oriented and satisfy their basic needs directly from nature: They participate only sparingly in the money or formal economy. Demographers generally agree that as the world's population approaches eight billion to ten billion during the next few decades, most of the growth will occur in the traditional markets. Because vibrant small communities in rural areas stem the pressures for mass migration and accompanying social, political, and environmental breakdown, focusing on the traditional market is both the key to sustainable development and an unprecedented business opportunity for visionary firms. Managers can identify sustainability-related opportunities in the traditional market by asking these questions:

- Can our existing products and services be modified to meet the needs of the poor?
- Can we apply state-of-the-art sustainable technology to meet the needs of those at the base of the economic pyramid?
- Have we overlooked market vacuums, where needs are fundamentally unmet?
- Are we blinded by our current business model?
- Can we build a customer base that can become more substantial over time?

Companies need to focus on developing technologies, products, and services geared specifically to the needs of those in the traditional market. Managers must understand four factors:

- Deep dialogue and mutual learning are necessary if products and services are to meet real needs and improve lives.
- Significant profits can be realized by meeting the needs of the poor and disenfranchised. Conventional wisdom holds that the poor do not make good customers, given their lack of money and education.
- Meeting those needs offers the opportunity to apply state-of-the-art (sustainable) technology in fundamentally new and disruptive ways. Simply transplanting business models from the consumer or even emerging markets will not work.
- Business models for the traditional market must leverage local talent, create livelihood opportunities, and build capacity in the local community.

Companies that recognize the business opportunity of the traditional market clearly understand and cater to the real needs of the poor but do so in a way that builds local capacity and self-esteem. For example, more than one billion people worldwide still lack access to safe drinking water. Another 2.4 billion have no access to proper sanitation. As a result, approximately four billion cases of diarrheal illness associated with contaminated water cause nearly three million deaths annually, mostly among poor children under the age of five.[40] This is the equivalent of 20 loaded jumbo jets plunging to Earth each day—an unprecedented human tragedy. For the traditional and emerging markets, then, access to clean water and improved sanitation are crucial elements of development and poverty alleviation. No one argues this point. The question is how to make the availability of clean water a reality.

Centralized water treatment and distribution systems are expensive and take years to complete. With population growing most rapidly in poor rural areas, providing water to the masses through infrastructure becomes increasingly untenable. Fortunately, other approaches exist: In-home (point-of-use) treatment of water allows individuals to control their own drinking water supply. Several companies have begun to focus commercial attention on this exciting—

and sorely needed—opportunity. For example, Procter & Gamble has pioneered the development of a combined chemical treatment technology called *PuR*. This technology, which is equivalent to a water treatment plant in an affordable sachet packet, has been field tested in Nicaragua and the Philippines by the U.S. Centers for Disease Control. The product, specifically designed for the low-income market, has demonstrated significant reductions in diarrheal disease, but the company has struggled to wrap a successful business model around it—evidence of how important it is to co-create businesses with the BoP communities to be served. After several unsuccessful commercialization attempts, PuR became a not-for-profit initiative of the company's philanthropic arm under the name "Children's Safe Drinking Water Program" and has been used extensively to aid disaster relief victims.

WaterHealth International (WHI) is another company that has developed a potentially viable commercial model for distributed water purification.[41] Using a proprietary ultraviolet light technology to treat and disinfect water, WHI sells their systems to small villages (with populations of 3,000 to 5,000) in rural India beyond the reach of centralized water treatment. A WaterHealth Center can provide a community of 7,000 people with up to 20 liters of safe, affordable drinking water per person per day for just 3 rupees (about US $0.06). ICICI Bank finances the purchase of these systems by the villages, and WHI has worked with the Naandi Foundation and other NGOs to establish a "turn-key" micro-utility model run by local entrepreneurs. User fees generated from the sale of water are split by the village and WHI until the loan is paid off (about eight years). At that point, the village water utility is completely owned and operated by the local players.

Given WHI's potential, Dow Venture Capital has invested an additional $7 million to enable the company to more rapidly increase its global presence and demonstrate the scalability of its business model. As of 2009, WHI had installed more than 250 village systems and serve more than 380,000 customers annually. As the business scales up, however, it has encountered new problems: Because WHI supplies water from a central village facility, transportation to and storage of water in the home present new risks of water recontamination. Addressing this "last mile" problem opens up a whole new domain for creative solutions and new business models. (See Chapter 9 for a case study on The Water Initiative, an innovative point-of-use drinking water company.)

Traditional markets thus challenge our assumptions about business and poverty. Companies that look at developing countries as dumping grounds for outdated technologies or dirty manufacturing facilities fail to identify market vacuums with minimal competition. Increasing numbers of telecommunication companies, for example, have recognized the benefit of avoiding prohibitively expensive landlines. Through satellite, cellular, and radio systems, they are reaching previously unserved rural areas with telecommunications comparable to those found in urban areas. Such wireless systems erase differences among regions and nations in their access to information, allowing smaller-scale economic development that reduces pressures on people to migrate to cities.

Firms succeed in the traditional market because their managers recognize the importance of developing markets and building future customer bases. Daewoo, for example, realizing the limits of competing head-on with U.S., Japanese, and European firms in overcrowded, technology-intensive markets in the consumer market, is relocating much of its industrial base to Burma, Iran, Uzbekistan, Russia, China, Vietnam, Brazil, and Tatarstan, where it can make long-term investments in economic infrastructure. Daewoo enters poor regions as a long-term development partner, offering skills in infrastructure planning, environmental management, and manufacturing. When hard currency is scarce, the company accepts barter. Uzbekistan, for example, is paying for its half of a joint venture factory with cotton, which Daewoo's trading arm sells on the world

market. By using first mover advantage to build relationships, Daewoo is implementing a long-range growth strategy that caters to the
world's poorest regions.

The Value Proposition

Recognizing global sustainability as a catalyst for new business
development will prove increasingly important to corporate survival
in the twenty-first century—the proverbial crossroads to the future.
Understanding the broad global dynamics associated with the three
economies outlined in this chapter is an important first step in identifying potentially innovative new strategies. To capture sustainable
opportunities, however, managers must rethink their prevailing views
about strategy, technology, and markets. Attention focused through
the three lenses—developed, emerging, and traditional markets—
should help in this regard.

Along with having such awareness and foresight, however, it is
crucial to understand how sustainability-related business strategies
can benefit a firm's economic and competitive position. Indeed,
unless they see an avenue for value creation, it is unlikely that senior
managers will commit the resources necessary to pursue such strategies. In the next chapter, a framework is developed showing how the
challenges associated with global sustainability can help to identify
distinctive strategies that contribute to a more sustainable world
while simultaneously driving shareholder value.

Notes

1. See, for example, Paul Ehrlich, *The Population Bomb* (New York: Ballantine,
   1968).

2. This example is borrowed from John McMillan, *Reinventing the Bazaar* (New
   York: W.W. Norton, 2002).

3. Erik Drexler, *Engines of Creation* (Garden City, NY: Anchor Press, 1986).

4. See Janine Benyus, *Biomimicry: Innovation Inspired by Nature* (New York: Morrow, 1997).

5. Diane Coyle, *Paradoxes of Prosperity* (New York: Texere Publishing, 2001).

6. This section draws from Stuart Hart, "Beyond Greening: Strategies for a Sustainable World," *Harvard Business Review*, 75(1) (1997): 66–76.

7. See Paul Hawken, Amory Lovins, and Hunter Lovins, *Natural Capitalism: Creating the Next Industrial Revolution* (Boston: Little Brown & Company, 1999).

8. G. Daily, *Nature's Services* (Washington, D.C.: Island Press, 1997); Millennium Ecosystem Assessment, *Ecosystems and Human Wellbeing* (Washington, D.C.: World Resources Institute, 2005).

9. Mathis Wackernagel and William Rees, *Our Ecological Footprint* (Gabriola Island, B.C.: New Society Publishers, 1996).

10. Allen Hammond, *Which World?* (Washington, D.C.: Island Press, 1998).

11. Robert Neuwirth, *Shadow Cities: A Billion Squatters, A New Urban World* (New York: Routledge, 2005).

12. Ibid.

13. Donella Meadows, Dennis Meadows, and Jorgen Randers, *Beyond the Limits* (Post Mills, VT: Chelsea Green Publishing, 1992).

14. See Helena Norberg-Hodge, *Ancient Futures* (San Francisco: Sierra Club Books, 1991), for a compelling description of how an ancient culture in the Himalayas (Ladakh) was disrupted fundamentally by the forces of "development."

15. Personal communication, Professor Nicholas Guttierez, EGADE Business School, Tec de Monterrey, Mexico.

16. Hernando De Soto, *The Mystery of Capital* (New York: Basic Books, 2000).

17. Allen Hammond, *Which World?*

18. This section is drawn from Lester Brown, *Eco-Economy* (New York: W.W. Norton, 2001). See also the Millenium Ecosystem Assessment, *Ecosystems and Human Wellbeing*.

19. Jennifer Reck and Stuart Hart, *Water for the Masses* (Chapel Hill, NC: Center for Sustainable Enterprise, 2004).

20. Erik Simanis and Stuart Hart, *Monsanto Company (A): Quest for Sustainability* (Washington, D.C.: World Resources Institute, 2000).

21. Stern Report, *The Economics of Climate Change* (Cambridge: Cambridge University Press, 2006); National Research Council, *Our Common Journey* (Washington, D.C.: National Academy Press, 1999).

22. Lester Brown, *Eco-Economy*.

23. National Research Council, *Our Common Journey*.

24. Peter Menzel, *Material World: A Global Family Portrait* (San Francisco: Sierra Club Books, 1999).

25. Wouter Van Dieren, *Taking Nature into Account* (New York: Springer-Verlag, 1995).

26. Tom Friedman, *Hot, Flat, and Crowded* (New York: Farrar, Straus, and Giroux, 2008).

27. Diane Coyle, *Paradoxes of Prosperity*.

28. This section is excerpted from Stuart Hart and Mark Milstein, "Global Sustainability and the Creative Destruction of Industries," *Sloan Management Review*, 41(1) (1999): 23–33.

29. John McMillan, *Reinventing the Bazaar*.

30. Remarks by Chad Holliday, Chemical Industry Conference, Washington, D.C., November 9, 1998.

31. Mark Milstein, Stuart Hart, and John Buffington, *Tandus 2010: Race to Sustainability (A)*, William Davidson Institute, www.globalens.com, 2009.

32. This description is based upon a presentation made by Scott Johnson of SC Johnson in April 2004 at Cornell's Society of Engineering Conference.

33. Lester Brown, *Eco-Economy*.

34. U.S. Asia Environmental Partnership, personal communication, April 1998.

35. Tom Friedman, *Hot, Flat and Crowded*.

36. Personal communication with Frank Liu, CEO of Redbud, December 2009.

37. Erik Simanis and Stuart Hart, *Monsanto Company (A): Quest for Sustainability*.

38. Personal communication with Paul Sellow, CEO of Fingerlakes Aquaculture, May 2004.

39. Lester Brown, *Eco-Economy*.

40. Jennifer Reck and Stuart Hart, *Water for the Masses*.

41. My thanks to Tralance Addy and Mark Edwards for their information about WaterHealth International.

3

The Sustainable Value Portfolio

Some years ago, William Ruckelshaus, former EPA administrator and CEO of Browning Ferris, made the following statement: "Sustainability is as foreign a concept to managers in capitalist societies as profits are to managers in the former Soviet Union." While intended to be at least partially tongue-in-cheek, I believe that this statement showed considerable insight. There can be little doubt that sustainability is one of the most frequently used but least understood terms of our time; it is right up there with the term strategy when it comes to overuse and lack of meaning. (I say this as a professor of both strategy and sustainability!) Indeed, it is with some regularity that I find myself engaged in a discussion with someone about sustainability, only to discover several minutes into the conversation that she is talking about something completely different from me.

This lack of precision in definition is often used by businesspeople to dismiss sustainability from consideration. I would be a rich man if I only had a nickel for every time I heard a manager say something like: "Until you can give me a clear definition of 'sustainability,' I'm not inclined to spend much time focusing on it in my business." To be sure, sustainability's ambiguous and multidimensional nature can be maddening at times, yet it is also one of its greatest attractions from a business perspective. A smart strategist gravitates toward ill-defined and ambiguous opportunities. That is because once everything has been defined and reduced to standard operating procedure, there is no money left to be made.

Yet, it is not possible to design a coherent strategy (there is that term again) without some broad guideposts, conceptual categories, and frameworks to work with. Without some broad agreement on constructs, we end up talking past each other. Accordingly, this chapter provides a business-oriented way of thinking about sustainability that organizes and rationalizes the many terms, issues, and communities of practice that are floating around out there. More important, the chapter seeks to connect these key dimensions of sustainability to drivers of shareholder value and financial performance. To this end, my colleague Mark Milstein and I have developed a sustainable value framework that directly links the societal challenges of global sustainability to the creation of shareholder value by the firm.[1] The framework shows how the global challenges associated with sustainability, viewed through the appropriate set of business lenses, can help to identify strategies and practices that contribute to a more sustainable world while simultaneously driving shareholder value. We define this "win-win" approach as the creation of sustainable value by the firm.

Sustainability Buzzwords

As the first two chapters suggest, the terms sustainability and sustainable enterprise encompass a mind-numbing range of ideas, issues, concepts, and practices. In an effort to map the conceptual territory, Mark Milstein and I brainstormed a lengthy (but I'm sure not exhaustive) list of buzzwords from the domain of sustainability. These are listed, in no particular order, in Exhibit 3.1. A quick scan of the exhibit will, no doubt, produce some familiar monikers (such as corporate social responsibility), but also some mysterious acronyms and labels (such as B24B). That is because the sustainability space is occupied by distinct and sometimes competing tribes of advocates, practitioners, and theoreticians. Further examination of the list will no doubt begin to produce frustration. You might be asking yourself, "How do I organize all of this stuff in any way that is useful or meaningful from a business point of view?"

Exhibit 3.1
Sustainability Buzzwords

- Environmental Management
- Corporate Social Responsibility
- Greening
- Industrial Ecology
- Stakeholder Management
- Life-Cycle Management
- Pollution Prevention (P ^{2})
- Sustainable Development
- Design for Environment (DfE)
- Green Design
- Urban Reinvestment
- Brownfield Redevelopment
- ISO 14001
- Waste Reduction
- Closed Loops
- Resource Productivity
- Sustainable Technology
- Radical Transactiveness
- Systems Thinking
- Corporate Governance

- Clean Technology
- Eco-Efficiency
- Eco-Effectiveness
- Biomimicry
- Triple Bottom Line
- Inclusive Capitalism
- Base of the Pyramid
- Pro-Poor Business
- Corporate Citizenship
- Voluntary Regulation
- Social Entrepreneurship
- Full Cost Accounting
- Environmental Mgmt Systems
- Risk Management
- Leapfrog Technology
- Cradle to Cradle
- Restorative Technology
- B24B
- Take-Back
- Transparency

Fortunately, we were able to import one of the most important analytical tools from the field of strategy to help make sense of this blooming, buzzing confusion: the 2 x 2 matrix. As anyone who has attended business school knows, the 2 x 2 matrix is what defines the field of strategy! In all seriousness, two dimensions combined in a framework help to provide conceptual clarity and enable one to cluster related sustainability buzzwords and practices. The framework also helps to organize the parameters that are important to firm performance and the creation of shareholder value. (See Exhibit 3.2 in the next section.)

Elements of Shareholder Value

The vertical axis of Exhibit 3.2 reflects the firm's need to manage today's business while simultaneously creating tomorrow's technology and markets. This dimension captures the tension created by the need to realize short-term results while simultaneously fulfilling expectations for future growth. The horizontal axis reflects the firm's need to nurture and protect internal organizational skills, technologies, and capabilities while simultaneously infusing the firm with new perspectives and knowledge from outside stakeholders. This dimension reflects the tension created by the need to buffer the technical core so that it can operate without distraction, while at the same time remaining open to fresh perspectives and new, disruptive models and technologies.

Exhibit 3.2
Shareholder Value Model

Source: Adapted from Hart, S. and Milstein, M. 2003. "Creating sustainable value." *Academy of Management Executive*, 17(2): 56-69.

Juxtaposing these two dimensions produces a matrix with four distinct dimensions of performance crucial to generating shareholder value—and understanding sustainability in terms relevant to the business. The lower-left quadrant focuses on those aspects of performance that are primarily internal and near-term in nature: cost and risk reduction. Quarterly earnings growth and reduction in exposure to liabilities and other potential losses are important drivers of wealth creation. Clearly, unless the firm can operate efficiently and reduce its risk commensurate with returns, shareholder value will be eroded.

The lower-right quadrant also focuses on performance dimensions that are focused on today's business but includes salient stakeholders external to the firm: suppliers and customers in the immediate value chain, as well as regulators, communities, nongovernmental organizations (NGOs), and the environment. Unless it respects these stakeholders' interests, the firm's right to operate might be called into question. But if it uses creativity to include their interests, the firm can differentiate itself, enhance its reputation, and establish the legitimacy it needs to preserve and increase shareholder value.

Shifting to the upper-left quadrant of the model, the firm must not only perform efficiently in today's businesses, but it should also be constantly mindful of generating the products and services of the future. This means developing or acquiring the skills, competencies, and technologies that reposition the firm for future growth. Without such a focus on innovation, it will be difficult for the firm to create the new product and service flow to ensure that it prospers well into the future. The creation of shareholder value thus depends upon the firm's ability to creatively destroy its current capabilities in favor of the innovations of tomorrow.

Finally, the upper-right quadrant focuses on identifying the needs that will define the growth markets of the future. Growth requires the firm to either offer new products to existing customers or tap into previously unserved markets. A convincing articulation of how and where the firm plans to grow in the future is crucial to the generation of shareholder value. The growth trajectory therefore provides guidance and direction for new technology and product development.

Firms must perform well in all four quadrants of the model if they are to continuously generate shareholder value over time.[2] Performing within only one or two quadrants is a prescription for suboptimal performance and even failure. Firms such as Kodak and Xerox, which failed to adequately invest in digital technology, illustrate how overemphasis on today's business (to the exclusion of tomorrow's technology and markets) might generate wealth for a time but will eventually erode shareholder value as competitors enter with superior products and services. The recent experience of many Internet companies also demonstrates how preoccupation with tomorrow's opportunity to the exclusion of performance today might be exciting and challenging but short-lived.[3] Companies such as Monsanto, which failed to adequately address stakeholder concerns over genetically modified food, show that overemphasis on the internal aspects of the firm might bring short-term results but will ultimately blind the firm to the constituencies and perspectives that are so important to both maintaining legitimacy and generating imaginative new ideas about how the firm might compete in the future. Finally, the subprime mortgage industry is perhaps the latest in a long litany of examples of how focusing on only one or two of the quadrants (in this case, short-term profits) can kill your success in the long run.

The Buzzword Sort

Just as the creation of sustained shareholder value requires performance on multiple dimensions, the societal challenges associated with sustainable development are also multidimensional. Accordingly, we can use the shareholder value model described earlier to cluster and organize the buzzwords enumerated in the previous section (see Exhibit 3.3).[4] This produces four distinct categories or constructs associated with the four quadrants of the framework. Each captures a conceptually distinct aspect of sustainability and connects to firm performance and shareholder value in a distinct manner. Understanding these conceptual distinctions is key to creating a more disciplined understanding of sustainability to transcend the current rhetoric that still plagues the field.

Exhibit 3.3
The Buzzword Sort

	Tomorrow	
•Eco-Effectiveness •Biomimicry •Leapfrog Technology •Sustainable Technology •Knowledge and Service Intensity •Cradle to Cradle •Closed Loops •Restorative Technology •Systems Thinking		•Sustainable Development •Base of the Pyramid •Urban Reinvestment •Brownfield Redevelopment •Inclusive Capitalism •Pro-Poor Business •Social Entrepreneurship •Radical Transactiveness •B24B
Internal		**External**
•Environmental Mgmt Systems •Greening •Pollution Prevention (P2) •Eco-Efficiency •Risk Management •Environmental Management •ISO 14001 •Waste Reduction •Resource Productivity		•Corporate Social Responsibility •Industrial Ecology •Stakeholder Management •Life-Cycle Management •Design for Environment (DfE) •Green Design •Corporate Citizenship •Full Cost Accounting •Take-Back •Transparency
	Today	

The lower-left quadrant is populated with the assortment of buzzwords that have to do with resource efficiency and pollution prevention—doing more with less. They enable the firm to squeeze more saleable product out of each pound of raw material that it buys. Recognizing that increasing industrialization, with its associated material consumption, pollution, and waste generation, is a key sustainability driver, the items in the lower-left quadrant are all geared toward the reduction of the waste and emissions associated with firms' current operations.

The lower-right quadrant is composed of buzzwords that focus on stakeholder engagement, transparency, and life-cycle management. These seemingly diverse items cluster together because they all challenge companies to access voices from beyond their immediate operational control. As we have seen, Internet-connected coalitions of NGOs are making it increasingly difficult for governments, corporations, or any large institutions to operate in secrecy.[5] Driven by the proliferation and interconnection of civil society stakeholders, the items in this quadrant help firms incorporate voices from the entire product lifecycle; this means more effective stakeholder engagement, new forms of governance, and a proactive approach to corporate social responsibility. Items in the lower-right quadrant thus challenge firms to operate in a transparent, responsive manner due to an increasingly well-informed, active stakeholder base.

The upper-left quadrant is populated by buzzwords that emphasize the development of new, inherently clean technologies and capabilities (through either internal development or acquisition). Specifically, this quadrant focuses on the emerging technologies (genomics, biomimicry, nanotechnology, information technology, and renewable energy) that could make many of today's energy- and material-intensive industries obsolete. New capability development in clean technology thus constitutes the key dimension of the upper-left quadrant.

Finally, the upper-right quadrant consists of the set of buzzwords that address the increases in population, poverty, and inequity associated with globalization. Whether we are dealing with disinvestment in urban cores, brownfield redevelopment, or the four billion poor at the base of the pyramid (B24B means "business to four billion"), this quadrant focuses on those who have been underserved or even exploited by capitalism to date. Social development and wealth creation on a massive scale, especially among the world's poorest, is thus the key aspect of the upper-right quadrant.

In sum, global sustainability is a complex, multidimensional concept that cannot be addressed by any single corporate action. Creating sustainable value requires that firms address each of the four quadrants—and be clear about how the strategies associated with each will help the firm build shareholder value. First, firms can create value by reducing the level of material consumption and pollution associated with its business. Second, they can create value by operating at greater levels of transparency and responsiveness, across the entire lifecycle of the product system. Third, they can create value through the development of new, disruptive technologies that hold the potential to greatly shrink the size of the human footprint on the planet. Finally, firms can create value by meeting the needs of those at the base of the world income pyramid in a way that facilitates inclusive wealth creation and distribution.

Connecting the Dots: The Sustainable Value Portfolio[6]

When viewed through the appropriate set of business lenses, the sustainability framework discussed previously presents opportunities for firms to improve performance in all four quadrants of the shareholder value model, as illustrated in Exhibit 3.4. Thinking systematically, through the full range of challenges and opportunities associated with sustainability, is the first important step managers can take toward the creation of sustainable value. Each of the four quadrants of the framework is explored in greater depth next.

Exhibit 3.4
The Sustainable Value Framework

Source: Adapted from Hart, S. and Milstein, M. 2003. "Creating sustainable value." *Academy of Management Executive*, 17(2): 56-69.

Growing Profits and Reducing Risk Through Pollution Prevention

Material consumption, waste, and pollution present an opportunity for firms to lower cost and risk by developing skills and capabilities in pollution prevention and eco-efficiency.[7] Pollution prevention is focused on reducing waste and emissions from current operations. Less waste means better utilization of inputs, resulting in lower costs for raw materials and waste disposal. Effective pollution prevention also requires extensive employee involvement, continuous improvement, and quality management capability.

Programs that reduce waste and emissions through eco-efficiency have been widely adopted by firms over the past two decades and include such notable cases as Dow Chemical's Waste Reduction Always Pays (WRAP) and Chevron's Save Money and Reduce Toxics (SMART). Pollution-prevention programs have proliferated at the industry level and receive a great deal of attention from regulatory bodies in the United States and Europe as potential alternatives to command-and-control regulation.[8] The well-publicized results of such pioneering programs as 3M's Pollution Prevention Pays (3P) illustrate the direct, bottom-line benefits of pollution prevention. Indeed, between 1975 and 1990, 3M reduced its total pollution by more than 530,000 tons (a 50 percent reduction in total emissions) and, according to company sources, saved more than $500 million through lower raw material, compliance, disposal, and liability costs. In 1990, 3M embarked on 3P+, which sought to reduce the remaining waste and emissions by 90 percent, with the ultimate goal being zero pollution.[9]

During the 1990s, DuPont's $1 billion Lycra business helped to further underscore the potentially sizeable financial payoff associated with pollution prevention.[10] Between 1991 and 1995, more than 50 million pounds of waste were eliminated from the business's nine plants worldwide. This saved roughly $5 million in compliance, liability, and waste disposal costs. However, a more thorough accounting revealed that yield improvements attributable to the pollution-prevention program increased process efficiency and reduced material costs by $45 million. Additional revenue associated with saleable by-product (which previously was waste) totaled $100 million. Furthermore, the business avoided making new capital investments in plant and facility as a result of greater up-time and faster cycle time in the existing capacity; this, they estimated, was worth another $100 million. Without even estimating the higher productivity of workers due to healthier working conditions and higher morale, these cost savings totaled a whopping $250 million for the business, a major contribution to the business's bottom line.

Evidence thus clearly shows that pollution-prevention and waste-reduction strategies actually do reduce cost and increase profits.[11] Pollution prevention provides managers with the clearest, fastest way to increase shareholder value by growing the bottom line for existing businesses through reductions in cost and liability.

Enhancing Reputation and Legitimacy Through Product Stewardship

Whereas pollution prevention focuses on internal operations, product stewardship extends beyond organizational boundaries to include the entire product life cycle, from raw material access through production processes, to product use and disposal of spent products.[12] Product stewardship integrates the voice of the stakeholder into business processes by allowing the firm to interact with external parties such as suppliers, customers, regulators, communities, NGOs, and the media. It thus offers a way to both lower environmental impacts across the value chain and enhance the firm's legitimacy and reputation by engaging stakeholders in the conduct of ongoing operations. Product stewardship enhances outsiders' confidence in the firm's intentions and activities, helping to enhance corporate reputation and encouraging other firms to follow suit.

Firms can take many actions to increase shareholder value through product stewardship. Cause-related marketing appeals to consumers' desires to purchase products that have positive social and environmental benefits.[13] Life-cycle management extends the value chain beyond traditional limits by including in the firm's responsibility the costs and benefits of products from raw materials to production and ultimately to disposal by consumers.[14] SC Johnson, for example, has developed Greenlist™, a patented raw material rating system that has transformed the way the company measures, tracks and advances the environmental profile of its products. The process rates raw materials according to their impact on the environment and human health, with each raw material receiving a rating from 3 to 0, with 3 being "best" and 0-rated materials used on a limited, approved basis. SC Johnson continues to improve the overall score for the raw materials used in the company's products and also publicly reports on its progress. With Greenlist™, SC Johnson is using ingredients that are the best available for the environment without impacting product performance, aesthetics, or consumer cost.[15]

Dofasco, one of the few profitable steel companies in North America, has hinged its strategy on product stewardship. By focusing on the production of ultralight steel auto bodies for the auto industry, the company has enabled its customers (the auto companies) to produce lighter-weight and less-costly vehicles that also realize better gas mileage. Because many of Dofasco's products also make use of scrap steel, the company has been able to boost its reputation—and its sales—through product stewardship.[16] At least in part because of its extraordinary reputation and performance, Dofasco was acquired in 2006 by Arcelor-Mittal, the world's largest steel company.

An increasingly active NGO community has led firms to pursue more collaborative approaches to business management. Together with industry, for example, European governments are pioneering take-back laws for electronics and appliances manufacturers, effectively closing the loop on the product life cycle.[17] Companies such as Shell have increased the use of stakeholder engagement through town hall–style meetings, facilitated dialogues, Internet-based comment boxes, and other tools designed to provide venues for stakeholders to voice their views about a firm's operations.

Under the leadership of Sam Palmisano, IBM has also emerged as a leader in leveraging their innovative technologies like grid computing, social networking, and virtual worlds to address problems in healthcare, transport, environment, and the plight of urban slum dwellers in the world's megacities. In fact, in 2006, IBM went where no other corporation had gone before with product stewardship: The company invited thousands of outsiders across all sectors into a "virtual" boardroom to discuss new product and service ideas with thousands of IBMers. That first "InnovationJam," held over an online platform, produced hundreds of ideas for new initiatives. As a result of the process, IBM has committed up to $100 million to support the strongest ideas.[18]

Nike also serves as a recent salient example of the value product stewardship creates for companies. Faced with growing backlash against its labor and environmental practices in the late 1990s, the company turned to product stewardship strategies to recover its reputation and preserve its right to operate. The company enacted a worldwide monitoring program for all contract factories, using both internal and third-party auditors such as PricewaterhouseCoopers. Nike also became a charter member of the Fair Labor Association (FLA), a nonprofit group that evolved out of an anti-sweatshop coalition of unions, human rights groups, and businesses. Nike also helped found the Global Alliance, a partnership among the International Youth Foundation, the MacArthur Foundation, and the World Bank, dedicated to improving workers' lives in emerging economies.[19]

Aside from taking action on the labor (social) front, Nike also took action environmentally. Its footwear designers started evaluating their new prototypes against a product stewardship scorecard, using life-cycle analysis. Nike also launched the Reuse a Shoe Project to recycle old, unwanted footwear. The company's retailers collected shoes and shipped them back to the company, which ground and separated the materials. Through partnerships with sports surfacing companies, the outsole rubber and midsole foam were turned into artificial athletic surfaces. Profits from this business generated income for the Nike Foundation and funded donations of sport surfaces made of the recycled material.

As the Nike case makes clear, firms can use product stewardship to demonstrate that stakeholder voices and opinions matter and can affect company behavior. As with pollution prevention, product stewardship is centered on improving existing products and services. As a consequence, changes are immediate, and value is quickly realized in the form of improved community relations, legitimacy, and brand reputation.

Accelerating Innovation and Repositioning Through Clean Technology

Clean technology refers not to the incremental improvement associated with pollution prevention, but to innovations that leapfrog standard routines and knowledge altogether. The rapid emergence of disruptive technologies such as genomics, biomimicry, information technology, nanotechnology, renewable energy, and close-loop systems presents the opportunity for firms—especially those heavily dependent upon fossil fuels, natural resources, and toxic materials—to reposition their internal competencies around more sustainable technologies. Thus, rather than simply seeking to reduce the negative impacts of their operations, firms can strive to solve social and environmental problems through the internal development or acquisition of new capabilities that address the sustainability challenge directly.[20]

A growing number of firms have begun to develop the next generation of clean technologies to drive future economic growth. For instance, BP and Shell have ramped up investments in solar, wind, and other renewable technologies that might ultimately replace their core petroleum businesses. In the automotive sector, Toyota and Honda were early entrants in the market for hybrid vehicles, which substantially increase fuel efficiency. Not long ago, most car makers talked of a transition to electric vehicles or alternative power taking 20 to 30 years. Today, in the wake of the Great Recession, GM, Ford, Toyota, and Honda are now committed to making it a commercial reality within a decade.

Firms such as Cargill and Dow are exploring the development of biologically based polymers to enable renewable feedstocks such as corn to replace petrochemical inputs in the manufacturing of plastics. Finally, General Electric's "Ecomagination" initiative—aimed at solving some of the world's most pressing environmental problems through technology—may be the most significant and visible new corporate commitment to clean technology (see Chapter 4). Each of these cases is notable for the firm's willingness to disrupt the very core technologies upon which its businesses currently depend.

Bold strategies in clean technology continue to be less common among large, established corporations than are activities in pollution prevention or product stewardship. Entrenched corporate mindsets and standard operating procedures inhibit the creation of structures that can catalyze innovation. The risks associated with such investments stand in stark contrast to the risk-reducing efforts associated with the pollution-prevention programs discussed previously. However, it is likely that future economic growth will be driven by those firms that are able to develop disruptive technologies that address society's needs. Firms that fail to lead the development and commercialization of such technologies are unlikely to be a part of tomorrow's economy.[21]

Crystallizing the Firm's Growth Path and Trajectory at the Base of the Pyramid

Too many corporate clean technology initiatives have floundered because the resulting technologies have stumbled in the marketplace—witness GM's failed effort to develop an electric car during the 1990s. To succeed, therefore, it is crucial to develop a vision not only for what needs the company is trying to address and how they relate to sustainability, but also for where the most appropriate markets can be found. The unmet needs of those at the base of the economic pyramid may present the best opportunity for firms to define a compelling trajectory for future growth. A more inclusive form of capitalism, characterized by collaboration with stakeholders previously overlooked or ignored by firms (such as radical environmentalists, shantytown dwellers, or the rural poor in developing countries), can help open new pathways for growth in previously unserved markets.

The case of the Grameen Bank in Bangladesh demonstrates how a vision aimed at those who had been bypassed by the financial system, opened a totally new pathway for business growth.[22] More than 30 years ago, Muhammad Yunus, then a professor of economics at Chittagong University in Bangladesh, conceived of the idea of a bank focused on offering "microcredit" loans to the poorest of the poor. This business concept was developed as a direct result of personal interactions that he and his students had with poor people in rural villages and shanty-towns. Most bankers assumed that laziness or lack of skill were the reasons that so many lived in abject poverty. As a result, they focused their attention on more affluent customers. But Yunus was personally motivated to understand what the poor felt they needed to change their lives for the better. Much to his surprise, he discovered, by traveling through villages and through extended personal interaction, that they were, for the most part, energetic and motivated and knew exactly what they needed to move forward. In almost every case, this involved gaining access to small amounts of credit to launch or expand small enterprises. Grameen Bank was established to serve this need.

To succeed, it was necessary for Grameen to turn most of the established assumptions about banking (loan size, need for collateral, contractual enforcement) upside down. Conventional banking is based on the principle that the more you have, the more you can get. Grameen Bank started with the belief that credit should be accepted as a human right. By focusing on making very small loans to poor women based upon a "peer lending" model, a system was built where those who possessed the least get the highest priority. Small groups of loan recipients ensure that everyone behaves in a responsible way and no one gets into repayment trouble. The bank's sales and service people visit villages frequently, getting to know the women who have the loans and the projects in which they are supposed to invest. In this way, lending due diligence is accomplished through trust-based interaction and exchange rather than mountains of paperwork and legal documentation characteristic of conventional banks. In fact, the individual loan amounts are often smaller than the document-processing charges of most financial institutions.

By 2009, Grameen was lending in excess of $8 billion each year to over 8 million poor borrowers in most villages throughout Bangladesh. Even more amazing, it achieved a better than 98 percent repayment rate, the highest of any bank on the Indian subcontinent, and indeed much higher than North American and European banks in the United States.[23] The competitive imagination of Yunus and the Grameen Bank has led to a global explosion of institutional interest in microlending over the past decade, including the recent entry of financial giants such as Citigroup. In recognition of his pioneering work, Muhammad Yunus received the Nobel Peace Prize in 2006. Later that year, he founded Grameen America, a 501(c)(3) microfinance organization based in New York. The non-profit opened its doors in 2008 in Jackson Heights, New York, where it provides loans (and other financial services) through the peer-group lending model to low-income entrepreneurs for income-generating activity. The bank now operates a second branch in Omaha, Nebraska, and is committed to opening a branch in any city or neighborhood that can commit $2 million of start-up capital.[24]

Increasingly, MNCs are recognizing that the voices of the poor and disenfranchised can be a source of creativity and innovation. Recognizing that information poverty may be the single biggest roadblock to sustainable development, Hewlett-Packard, under previous CEO Carly Fiorina, focused attention on the needs of the isolated and disconnected through its World e-Inclusion initiative. HP created an "i-community," a living laboratory, in rural India with the express purpose of coming to understand the particular needs of the rural poor. The firm quickly realized that this was not unoccupied space: Local companies such as N-Logue, Tarahaat, (and now Drishtee) were also developing information technology and business models to serve this enormous potential market. Through shared access (for example, Internet kiosks), wireless infrastructure, and R&D focused on cost reduction, these companies are dramatically reducing the cost of being connected.

Despite the efforts of organizations such as Grameen and HP, however, most companies continue to mistakenly assume that poor markets possess no value opportunities. Such companies have yet to try to understand the possibilities of serving the spaces they are used to ignoring. Indeed, BoP initiatives must overcome powerful "corporate antibodies" that seek to surround and kill any innovation that does not appear proximal and familiar. Senior executive protection is especially important, as BoP innovators in HP discovered upon Carly Fiorina's departure. Firms that do find a way usually recognize that those at the base of the pyramid lack attention and capital, not ingenuity and aspiration. Thus, these firms have the potential to unlock future markets of immense scale and scope.

Charting the Sustainable Value Portfolio

By now, the core dimensions of sustainability and their linkages to firm performance and value creation should be clear: Firms are challenged to minimize waste from current operations (pollution prevention), while simultaneously acquiring or developing more sustainable technologies and skill sets (clean technology). Firms are also challenged to engage in extensive interaction and dialogue with external stakeholders, regarding both current offerings (product stewardship) and economically sound new solutions to social and environmental problems for the future (base of the pyramid).

Taken together as a portfolio, these strategies and practices hold the potential to reduce cost and risk, enhance reputation and legitimacy, accelerate innovation and repositioning, and crystallize growth path and trajectory, all of which are crucial to the creation of shareholder value. The challenge for the firm is to decide which actions and initiatives to pursue and how best to manage them. Companies can begin by taking stock of each component of what I call their sustainable value portfolio (see Exhibit 3.5). This simple diagnostic tool can help any company determine whether its strategy has the potential to truly create sustainable value.

Exhibit 3.5
The Sustainable Value Portfolio

	Internal	External
Tomorrow	**Clean Technology** Is the sustainability of our products limited by our existing competency base? Is there potential to realize major improvements through new disruptive technology?	**Base of the Pyramid** Does our corporate vision direct us toward the solution of social and environmental problems? Does our vision focus us on serving the unmet needs at the base of the economic pyramid?
Today	**Pollution Prevention** Where are the most significant waste and emission streams from our current operations? Can we lower costs and risks by eliminating waste at the source or by using it as useful input?	**Product Stewardship** What are the implications for product design and development if we assume responsibility for a product's entire life cycle? Can we build reputation and legitimacy by engaging a broader range of stakeholders?

Source: Adapted from Hart, S. 1997. "Beyond greening: Strategies for a sustainable world." *Harvard Business Review*, January-February: 66-76.

First, assess your company's (or your business unit's) capability in each of the four quadrants by answering the questions in Exhibit 3.5. Then rate your capability on the following scale for each quadrant: 1) nonexistent, 2) emerging, 3) established, or 4) institutionalized. Unbalanced portfolios spell missed opportunity and vulnerability: A bottom-heavy portfolio suggests a good position today but future vulnerability. A top-heavy portfolio indicates a vision of sustainability without the operational or analytical skills needed to implement it. A portfolio skewed to the left side of the chart indicates an inward focus that could lead to myopia and might ignore important perspectives from external constituencies. Finally, a portfolio skewed to the right side, although highly open and public, runs the risk of being labeled "greenwash" because the underlying plant operations and core technology still cause significant harm.

Programs in pollution prevention and product stewardship are well institutionalized within most MNCs today and have saved hundreds of millions of dollars over the past decade. U.S.-based companies have been especially focused on the efficiency gains and cost savings associated with pollution prevention. Highly publicized crises at companies such as Monsanto and Nike that failed to successfully engage the views of stakeholders have also caused growing numbers of firms to explore strategies for product stewardship. European companies have been particularly active in engaging in more stakeholder dialogue, extending producer responsibility for products, and adopting more inclusive forms of corporate governance. Research and consulting experience, however, suggest that few firms seem to recognize, let alone exploit, the full range of sustainable business opportunities available.[25] Rather, most focus their time and attention primarily on the bottom half of the matrix: short-term solutions tied to existing products and stakeholder groups.

The Road to Sustainability

Consider the auto industry. During the 1970s, government regulation and dirty tailpipe emissions forced the industry to focus on pollution control. In the 1980s, the industry began to tackle pollution prevention. Initiatives such as the Corporate Average Fuel Efficiency requirement and the Toxic Release Inventory led auto companies to examine their product designs and manufacturing processes to improve fuel economy and lower emissions from their plants. The 1990s witnessed the first signs of product stewardship. In Germany, the 1990 "take-back" law required auto manufacturers to take responsibility for their vehicles at the end of their useful lives. Innovators such as BMW influenced the design of new cars with "design for disassembly" efforts. Industry-led consortia such as the Partnership for a New Generation of Vehicles were driven largely by the product stewardship logic of lowering the environmental impact of automobiles throughout their life cycles.

Early attempts to promote clean technology were driven by initiatives such as California's Zero-Emission Vehicle Law and the U.N.

Climate Change Convention, which sought to limit greenhouse gas emissions on a global scale. But early efforts by industry incumbents were either incremental—for example, the development of natural gas vehicles—or defensive in nature. Electric vehicle programs, for instance, were used primarily to demonstrate the infeasibility of the California law rather than to lead the industry to fundamentally cleaner technology. It came as no surprise that GM chose to shutter its electric vehicle program, the Impact. While stylish and successful at generating a cult following, the Impact featured over 1,000 pounds of batteries, a range of less than 100 miles, and a price tag nearly double that of other vehicles in its class. Similarly, the issue of climate change, perhaps the single biggest threat to the internal combustion engine as we know it, was addressed primarily through stakeholder dialogue and the establishment of incremental reduction goals for greenhouse gas emissions. These initiatives, while laudable as far as they went, were motivated primarily by a desire to maintain legitimacy and the right to operate in the face of a product fleet that was becoming increasingly dominated by behemoth, gas-guzzling SUVs and oversize pickup trucks.

The early 2000s saw the introduction of the first serious new product entries containing alternative power plants. Hybrid-electric vehicles such as the Prius and the Civic, from Toyota and Honda, respectively, were introduced at premium prices with fuel efficiencies 50% better than those of conventional vehicles. Despite clear signals of demand by a growing "green" consumer base, however, production capacity lagged far behind demand and by 2006 was still focused on vehicles at the low end of the market, where conventional cars were already quite fuel-efficient. Only in the past few years have these companies begun to produce hybrid options in the large car, minivan, SUV, or pickup truck segments, which are, by far, the most polluting and least energy-efficient. With a surge in gasoline prices during 2006 and again in 2008, Toyota and Honda's clear dominance in both hybrid technology and fuel efficiency all but brought Ford, GM, and Chrysler to their knees. Indeed, both GM and Chrysler required government bailout money in 2009 to avoid outright failure, with potentially devastating social and economic consequences.

The advent of the new century also saw a rush by car companies into hydrogen fuel cell development programs. Some automakers (such as Ford) sought joint ventures with existing fuel cell companies; others (such as GM) initiated their own programs of technology development. Most targeted the United States as the entry market for this revolutionary new technology. Unfortunately, because there are no alternative fuels for sale to consumers in the United States, it will be necessary to outfit these fuel-cell vehicles with expensive gasoline reformers well into the future. Converting gasoline into hydrogen does not solve the problem of fossil fuel dependence or greenhouse gas emissions.

Indeed, it is staggering that none of the incumbent auto companies has connected the challenge of clean technology development to its strategies for emerging markets (such as China and India, where there will be massive transportation needs in the coming decades). Consider the impact of automobiles on China alone. In the mid-1990s, there were fewer than one million cars on the road in China. However, with a population of more than one billion, it would take less than 30 percent market penetration to equal the current size of the U.S. car market (12 million to 15 million units per year). Ultimately, China might demand 50 million or more units annually. Because China's energy and transportation infrastructures are still being defined, there is an opportunity to leapfrog to clean technology, yielding important environmental, public health, and competitive benefits.

Emerging players from the developing world such as the Tata Group in India and BYD in China seem to see the logic of such a strategy. In 2008, for example, Warren Buffet invested $230 million in BYD, which is focused on producing an affordable, mainstream electric car, and his 10% stake is now worth nearly $2 billion. That same year, Tata Motors launched the "Nano" in India—a $2,000 vehicle that seats four, passes European safety and emission standards, and gets 55 miles to the gallon. Compare this car to the vaunted Toyota Prius, which has a similar profile but gets only 45 miles to the gallon and costs $25,000![26] To achieve these radical goals, Tata Motors started with a clean sheet design that radically simplified the number of parts and components, requiring a reinvention of the upstream supply chain. In addition, this simplified design made "kit" assembly by dealers and distributors possible, eliminating the need for expensive final assembly plants, while also creating jobs in small cities and rural areas where the vehicle could be assembled, sold, and serviced directly by microentrepreneurs.

Furthermore, within the next two years, Tata Motors has committed to launching an electric version of the Nano and is working on the launch of a vehicle that runs on compressed air.[27] Can we possibly imagine Ford or GM (or for that matter, Toyota or Honda) achieving this combination of innovation in fuel efficiency, radical simplicity, and affordability? By "shattering the trade-offs," Tata Motors and other players like them are staking out the future, with potentially dire consequences for the established players.

Now assume for a moment that these innovators succeed in creating a commercially viable next generation of affordable (and renewable) vehicles using emerging markets as the incubator. Try, then, to envision a transportation infrastructure capable of accommodating so many vehicles. How long will it take before gridlock and traffic jams force the auto industry to a halt? Sustainability will require new transportation solutions for the needs of emerging economies with huge populations. This might feature entirely new products and services designed to make smaller cities and villages more economically viable so that mass migration to megacities becomes unnecessary and even undesirable.

Skylite Aeronautics, for example, is a start-up company focused on the commercial deployment of next-generation airship technology—the GeoShip.[28] We are not talking here about a modern-day version of the Hindenburg! Instead, the GeoShip includes several technological and design innovations that make it quite distinct from traditional blimps. The structure is based on a geodesic tetrahedral truss, providing tremendous strength. The airship does not use tail fins (which means less drag and lighter weight) and is powered by quiet and efficient electric motors (rather than jet engines). The result is an airship that can haul enormous amounts of cargo and/or people with a minimal environmental footprint at very low cost: Each GeoShip can carry up to ten 747s' worth of cargo while using less than 10% of the fuel required by jet aircraft. And by using both solar power and select biofuels, the carbon footprint of the GeoShip could be taken to near zero.

Because it can take off and land vertically, with no landing gear and minimal need for ground-based infrastructure, the GeoShip can link remote communities, regions, and countries directly to global markets. Just as cellular telephony leap-frogged the need for expensive land lines, the airship can leap-frog the need for expensive and environmentally damaging transportation infrastructure such as roads, rail lines, bridges, ports, and airports.[29] Most of us have forgotten that Ford was once in the airplane business (or that SAAB still is). Can "car" companies expand their conception of sustainable mobility to include the development of technologies like the GeoShip? Will the giants in the auto industry be prepared for such radical change, or will they leave the field to new ventures that are not encumbered by the competencies of the past?

In summary, although the auto industry has made progress, most auto companies fall far short of creating truly sustainable value. While most have succeeded in implementing some version of pollution prevention and product stewardship, few have ventured very far beyond the safe confines of the current technology and business model. Initiatives in the clean technology and base of the pyramid quadrants have been fragmentary, at best, leaving open a future opportunity of potentially vast proportions. Unfortunately for the incumbents, the firms best positioned to seize this opportunity are new entrants or emerging players from the developing world.

Pursuing the White Space

As the case of the auto industry suggests, relatively few firms have begun to explore seriously the opportunities associated with the upper half of the sustainable value portfolio, the portion focused on building new capabilities and markets. Indeed, most clean technologies today are being developed and commercialized by small, often undercapitalized new ventures, not by the MNCs that possess the financial resources for doing so successfully. Similarly, most business experiments at the base of the economic pyramid have been initiated by NGOs or small local firms, while MNCs' emerging market plays have been limited largely to the elites or emerging middle classes in the developing world. Given that pursuit of clean technology and markets at the base of the pyramid is disruptive in character, perhaps we should not be surprised that large firms have not actively blazed these trails. As we have seen "corporate antibodies" serve to effectively kill any innovation that departs too much from the norm.

Yet it need not be this way. Just as particular competencies (for example, quality management, continuous improvement, boundary-spanning capability) predispose some companies to be more effective than others in implementing pollution prevention and product stewardship, some MNCs will be better positioned than others to pursue clean technologies and markets at the base of the pyramid—those with demonstrated ability in acquiring new skills, working with unconventional partners, incubating disruptive innovations, shedding obsolete businesses, and creatively destroying existing product portfolios, to name just a few. Incumbent firms with these skill sets possess a potentially powerful first-mover advantage.

The opportunity to create sustainable value—shareholder wealth that simultaneously drives us toward a more sustainable world—is huge but yet to be fully exploited. The sustainable value portfolio outlined in this chapter shows the nature and magnitude of the opportunities in sustainable business development and connects them to ways for the firm to create value. The strategies associated with the four quadrants also enable a sustainable competitive advantage because they cannot be easily or quickly copied by competitors. The framework's simplicity, however, should not be mistaken for ease of execution: Understanding the connections is not the same thing as successfully implementing the necessary strategies and practices. This task is very challenging and complex indeed. Only a few firms will be able to successfully carry out activities in all four quadrants simultaneously, especially those in the upper part of the portfolio that require the greatest efforts in terms of vision, creativity, and patience.

Stagnant or negative economic growth at the top of the income pyramid and stale business models will present formidable challenges to corporations in the years ahead. Focusing on incremental improvements to existing products and businesses is an important step, but it neglects the vastly larger opportunities associated with clean technology and the underserved markets at the base of the economic pyramid. Indeed, addressing the full range of sustainability challenges by moving "beyond greening" can help to create shareholder value and could represent one of the most underappreciated avenues for profitable growth in the future. It is to this prospect that we turn our attention in the next section of the book.

Notes

1. The discussion of the sustainable value framework in this chapter is excerpted from Stuart Hart and Mark Milstein, "Creating Sustainable Value," *Academy of Management Executive* 17(2) (2003): 56–69.

2. This idea is similar to the balanced scorecard (see Robert Kaplan and David Norton, "The Balanced Scorecard—Measures That Drive Performance," *Harvard Business Review* 72(1) (1992): 71–79) and other tools that emphasize the need to balance a portfolio of actions to drive firm value over time.

3. The experiences of Enron and the numerous dot-bombs of the tech wreck serve as the most recent illustrations that, although it can be very glamorous to be viewed as on the cutting edge of the business world, bankruptcy provides a particularly ineffective platform from which to generate future growth.

4. Admittedly, the clustering of these terms represents our interpretation of where each belongs. Others may well take issue with our choice of placement.

5. Howard Rheingold, *Smart Mobs: The Next Social Revolution* (Cambridge, MA: Perseus Publishing, 2002).

6. The four strategies developed in this section were first articulated in: Stuart Hart, "Beyond Greening: Strategies for a Sustainable World," *Harvard Business Review* 75(1) (1997): 66–76. I would also like to thank my colleagues at the Sustainable Enterprise Academy—in particular, Brian Kelly, David Wheeler, Bryan Smith, John Ehrenfeld, Chris Galea, Art Hanson, David Bell, Nigel Roome, Jim Leslie, and Pat Delbridge—for helping us to clarify our thinking regarding how the drivers of sustainability, viewed through the proper set of business lenses, influence shareholder value.

7. The most comprehensive treatment of eco-efficiency was done by the World Business Council for Sustainable Development in Livio DeSimone and Frank Popoff, *Eco-efficiency: The Business Link to Sustainable Development* (Cambridge: MIT Press, 1997).

8. See Alfred Marcus, *Reinventing Environmental Regulation* (Washington, D.C.: Resources for the Future Press, 2002).

9. 3M Company, Pollution Prevention Pays, 1992 videotape.

10. Personal communication, Paul Tebo, Executive VP, DuPont, April 1998.

11. See, for example, Petra Christmann, "Effects of 'Best Practices' of Environmental Management on Cost Advantage: The Role of Complementary Assets," *Academy of Management Journal* 43(4) (1998): 663–680; and Sanjay Sharma, and Harrie Vredenburg, "Proactive Corporate Environmental Strategy and the Development of Competitively Valuable Organizational Capabilities," *Strategic Management Journal* 19(8) (1998): 729–753.

12. See, for example, Ulrich Steger, "Managerial Issues in Closing the Loop," *Business Strategy and the Environment* 5(4) (1996): 252–268.

13. Steve Hoeffler and Ken Keller, "Building Brand Equity Through Corporate Societal Marketing," *Journal of Public Policy and Marketing* 21(1) (2002): 78–89.

14. Joseph Fiksel, *Design for Environment: A Guide to Sustainable Product Development* (New York: McGraw-Hill, 2009).

15. Stuart Hart and May Matthews, *SC Johnson and the GreenList Opportunity*, www.globalens.com, 2009.

16. Personal communication, Don Pether, CEO of Dofasco, Inc., November 2003.

17. See Proposal for a Directive of the European Parliament and of the Council on Waste Electrical and Electronic Equipment and on the Restriction of the Use of Certain Hazardous Substances in Electrical and Electronic Equipment, COM #(2000)347, available at http://europa.eu.int/comm/environment/docum/00347_en.htm.

18. For more detail, see Bradley Googins, Philip Mirvis, and Steven Rochlin, *Beyond Good Company* (New York: Palmgrave-MacMillan, 2007).

19. The Nike example is drawn from Heather McDonald, Ted London, and Stuart Hart, *Expanding the Playing Field: Nike's World Shoe Project,* www.globalens.com, 2009.

20. William McDonough and Michael Braungart, *Cradle to Cradle* (New York: North Point Press, 2002).

21. Gary Hamel, *Leading the Revolution* (Boston: Harvard Business School Press, 2000); Clay Christensen, Thomas Craig, and Stuart Hart, "The Great Disruption," *Foreign Affairs* 80(2) (2001): 80–95; and Robert Foster and Sarah Kaplan, *Creative Destruction* (New York: Currency Books, 2001).

22. Alex Counts, *Give Us Credit* (New York: Times Books, 1996).

23. Steven Vogel, President of Grameen America, presentation at McGill University, November 2009.

24. www.grameenamerica.com.

25. Stuart Hart and Mark Milstein, "Global Sustainability and the Creative Destruction of Industries," *Sloan Management Review* 41(1) (1999): 23–33; Stuart Hart and Clay Christensen, "The Great Leap: Driving Innovation from the Base of the Pyramid," *Sloan Management Review* 44(1) (2002): 51–56; and C. K. Prahalad and Stuart Hart, "The Fortune at the Bottom of the Pyramid," *Strategy+Business* 26 (2002): 54–67.

26. R. Chandrasekar and Oana Branzei, *Nano Tata-logy: The People's Car*. The University of Western Ontario, Case #9B08M074, 2008.

27. Ratan Tata, personal communication, 2009.

28. Mike Voorhees, "The Sustainable Transportation Revolution," *Skylite Aeronautics,* 2009.

29. Thanks to Mike Voorhees, Founder and CEO of Skylite Aeronatics, for this metaphor.

Part Two

Beyond Greening

4

Clean Technology and Creative Destruction

More than 50 years ago, economist Joseph Schumpeter described the dynamic pattern in which innovative upstarts unseat established firms as "creative destruction."[1] Whereas most twentieth-century economists focused on competition under conditions of static equilibrium, Schumpeter insisted that disequilibrium was the driving force of capitalism. There is now little doubt that the economy is driven by firms that are able to capitalize on the "new combinations" described by Schumpeter: Coal Age technologies gave way to Oil Age technologies that are now giving way to Information Age technologies. With each change, the technological and socio-economic infrastructure of society experiences dramatic transformation, with new institutions, enterprises, and geographic patterns of development.

Not surprisingly, the notion of creative destruction makes many managers uncomfortable—and it should. Frequently, incumbent firms either have discounted the significance of emerging technology or have reacted to changes by becoming more committed to existing products and markets. Incumbents that survive episodes of creative destruction do so because they display more foresight than their peers; they invest and form partnerships to acquire new competencies and experiment in new, untested markets.[2] They are not held hostage by their current technology or market position.[3]

Mark Milstein and I have argued that the emerging challenges associated with global sustainability are, in reality, catalysts for a new round of creative destruction that offers unprecedented business opportunities.[4] Today's corporations can seize the opportunity for sustainable development, but to do so, they must look beyond the incremental improvements associated with pollution prevention and product stewardship in the current business. Instead, companies must make obsolete the very technologies and product systems upon which they currently depend.[5]

Continuous Improvement Versus Creative Destruction

Episodes of creative destruction are usually driven by waves of scientific and technological discovery and/or major periods of sociopolitical upheaval. We are now in the early stages of such a revolution—the transformation toward a sustainable world. Most existing large corporations evolved in an era of abundant raw materials, cheap energy, and seemingly limitless sinks for waste disposal. During the past few decades, however, it has become increasingly clear that many of the technologies developed during this period are unsustainable. Indeed, the specters of toxic contamination, depleted forests and fisheries, eroded soils, loss of biodiversity, global climate change, burgeoning populations, a widening gap between rich and poor, and growing civil strife are explicit signals that companies must take more seriously the social and environmental impacts of their technologies and businesses.

In fact, only by replacing many of today's unsustainable technologies with those that are inherently clean, renewable, and nontoxic can we make rapid progress toward a more sustainable world. Just as nature enables some species to out-compete others through a process of natural selection and succession, so the sustainability revolution will enable those firms with more sustainable strategies to outperform—and, ultimately, replace—those with outmoded strategies and damaging technologies. No amount of greening will save firms from the gales of creative destruction that are likely to ensue in the coming decades. In short, most truly sustainable technologies are likely to be disruptive—but not all disruptive technologies will be sustainable. Learning the difference could hold the key to long-term survival.

Greening = Continuous Improvement

Strategies for greening generally serve to incrementally improve the performance of existing products and processes (see Exhibit 4.1). Initiatives in pollution prevention and product stewardship solidify incumbents' competitive positions by rewriting the rules of the game in their favor. Greening perpetuates the current industry structure; it fosters continuous improvement rather than reinvention or fundamental innovation. In the long run, however, the dynamics of creative destruction will work against firms that rely only on incremental improvements and fail to change the fundamental manner in which they provide products, processes, and services.

Exhibit 4.1
Continuous Improvement Versus Creative Destruction

Strategies for Greening	Strategies for Beyond Greening
Focus on Existing:	**Focus on Emerging:**
products	technologies
processes	markets
suppliers	partners
customers	needs
shareholders	stakeholders
Characteristics:	**Characteristics:**
Incremental	Discontinuous
Continuous Improvement	Creative Destruction
Rationalizes Industry	Restructures Industry
Example: Responsible Care	Example: Biotech Revolution

Source: Adapted from Hart, S. and Milstein, M. 1999. "Global sustainability and the creative destruction of industries." *Sloan Management Review*, 41(1): 23-33.

An example of incremental innovation is the Chemical Manufacturers Association's (CMA) Responsible Care program, which helped rescue the industry from near oblivion but has not led its members to revolutionize practices. Following the Bhopal disaster in 1984 (in which 3,000 residents of Bhopal, India, died as a result of a toxic chemical explosion at a Union Carbide plant), leading chemical companies, including Dow, DuPont, and Monsanto, pressed for self-regulation in the face of public hostility and calls for stricter regulatory measures that threatened industry survival. In 1988, the CMA adopted Responsible Care, a statement of environmental principles and codes of management practices that included provisions for pollution prevention, product stewardship, and community advisory panels. To strengthen the program, the principles and codes were made mandatory for CMA member companies, which make up 90 percent of the chemical capacity in the United States; noncompliance was grounds for expulsion from the CMA. Since 1988, Responsible Care has transformed the chemical industry's environmental behavior and helped to change the public's perception of the industry from shameless polluter to more responsible actor.

But although it has been successful in reestablishing the legitimacy of an industry under tremendous public pressure, Responsible Care has failed to address the fundamental underlying problems associated with the chemical industry: Many of its products and processes are highly toxic, resource-intensive, and inherently unsustainable. As an industry-level collaborative process, the Responsible Care program has fostered incremental improvement by forcing hundreds of smaller chemical firms to mimic the leaders in terms of environmental management and community involvement. This has left the leading firms in a stronger competitive position by helping to shore up support for their right to operate but, ironically, has reduced the likelihood of fundamental innovation by chemical company incumbents. Indeed, research now shows that the biggest gains in environmental performance occurred not within the Responsible Care firms, but among those firms that decided not to join.[6]

Beyond Greening = Creative Destruction

If we reflect on the generally accepted definition of sustainable development as the ability of the current generation to meet its needs without compromising the ability of future generations to meet theirs, we can see how most existing products and processes fail to meet this criterion.[7] Growing data suggest that today's extractive and material-intensive industries (for example, mining, energy, chemicals, forest products, agriculture, and transportation) are not sustainable. If the entire world were as material-intensive as North America, it would take more than three planet Earths to support the material requirements of the current world population.[8] We should therefore see global sustainability as a major disruptive force, with the power to radically transform the structure of many industries.

Visionary companies have an opportunity to drive the redefinition and redesign of their industries. Material- and energy-intensive industries will find global sustainability to be a competency-destroying challenge that calls for radical repositioning and new competency development. Information- and service-intensive industries will find global sustainability to be a competency-enhancing challenge that offers significant potential for substitution and leapfrogging over existing unsustainable technologies.

Unlike greening, which works through the existing supply chain to effect continuous improvement in the current business system, "beyond greening" strategies focus on emerging technologies, new markets, and unconventional partners and stakeholders. Such strategies are thus disruptive to current industry structure and raise the possibility of significant repositioning, enabling new players to establish leading positions as the process of creative destruction unfolds.

In the chemical industry, we can also see the early stages of creative destruction, as key incumbents begin to reposition themselves for the clean technology revolution. Consider the case of DuPont. In the late 1800s, the company transformed itself from a manufacturer of gunpowder and explosives into a chemical company focused on the production of synthetic materials using petroleum feedstocks. This strategy produced nearly a century of success, with such well-known blockbuster products as Nylon, Lycra, Teflon, Corian, and Kevlar.

In the late 1900s, DuPont embarked on its second major transformation—from an energy-intensive petrochemical company to a renewable resource company focused on sustainable growth.[9] To realize this transformation, the company has pursued a strategy of acquisition, divestiture, and internal technology development. Between 1995 and 2005, for example, DuPont invested more than $15 billion in biotechnology, including the acquisition of Pioneer Hi-Bred, a major player in the agricultural biotech business. It also divested resource- and energy-intensive businesses such as its oil subsidiary (Conoco) in the 1990s and, most recently, its core Nylon and Lycra businesses in 2004.

In an effort to dramatically shrink its footprint, the company established two energy goals in late 1999 for 2010: to hold total energy use flat (with 1990 levels) and to increase its use of renewable resources to 10 percent at a cost competitive with best available fossil fuels. To hit such ambitious targets while continuing to grow as a company, the firm sought to reorient its technology base toward biology (genomics and biomimicry, for example), renewable energy (fuel cells), and information (knowledge-intensive rather than resource-intensive products). And to accelerate this process, DuPont is seeding internal ventures focused on sustainable technology development and innovations aimed at the developing world.[10]

In its 2008 Sustainability Progress Report, DuPont declared that its energy use was down 7 percent through "Energy Breakout Initiatives" that were launched at 47 participating plants in 2005 and 2006; this reduction saved an estimated $60 million. In addition, it had obtained 6 percent of overall energy needs from renewable sources through, for instance, landfill gas projects. The company is now working toward a set of lofty environmental footprint reduction targets for 2015.[11]

During the past decade, de-mergers, spin-offs, acquisitions, and significant new technology developments have structurally transformed the chemical industry. Monsanto, Hoechst, and Rhone-Poulenc have spun off their chemical businesses to concentrate on life sciences, food, pharmaceuticals, and biotechnology. ICI, Sandoz, and Ciba-Geigy have refocused on chemicals by spinning off their life sciences and biotechnology investments (for example, the creation of Zeneca and Novartis). Dow is ramping up significant investments in biotechnology. Other firms, such as Novo Nordisk, the fast-growing Danish pharmaceutical and biotechnology company, and Empresas La Moderna, an emerging life sciences powerhouse, are exploring "green chemistry" and finding biological substitutes for synthetic chemicals. In fact, many of the new technologies being developed by these firms will make existing petrochemically based products and applications obsolete.

Almost every energy- and material-intensive industry, from energy and automobiles to food and forest products, is experiencing similar changes. Every firm must strike a balance between the incremental change and continuous improvement associated with greening, and the disruptive innovation and creative destruction associated with beyond greening. In the past, competitive advantage was based largely upon lowering cost or gaining differentiation in existing industries and businesses. In the future, however, it appears that competitive advantage will depend more upon the capacity to generate disruptive innovation and creative destruction through competitive imagination. A growing body of scholarly work affirms Joseph Schumpeter's assertion over a half-century ago that "the problem that is usually being visualized is how capitalism administers existing [industrial] structures, whereas the relevant problem is how it creates and destroys them."[12] Disruption and innovation are more important to corporate success than it has ever been.[13]

In their book *Creative Destruction*, Foster and Kaplan demonstrate empirically that the base rate of change in the economy has been accelerating over the past 80 years, with dire consequences for industry incumbents: The turnover rate for the S&P 500 has increased from about 1.5 percent per year in the 1920s to nearly 10 percent in 2000. This implies that the average number of years a firm spends on the Standard and Poor index declined from 65 in the 1920s and 1930s (S&P 90) to 10 in the 1990s (S&P 500). By 2020, they state, "more than three-quarters of the S&P 500 will consist of companies we don't know today—new companies drawn into the maelstrom of economic activity from the periphery, springing from insights unrecognized today."[14]

To date, unfortunately, the lion's share of effort and activity in most companies has focused on greening—the continuous improvement of existing products and processes. Given the velocity of technological change and the growing significance of sustainability, however, this no longer appears to be a viable strategy. In fact, investment in clean technology has mushroomed over the past decade. Venture capitalists around the world have pumped in excess of $20 billion into clean-tech companies since 2005. Indeed, clean-tech is now the largest venture capital category in the US.[15] Increasingly, creative destruction appears to hold the key not only to the growth industries of the future, but to corporate survival.

From Textile Dyes to Biomaterials

Burlington Chemical Company provides a vivid illustration of difference between continuous improvement and creative destruction.[16] Founded in the early 1950s in the heart of North Carolina's textile belt, Burlington focused on producing chemicals and dyes for the many textile companies in the region. The company grew steadily throughout the 1960s and '70s until the early 1980s, when the State of North Carolina passed a stringent new regulation requiring that fish be able to successfully reproduce in the effluent water coming from textile mills. This requirement presented a formidable challenge to the textile companies in the state. Recognizing that its customers' problems were its problems, too, Burlington seized the opportunity and began to focus on producing more environmentally friendly textile chemicals and dyes.

Led by Sam Moore, the grandson of the company's founder, Burlington's management team adopted the ideals of product stewardship and industrial ecology in 1983. This revolutionary approach led the company into a whole new line of textile chemical products that were low in toxicity, biodegradable, and much more energy-efficient. Despite the textile industry's steady decline, by the early 1990s, Burlington had grown to more than $50 million in annual sales and employed more than 150 people. Product stewardship and design-for-environment had enabled the company to thrive in what was otherwise a highly cost-competitive, commodity business. Then came the passage of the North American Free Trade Agreement (NAFTA) in 1995.

With NAFTA, the slow decline of the textile industry in North Carolina turned into a mass exodus. Textile mills across the state shut down and moved to Mexico to take advantage of the dramatically lower labor costs there. Between 1995 and 2000, Burlington's revenue declined by more than 50 percent, and more than 60 percent of its customers went out of business. Even worse, the average selling price of its products dropped by more than half. Burlington was forced to lay off more than 100 of its employees. Fortunately, given the company's strong focus on employee training and advanced technological competence, laid-off workers found jobs that paid at least as well within a few months. It was clear, however, that if the company were to survive, it would need new "lifeboat" businesses outside the textile industry. The company's managers thus committed themselves to a strategy of "creative destruction."

Burlington's investment in product stewardship and industrial ecology during the 1980s paid off: After two failed attempts to sell its textile chemical and dyes business (one acquirer would have shut down the operation, displacing the remaining workers), the firm succeeded in selling it to a German company in 2003. Under the terms of the agreement, Burlington retained exclusive manufacturing rights, and the new owner agreed to hire all Burlington's salespeople. The German firm was then able to leverage Burlington's clean textile dye technology throughout its extensive textile operations in Asia—a win-win, both financially and environmentally.

During the same period, Burlington built manufacturing facilities to focus on the development and production of new, bio-based lubricants, catalysts, and additives. In 2000, it launched a new Luberos lubricants division. The sale of the textile chemicals business freed assets with which to expand the new vision, which is focused on bio-based sustainable chemistry for manufacturing and service industries. New products include lubricants manufactured from used vegetable oils, soy-based fabric softeners, and new cleaning systems for the transportation industry.

By 2004, the company had begun to turn the corner, realizing a positive cash flow for the first time in six years and an improving balance sheet. The new vision provided vast opportunities for future growth in emerging industries, with tremendous upside potential. The company's early commitment to industrial ecology had provided it the intellectual and physical capital to make the leap into a whole new technology and business space. In short, the early commitment to clean technology provided the platform for creative destruction that saved the company.[17]

Using Carbon Dioxide to Change the World

During the mid-1990s, an innovative new venture was spun out of the University of North Carolina at Chapel Hill. Spearheaded by chemistry professor Joe DeSimone, Micell Technologies and its research arm, the Kenan Center for the Utilization of Carbon Dioxide in Manufacturing, focused on the growing demand for green manufacturing methods. Creative destruction has been the company's stock and trade. Micell Technologies is dedicated to the vision that liquid (supercritical) carbon dioxide can reduce water-based waste streams and replace a significant amount of the 30 billion pounds of organic and halogenated solvents used and released each year. DuPont has already benefited directly from this work—it has developed a new process for making Teflon in carbon dioxide in place of the current method, which is water- and solvent-intensive.

Micell is also seeking to revolutionize the semiconductor industry, in which chip fabrication currently uses massive quantities of both water and toxic solvents. Through its innovative technology, the company has developed applications that complete the most chemical- and water-intensive steps of the chip-production in a liquid carbon dioxide environment, eliminating the use of water and solvents for cleaning—and reducing the costs of production in the process. Ultimately, the company aims to creatively destroy the entire chip-fabrication process through its carbon dioxide-based approach, making the process a virtually closed system and eliminating entirely the need for expensive clean room technology.

One of Micell's most interesting business applications is in dry cleaning. Current dry cleaning technology uses a highly toxic chemical, perchloroethelene, as the cleaning agent. This chemical not only contaminates the sites where it is used (making virtually every dry cleaning shop a hazardous waste site), but it is also very hard on fabrics, shortening the useful life of clothing items. DeSimone and Micell have designed a set of soaps and surfactants that work especially well in a liquid carbon dioxide environment. Under pressure in a specially designed washing machine, carbon dioxide turns to a supercritical liquid; clothes are then "washed" with the specially designed surfactants. Upon completion of the process, the pressure is released, allowing the carbon dioxide to return to a gas; the surfactants are separated from the dirt and captured for reuse. The clean clothes are ready, without the need for any form of drying. The entire process is a closed system, eliminating all forms of waste, pollution, and emissions.

Micell's franchise operation, Hanger's Cleaners, is now being rolled out across North America. The clean and safe nature of the workplace, combined with the more sophisticated nature of the technology, enables Hangers to create jobs with a higher skill and wage base. There are now a handful of other carbon dioxide-based dry cleaning plays on the market. It is only a matter of time before the toxic dry cleaning sweatshops of today are relegated to the scrap heap of history.

Developing an Ecomagination

It may indeed be possible for small, start-up ventures like Micell Technologies to creatively destroy the dry cleaning industry in the United States: The industry has not consolidated, at least in part because acquiring current players would mean amassing a huge portfolio of toxic sites! Thus, given the fragmented "mom-and-pop" nature of the industry, there are no large incumbent dry cleaning corporations with established positions to protect. In most other industries, however, it is a different story given that creative destruction means some large incumbents' core businesses end up on the chopping block. It is this reality that makes General Electric's initiative in clean technology so interesting—and important.

Indeed, May 2005 may have marked an important turning point for General Electric, the venerable 127-year-old corporate titan. It was then that chairman and CEO Jeffrey Immelt publicly announced that the $150 billion company was betting its future on clean technology. Immelt unveiled a company-wide growth plan—dubbed "Ecomagination"—aimed at solving some of the world's most pressing environmental problems through the aggressive commercialization of new technologies such as wind power, solar energy, fuel cells, high-efficiency gas turbines, hybrid locomotives, lower-emission aircraft engines, lighter and stronger materials, energy-efficient lighting, and water purification technologies.[18]

As part of the Ecomagination initiative, GE has committed to: 1) doubling its annual research investment in cleaner technologies, from $700 million in 2004 to $1.5 billion in 2010; 2) doubling its current $10 billion in annual revenue from clean tech products and services to at least $20 billion by 2010; 3) reducing its greenhouse gas intensity 40 percent by 2012 (a 1 percent real reduction in emissions versus a 40 percent rise without further action); and 4) reporting publicly on its progress toward meeting these goals. As of 2009, the company was on track to meet or exceed all of these goals.

While May 2005 marked the official launch of the Ecomagination initiative, it clearly built on decades of investment in technology and product development at the company. Indeed, GE's aggressive, risk-taking style and innovative technical culture made it perfectly suited to the melding of societal and financial goals. Immelt stated this succinctly in his May 2005 address: "Ecomagination, which is based on GE's belief that solving environmental problems is good business, constitutes a significant growth strategy for the company." The message seems clear: There need not be an inherent trade-off between environmental and financial performance. Rather, with creativity and imagination, it is possible to solve some of the world's most difficult environmental problems and make money doing it.

Working with the NGO Green Order and other third-party environmental groups, GE developed a scorecard system for evaluating products and technologies. To qualify for Ecomagination, products must not only outperform environmentally, but also economically—both for GE and its customers. Under this system, "green products" that deliver a lower level of functionality at a premium price using environmental performance as an excuse would never see the light of day. Only those products and technologies that break free from the tyranny of trade-off thinking would achieve Ecomagination status.

Individual businesses propose products for Ecomagination consideration. The evaluation process is audited by a third party and can take up to a month and a half to complete. Interestingly, potential products are not limited to those produced by the company's manufacturing businesses. The program extends to the products and services of the organization's vast financial business as well. By the end of 2008, GE had 80 Ecomagination products, up from just 17 in 2005. Revenue derived from Ecomagination products had also surpassed the $17 billion mark with a backlog of nearly $100 billion.

Is Ecomagination a bold move? The truth is that the majority of Ecomagination products thus far have been "greening" improvements to existing products. However, Ecomagination also includes an important though less visible process for fostering corporate investment in disruptive technologies such as biomimicry, nanotechnology, renewable energy, point-of-use water treatment, and other emerging clean technologies. At a time when most other corporations are cutting back central R&D funding for projects that lack clear market application with existing customers, the Ecomagination initiative goes in a different direction. Through the initiative, GE is creating options to pursue more radical technologies that may take longer to develop but promise the potential for step function improvements with large payoffs. Indeed, in 2008, the company invested $1.4 billion in clean-tech R&D.

Whole-Systems Thinking

As the cases of General Electric, Burlington Chemical, and Micell Technologies make clear, managing for continuity and efficiency—through cost or differentiation advantages in existing industries and businesses—is no longer enough. In the future, competitive advantage will increasingly shift to the capacity for exploration, disruptive innovation, creative destruction, and corporate "blue ocean" strategy.[19] This shift necessitates moving beyond the conventional modes of business analysis, those emphasizing comparison of existing alternatives so prevalent in business schools and firms today.

The logic of marginal analysis—the tracking of incremental changes in costs and benefits—holds that there is an optimum point beyond which it makes no sense to seek additional performance improvements in, say, quality or emissions reduction. Beyond a certain point, in other words, it costs more to achieve an additional increment of improvement than it is worth. Although this form of analysis makes implicit sense in a world of predetermined alternatives and incremental adjustments, it becomes self-defeating when the objective is disruptive change. To succeed in this space, a new logic is required, one based upon whole-systems thinking.

In their encyclopedic treatise *Natural Capitalism*, Paul Hawken, Amory Lovins, and Hunter Lovins make a persuasive case for the logic of whole-systems thinking in connection with sustainability.[20] They demonstrate how incremental thinking can blind us to the potential for leapfrog innovation. Using the familiar example of home construction, they show how component-based, marginal analysis leads us to design buildings that fail to realize their full potential. For example, the energy efficiency of buildings is usually determined after the basic structure and utilities have already been put in place by how much insulation is used, what grade of windows are installed, what types of appliances are purchased, and so on. Each of these decisions is made separately using marginal analysis: Additional insulation becomes "uneconomic" beyond a certain point because the initial capital cost will never be recouped through energy savings. This style of analysis has trained us to believe that the only way to realize more energy-efficient homes is to pay the additional cost required to install the necessary conservation technology. Incremental benefits must exceed incremental costs.

But what happens if we step outside the artificial cage imposed by component-based, marginal thinking? To do this, we must abandon the existing design conventions associated with home construction (which means we also have to set aside existing building codes, regulations, and industry best practices). We must start with a clean sheet and embrace the logic of whole-systems thinking. When we do this, however, we can readily see that it is possible to "have our cake and eat it too." That is, we can design superefficient houses and even cars that actually cost less to build than the original unimproved versions.

How is this possible? The fatal flaw of marginal analysis is its tacit acceptance of current designs and products as given. By accepting the world as it currently exists, we ensure that only incremental improvements are possible. Thus, in seeking a more energy-efficient home, we accept that the current convention (indeed, requirement in most localities in the United States) of having heating systems, ductwork, blowers, air compressors, and so on is necessary and appropriate. The aim is simply to reduce the extent of their use through add-on energy-conservation investments. (It should be apparent that this is nothing more than a glorified form of end-of-pipe thinking.)

But what if we question the very need for these expensive and potentially unnecessary pieces of capital equipment? What if we invest more in building a well-insulated, passively heated and cooled structure powered by solar energy so that we can eliminate the need for a conventional heating and cooling system altogether? Might this not produce a home of superior functionality, energy efficiency, and cost? Ample evidence demonstrates that, indeed, such a design philosophy can and does work. What holds it back is not technology, but rather restrictive rules, laws, and building codes, and the inertia associated with the current construction industry, particularly material suppliers and contractors, who only know how to build one way: the unsustainable way.

Make It Right (MIR) Foundation in New Orleans demonstrates the potential for such a whole-systems design philosophy.[21] In the wake of Hurricane Katrina, Brad Pitt engaged William McDonough, Cherokee Gives Back, and the architectural firm Graft to design a safe, sustainable, and affordable form of housing for the redevelopment of the Lower 9th Ward—the area that was completely devastated by the flood. Inspired by "cradle-to-cradle" thinking, MIR has been able to "shatter the trade-off" by designing homes that are virtually energy self-sufficient (as well as storm resistant) while keeping the cost per square foot competitive with standard construction. Because the new homes are so cheap to operate, they turn out to be *more* affordable for returning residents than either existing homes or conventional new construction.

Implementing the logic of whole-systems thinking in a fragmented industry like home construction is difficult, but it may be easier to achieve in industries dominated by large incumbent players with the bargaining power to change the rules of the game. Walmart, for example, in its recent shift to sustainability as a core business strategy, has shown just how much power and leverage large retailers can have over the companies they purchase from. In 2005, Walmart, the second largest corporation in the world, announced three quite audacious environmental goals: 1) to be supplied 100 percent by renewable energy; 2) to create zero waste; and 3) to sell products that sustain resources and the environment. At the same time, the company remained totally committed to its promise of Every Day Low Prices.

Clearly, these goals cannot be reconciled through greening alone. It will be necessary for suppliers and vendors to "shatter the trade-off myth" through beyond greening initiatives that foster creative destruction. Rather than simply squeezing current suppliers, Walmart is using whole-systems thinking to restructure entire value chains. The company's organic cotton strategy provides a case in point: Walmart is working with farmers to assist them in the transition to organic farming practices. In the short term, however, this has the effect of raising the price of cotton, considering it takes several years for farmers to achieve organic certification. To offset this added cost, the company is using its leverage to lower costs elsewhere by eliminating middle men and simplifying the cotton supply chain. The end result is natural apparel on sale at Every Day Low Prices—and the prospect of moving the mass market toward organic cotton. This is especially significant considering that conventional cotton agriculture accounts for over one-quarter of total pesticide use in the world![22]

Thinking like a disruptive innovator through the logic of whole-systems thinking may also hold the key to future growth for incumbents in industries currently mired in low-growth, commodity competition. It may also hold the key to moving us toward a more sustainable form of mobility for the twenty-first century. Consider the possibilities.

Reinventing the Wheels

Chapter 3, "The Sustainable Value Portfolio," analyzed the automobile industry's evolution over the past 50 years in terms of the sustainable value portfolio. It traced the industry's path from a strictly adversarial command-and-control approach to the pollution-prevention and product stewardship initiatives of the 1980s and 1990s. By the early twenty-first century, all major car companies had initiated clean technology (fuel cell or alternative) vehicle programs. Unfortunately, all had continued to use the logic of component-based, incremental thinking in these clean technology initiatives, except one: General Motors.

Most fuel cell vehicle programs, like their hybrid vehicle cousins, still envisioned the product in conventional terms: a heavy metal chassis and body with thousands of component parts. Unfortunately, in the early twenty-first century, fuel cells were still many times more expensive to produce than internal-combustion engines. Thus, when a fuel cell (with an electric motor) is seen as a simple replacement for the internal-combustion engine, the result is an overpriced product that few consumers (save the ultragreen) would ever consider purchasing. GM had already been down this path with its overpriced and underperforming electric vehicle, the Impact, in the 1990s. With more than 1,000 pounds of batteries, it failed to gain sufficient commercial traction, even in the regulation-driven California market, where a certain percentage of zero-emission vehicles was required by law. As Amory Lovins likes to say, "Optimizing one element in isolation pessimizes the whole system."

In 2002, General Motors launched the AUTOnomy project, a bold $1 billion initiative to reinvent the automobile around hydrogen fuel cell technology. Unlike its competitors, GM took a clean-sheet approach not only to vehicle design, but to the entire manufacturing system. Rather than thinking of the fuel cell as a simple replacement for the engine, GM tried to imagine a different approach. Who said that fuel cells have to be boxlike contraptions that look like batteries or engines? Why couldn't the fuel cell be integrated into the design of the vehicle in a more functional way? Accordingly, the design team devised a way to build a fuel cell that doubles as the vehicle's chassis—a fuel cell "skateboard" with four small electric motors to power each of the four wheels independently (see Exhibit 4.2). This design not only delivers superior power and torque, especially at the low end, but it also allows the wheels to be controlled independently, enabling the vehicle to be driven sideways into a parallel parking place.

Exhibit 4.2
GM's Autonomy

Wireless steering controls, fuel cell
"skateboard" mean more flexible
body design

The skateboard forms the backbone for the product concept, which can then take on virtually any form or functionality. Body types and seating capacity can be modularly designed and installed on the skateboard in a way that allows for maximum flexibility. Want an SUV? Lease an SUV body and interior. Want a sedan? Switch to this body type as you see fit. What's more, GM has moved to radically simplify the vehicle's design. Apart from the electric motors and the wheels, there are virtually no moving parts: The steering and all the vehicle's functions are controlled electronically using wireless technology. This so-called Hy-wire approach has allowed GM engineers to reduce the number of component parts from thousands to hundreds, drastically simplifying the supply chain and cycle time of the product. Thus, by radically simplifying the design around a fuel cell that doubles as the vehicle's chassis, GM hopes to compensate for the higher cost of the fuel cell with much lower sourcing and production costs.[23] This is whole-systems thinking at its best.

Yet conceptualizing and building the innovative new product is not enough. Commercialization strategy is also a crucial piece of the puzzle. Here it is not clear that GM, which is famous for creating impressive new technologies only to have them fail in the marketplace, has a compelling lead. GM's plan is to launch the AUTOnomy in the highly competitive United States market. Unfortunately, given the widespread availability of gasoline in the U.S., it is highly unlikely that a hydrogen fuel infrastructure will be developed anytime soon, unless the federal government has a significant change of heart. Because fuel cells depend on hydrogen for fuel, the only way that GM can bring its product to market in the United States is to add an expensive piece of equipment that "reforms" gasoline into hydrogen to power the fuel cell. Thus, even though the vehicle would be powered by a fuel cell, it would use fossil fuels to supply hydrogen to the cell, effectively nullifying the alternative nature of the technology. In a carbon-constrained world with significant dependence on oil from the Middle East, this would not seem to be a very sustainable strategy.

Unfortunately, most car companies persist in viewing the developing world market as consisting only of the rich at the top of the pyramid. GM's China strategy consists largely of producing Buicks to compete against prestige brands such as Mercedes, BMW, and Lexus in a battle to win the business of China's wealthiest and most sophisticated consumers. But what if GM connected its recently announced joint venture to produce "minivehicles" in China to its billion-dollar strategy to produce fuel-cell vehicles in the United States? Might it be possible to invent a whole new product category while simultaneously incubating a renewable fuel infrastructure in China? As noted in Chapter 3, aspiring companies from the developing world such as Tata Motors appear to have already set these wheels in motion. The winds of creative destruction are gaining strength, and they appear to blowing from the East.

Technologies of Liberation

Since the dawn of the Industrial Revolution, Western economies have relied on the unsustainable use of raw materials and energy from lesser-developed countries to prosper: timber from South America, oil from the Middle East, minerals from Africa. Economies of scale ruled the day, with massive investments in power plants, pipelines, factories, dams, and highways to more efficiently serve the burgeoning consumption needs of those at the top of the economic pyramid. Industrial-era technologies (such as electricity, petrochemicals, and automobiles) were also closely associated with mass production, the assembly line, and centralized, bureaucratic organization, resulting in the rise of organized labor, worker alienation, and growing social stratification. As Diane Coyle points out in her book *Paradoxes of Prosperity*, society both shapes the dominant technology and is, in turn, shaped by it.[24]

As we enter the second decade of the new century, the "dark satanic mills" of the Industrial Revolution are giving way to a new generation of technologies that promise to change dramatically the societal, economic, and environmental landscape. The information economy powered by the microchip has already begun to revolutionize society by democratizing access to information, empowering workers, and increasing productivity. Indeed, Facebook, U-Tube, Twitter, and the rapid emergence of the "Blogosphere" have spawned a bottom-up revolution in user-generated content. In the coming years, bioscience, nanotechnology, new materials, wireless IT, solar, fuel cells, and other forms of distributed energy generation could also dramatically reduce the size of the human footprint on the planet.

Indeed, there are two fundamentally different types of clean technology—large-scale, centralized applications and small-scale, distributed solutions.[25] The first variety, which I call "Green Giant," typically requires policy change, public investment, and a centralized deployment strategy to implement. Because of their scale and scope, Green Giant technologies are more readily developed by large, incumbent firms with much to gain through government subsidy or procurement; think big wind, centralized water treatment, and massive solar wind farms. The "go big" approach is also politically advantageous because it gives the appearance of confronting big problems with big and bold solutions. The problem, of course, is that there is little margin for error: Betting on a few big solutions in unexplored territory almost always produces nasty surprises. Remember nuclear power in the 1960s and '70s? Electricity too cheap to meter short-circuited with Three Mile Island and Chernobyl. In the end, the Law of Unintended Consequences almost always wins. We are just not that smart.

In contrast, the second variety of clean-tech, which I call "Green Sprout," is typically distributed in character and disruptive to incumbent firms and institutions. Because existing players in the utility, energy, transport, food, and material sectors have so much to lose, it is enormously difficult for the entrepreneurs developing small wind, decentralized solar, point-of-use water, and other distributed solutions to gain traction in established markets. Yet given their small scale and distributed nature, such clean technologies hold the potential to creatively destroy existing hierarchies, bypass corrupt governments and regimes, and usher in an entirely new age of capitalism that brings widely distributed benefits to the entire human community. And rather than depending on national governments or paternalistic social engineers to design the future for the aspiring masses, these disruptive new technologies may be best brought forward through the power of capitalism—not the capitalism of the Industrial Revolution, which enriched a few at the expense of many, but rather a new, more dynamic form of global capitalism that will uproot established elites and unseat incumbents by creating opportunity at the base of the economic pyramid on a previously unimagined scale.

Eating Your Own Lunch

Joseph Schumpeter was skeptical of the ability and motivation of large, incumbent corporations to drive the process of creative destruction, but he did not dismiss them entirely. He thought that large investments in an installed asset base and misaligned managerial incentives would reduce incumbents' motivation to make their established positions obsolete. Yet he also recognized that, paradoxically, large corporations have financial, technical, and organizational resources that cannot be matched by small, entrepreneurial new entrants: "[I]t may happen that new combinations should be carried out by the same people who control the productive or commercial process which is to be displaced by the new."[26]

Clearly, incumbents in certain industries are structurally more likely than others to pursue the path of creative destruction. Industries characterized by high asset intensity and long asset life (for example, utilities, mining, oil, petrochemicals, and automobiles) may find it the most difficult to engage in the sort of self-disruption described in this chapter. Greening clearly presents the path of least resistance for these incumbents, given their heavy commitment to existing assets in the ground. Why? Fully depreciated assets are very profitable to run; shutting them down prematurely results in a significant performance penalty in the short term.

At the other end of the spectrum are service industries, retailers, and firms based on the emerging "technologies of liberation" described previously. Players in these industries are in a prime position to focus their strategic energy on disruption for sustainability. Because they are not wed to long-lived assets in the ground, firms in these industries can purposefully skip over emphasis on the incremental improvements to current technologies associated with greening. Witness, for example, Walmart's recent conversion to sustainability. Given its size and buyer power, the company is not only "greening" its entire supply chain, but, increasingly, it is seeking out the clean technologies and products of tomorrow.

Between these two extremes are industries with intermediate levels of asset life and intensity—electronics, computers, information technology, health care, and consumer products, for example. Incumbents in these industries are well positioned to pursue hybrid strategies of both continuous improvement and creative destruction, given their shorter technology life cycles and more rapid turnover of assets.

Industry structure thus determines, at least to some extent, the proclivity of incumbents to pursue beyond greening strategies. Although firms in asset-intensive industries may be the least likely to pursue this path, they paradoxically face the biggest threat if they ignore the challenge: For these firms, continued blind adherence to yesterday's technology could spell doom, not just a missed opportunity. The recent bankruptcy and bailout of GM could not provide clearer evidence of this assertion. It is therefore crucial that all firms, especially incumbents in pollution- and asset-intensive industries, begin to accelerate the process of creative destruction for sustainability.

To succeed at creative destruction, innovators—be they large corporations or entrepreneurial startups—will need to find the appropriate early markets for the sustainable technologies of the future. As we saw with the GM fuel cell case, forcing clean technologies into the established market at the top of the pyramid may not be the best course of action. Building the early markets for clean technologies with the potential for creative destruction may instead require a fundamentally different approach. As we will see, the base of the economic pyramid, where four billion people's needs are still unmet, may be the best place to incubate the technologies of the future.

Notes

1. Joseph Schumpeter, *The Theory of Economic Development* (Cambridge, MA: Harvard University Press, 1934).

2. Clayton Christensen, *The Innovator's Dilemma: When New Technologies Cause Great Firms to Fail* (Boston: Harvard Business School Press, 1997).

3. Ibid.

4. Portions of the next section are excerpted from Stuart Hart and Mark Milstein, "Global Sustainability and the Creative Destruction of Industries," *Sloan Management Review* 41(1) (1999): 23–33.

5. Stuart Hart and Clayton Christensen, "The Great Leap: Driving Innovation from the Base of the Pyramid," *Sloan Management Review* 44(1) (2002): 51–56.

6. Andy King and Michael Lenox, "Exploring the Locus of Profitable Pollution Reduction," *Management Science* 47(2) (2002): 289–299.

7. World Commission on Environment and Development, *Our Common Future* (Oxford: Oxford University Press, 1987).

8. Mathis Wackernagel and William Rees, *Our Ecological Footprint* (Gabriola Island, B.C.: New Society Publishers, 1996).

9. Chad Holliday, "Sustainable Growth, the DuPont Way," *Harvard Business Review* 79(8) (2001): 129–132.

10. The information about DuPont comes from personal communications with key executives, including Paul Tebo, Corporate Vice President for Safety, Health, and Environment; and Eduardo Wanick, President of DuPont Latin America.

11. "2008 Sustainability Progress Report," DuPont, 2008.

12. Joseph Schumpeter, *Theory of Economic Development*.

13. See, for example, Richard Foster and Sarah Kaplan, *Creative Destruction* (New York: Doubleday, 2001); Gary Hamel and C.K. Prahalad, *Competing for the Future* (Boston: Harvard Business School Press, 1994); and Clayton Christensen, *The Innovator's Dilemma*.

14. Richard Foster and Sarah Kaplan, *Creative Destruction*.

15. See www.cleantech.com. See also Mark Johnson and Josh Suskewicz, "How to Jump Start the Clean Tech Economy," *Harvard Business Review*, November (2009).

16. Many thanks to Sam Moore, Chief Technologist for Burlington Chemical, for the information cited in this case.

17. Unfortunately, the company could not make the transition from textiles into specialty lubricant additives and green surfactants rapidly enough. In hindsight, although some short-term improvements occurred, the long timeframe required to gain credibility with clean technologies in the incumbent markets was underestimated. Had the company divested the textile segments of its business sooner, recognizing the need for "creative destruction" of this business in order to free up cash flows and organizational energy targeting new markets, the strategy could have succeeded. Unfortunately, the economic environment and the slow adoption of green lubricant and surfactant additives caught up with the company in 2007, and it was forced to divest its assets.

18. This section is summarized from: Stuart Hart and Mark Milstein, "In Search of Sustainable Enterprise: The Case of GE's Ecomagination Initiative," *Value* 1(1) (2006): 36–42.

19. James March, "Exploration and Exploitation in Organizational Learning," *Organization Science* 2(1) (1991): 71–87; Clayton Christensen, *The Innovator's Dilemma*; Stuart Hart and Mark Milstein, "Global Sustainability;" Chan Kim and Renée Mauborgne, *Blue Ocean Strategy* (Boston: Harvard Business School Press, 2005).

20. Paul Hawken, Amory Lovins, and Hunter Lovins, *Natural Capitalism* (Boston: Little Brown and Co., 1999).

21. www.makeitrightnola.org.

22. Lyn Denend and Erica Plambeck, *Wal-Mart's Sustainability Strategy*, Stanford Graduate School of Business Case, 2007.

23. David Baum, "GM's Billion-Dollar Bet," Wired.com, www.wired.com/wired/archive/10.08/fuelcellcars.html, 2002.

24. D. Coyle, *Paradoxes of Prosperity* (New York: Texere Publishing, 2001).

25. These ideas are adapted from Stuart Hart, "Taking the Green Leap," Cornell University Working Paper, 2009.

26. Joseph Schumpeter, *Theory of Economic Development*, p. 66.

5

Innovation from the Bottom-Up

The dual financial and climate crises have finally awakened the sleeping giant. *New York Times* columnist Tom Friedman argues that the best way for America to "get its groove back" is to take the lead in solving the world's big problems—to issue what he calls a "Code Green:" "In a world that is getting hot, flat, and crowded, the task of creating the tools, systems, energy sources, and ethics that will allow the planet to grow in cleaner, more sustainable ways is going to be the biggest challenge of our lifetime."[1] Activist Van Jones, Founder of Green for All, agrees: America's challenge is to build the "green collar economy" where ordinary people benefit from the rapid deployment of energy efficiency and green technology: "That's why the government needs to immediately launch a massive initiative like the Manhattan Project...or the Apollo Mission...to solve the riddles of clean energy and perfect these technologies."[2]

And the good news is that after decades of denial, inaction, or, at best, incremental policy prescriptions, the alarm bell has now sounded in government. The Obama administration in the U.S. has now made green technology (and the creation of "green collar" jobs) a national priority, along with scores of other countries around the world, including China, Brazil, and India. Indeed, we are now flooded with proposals for massive government programs, corporate restructurings, stimulus packages, and moon-shot-style initiatives for green technology development. During times of crisis, the temptation is great to believe that a few smart people can design the Big

Solution. The metaphor of "war" is often invoked—the war on terrorism, drugs, poverty, global warming, etc. Yet, with the exception of actual wartime military mobilizations, seldom have massive, centrally-directed initiatives succeeded.[3]

So if incremental governmental policies are insufficient, and large-scale, crash programs are likely to fail, then what can be done? Fortunately, there is a third way—a strategy for incubating thousands of small-scale, yet radical business experiments aimed at leapfrogging today's unsustainable practices, each with the opportunity to grow and become one of tomorrow's sustainable corporations. In order for the vision of a sustainable future to flourish, it will take an engaged private sector and entrepreneurship on an unprecedented scale. It is a strategy that taps into the entrepreneurial spirit in all of us—change agents in global corporations and NGOs, social entrepreneurs, the poor in underserved communities, investors, and public servants; a strategy that can unite the world—East and West, North and South, Rich and Poor—in a common cause, fostering peace and shared prosperity. But perhaps most importantly, it is a strategy that starts small and grows from the bottom up, starting from the base of the pyramid.

On the Horns of a Dilemma

Just as countries are struggling to find their way in this new world, so too are corporations searching for new strategies. Indeed, the majority of large companies seem to be mired in saturated markets that have few significant growth opportunities. Before the financial crisis plunged the world into a global economic slow-down, corporate leaders were content with the centralized globalization and "emerging market" strategies that had served them well throughout much of previous two decades. During this time, rich countries and rising middle classes in the developing world accounted for the majority of the market opportunity. Now, however, with the rich world likely to be mired in a prolonged period of slow growth, companies must turn their attention elsewhere—to the low-end segments that they previously ignored.

However, as we have seen, the rapid rise of global capitalism over the past two decades has been accompanied by mounting concerns over environmental degradation, labor exploitation, cultural hegemony, and loss of local autonomy, particularly in the Third World. The rising tide of antiglobalization, along with civil strife and growing insurrection throughout the developing world, make it apparent that corporate expansion at the expense of the poor and the environment will encounter vigorous resistance. This raises the question: Must corporations' quest for future growth serve only to fan the flames of the antiglobalization movement?

Fortunately, there is a way out of this global "Catch-22": The best way to both generate growth and satisfy social and environmental stakeholders is to focus on emerging markets. By this, I do not refer to incremental market expansion targeted at the wealthy few or rising middle classes in the developing world. Instead, I argue that the best path will be through a Great Leap Downward—to the base of the economic pyramid, where more than four billion people have been bypassed or damaged by globalization.[4] It is here that companies will find the most exciting growth markets of the future—and the basis for a formidable future vision. It is here that the disruptive technologies needed to address the social and environmental challenges associated with economic growth can best be incubated and developed. And it is here where the solutions to the rich world's environmental and economic problems will first be incubated.

Birth of BoP

I still vividly recall the conversation that started it all. It was the fall of 1997, and I had recently published an article in the *Harvard Business Review* (HBR) that examined the opportunity for the corporate sector to profitably pursue strategies for a more sustainable world. Global poverty, rising inequity, and environmental degradation in the Third World led the list of problems to be solved. The article, "Beyond Greening: Strategies for a Sustainable World," went on to win the McKinsey Award as the best article in HBR that year. My strategy colleague at Michigan, the late C.K. Prahalad, had just completed a draft manuscript with Ken Lieberthal that would ultimately appear in HBR in 1998 as "The End of Corporate Imperialism."[5] He shared a copy of the paper and asked for comments and suggestions.

I remember being absolutely struck by the complementary nature of our thinking. In the paper, Prahalad and Lieberthal make a compelling argument for both the challenge and opportunity of serving the emerging markets in China and India, especially the tier below the wealthiest consumers in these countries that most multinationals had been preoccupied with up to that point. In our ensuing discussion about the paper, I remember making the comment that serving the next tier down from the top was indeed important, but this still left unexamined (and unserved) the vast majority of humanity in the lowest tiers of the global economic pyramid. Neither government (including the multilaterals) nor the nonprofit sector had been particularly successful in addressing this mounting problem over the past half-century. Aid and philanthropy were clearly insufficient to solve the problem.

At that moment, it became apparent to both of us that what was missing (and critically needed) was a logic for why (and how) the corporate sector might focus attention on understanding and serving the four billion poorest people at the bottom (or base) of the economic pyramid (BoP, for short). We developed a working paper in 1998 that went through literally dozens of revisions over the next four years before it was published in January 2002 as "The Fortune at the Bottom of the Pyramid."[6] (C.K. later published a book by the same title.) The concept of the BoP was born.

Significant momentum has now been established around this agenda, with literally dozens of colleagues from around the world now working actively in this arena.[7] In 2000, the Base of the Pyramid

(BoP) Learning Laboratory was founded at UNC's Kenan-Flagler Business School.[8] The BoP Learning Lab is a consortium of corporations, NGOs, and academics interested in learning how to serve the needs of the poor in a way that is culturally appropriate, environmentally sustainable, and profitable.[9] A global network of BoP Learning Labs has since been spawned with partners in Mexico, Brazil, Argentina, Spain, the Netherlands, Denmark, India, China, and South Africa.[10]

In 2004, the BoP Learning Laboratory moved to Cornell University as part of the new center for Sustainable Global Enterprise at the Johnson School. Since the advent of the BoP Learning Lab, the World Resources Institute, the World Business Council for Sustainable Development, International Finance Corporation, the United Nations Development Program, U.S. AID, and the Inter-American Development Bank, among others, have launched major programs focused on the role of the private sector in alleviating poverty and catalyzing sustainable development. Over the past decade, it has thus become apparent that the BoP offers both enormous opportunities and challenges for companies accustomed to serving the wealthy at the top of the economic pyramid.

The Tip of the Iceberg

As just noted, for much of the past half-century, corporations have chosen to focus their attention exclusively at the top of the world economic pyramid, especially the very top where 75 million to 100 million highly affluent "Tier 1" consumers reside.[11] This is a cosmopolitan group, to be sure, composed of upper-income people in developed countries, especially the U.S., Western Europe, and Japan, and the few rich elites from the developing world.

With the fall of communism in the late 1980s, however, multinational corporations rushed into so-called "emerging markets"—Russia and its former allies, along with China, India, and Latin America—with the expectation that they would be the next great business bonanza. Unfortunately, by the early twenty-first century, corporate momentum in emerging markets had slowed considerably. The prospect for hundreds of millions of new middle-class consumers in the developing world had been oversold. The Asian and Latin American financial crises in the late 1990s put a damper on the rate of foreign direct investment (FDI). The events of September 11, 2001, further slowed the advance. And the recent global financial crisis all but flattened what Tom Friedman refers to as the emerging "flat world" of the global middle class.[12]

With the benefit of hindsight, we can now see more clearly why most multinationals' global and emerging market strategies have not realized their full potential: They were neither very global nor particularly oriented toward emerging markets. In the developing world, most FDI has targeted only the few "large market" countries, such as China, India, and Brazil. And even there, most MNC emerging market strategies have focused exclusively on the 800 million or so wealthy customers or perhaps the rising middle classes, ignoring the vast majority of people considered too poor to do business with (see Exhibit 5.1).

Many reasons have been offered to justify and explain corporate preoccupation with the top of the economic pyramid in emerging economies. Some, for example, have suggested that such customers are more similar to American, European, and Japanese consumers, which MNCs are accustomed to serving, and thus present less "psychic distance" than do the impoverished inhabitants of shantytowns and rural villages. Others point to the lack of important institutions in the developing world (such as rule of law and intellectual property), which makes conventional MNC operations all but impossible.[13]

Not surprisingly, then, most MNC strategies have aimed to tailor existing products to fit the needs of the top of the pyramid in the developing world. The incremental product changes and modest cost reductions associated with this strategy, however, have not succeeded in reaching the vast majority of people. The net result is that the four billion plus people at the base of the economic pyramid—fully two-thirds of humanity—have been largely ignored by corporations. They have been bypassed by globalization, their needs are being poorly met by local vendors, and they are increasingly the victims of corruption and active exploitation by predatory suppliers and intermediaries.[14] Much like the proverbial iceberg with only its tip in plain view, this huge segment of the global population—along with its massive potential market—has remained largely invisible to the corporate sector.

Exhibit 5.1
The Global Pyramid

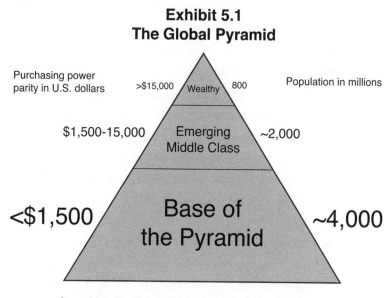

Source: Adapted from Prahalad, C.K. and Hart, S. 2002. "The fortune at the bottom of the pyramid." *Strategy+Business*, 26: 54-67, with assistance from Ted London.

GE's Ecomagination initiative (described in detail in Chapter 4, "Clean Technology and Creative Destruction") provides a case in point. Without detracting from Ecomagination's bold intent and clear, rigorous process, it is also important to point out its limitations. Indeed, virtually all of the Ecomagination products serve the needs of current, wealthy (or emerging middle class) customers at the top of the economic pyramid. Comparatively little attention has been given to the world's 4 billion poor at the base of the economic pyramid who lack reliable, affordable solutions related to energy, transportation, water, materials, and financial services.

Where GE's new technologies might apply to solving the problems of the world's poor (e.g., desalination technology, wind energy, advanced membrane technology), they have typically been large-scale, capital-intensive applications premised on existing business models. In fact, most Ecomagination products and technologies continue to focus on centralized solutions. This should not come as a great surprise given the company's large-scale, industrial past, but it does represent a potential blind spot in the Ecomagination strategy. For example, the wind energy business seems to be organized exclusively around "big wind"—the massive utility-scale wind turbines that lend themselves to connection to the existing grid system.

Only recently has the company begun to entertain the commercialization of small-scale, distributed technologies such as distributed solar, point-of-use water treatment, and portable, small-scale health devices—what I refer to as "Green Sprout" technologies. In fact, in a 2009 *Harvard Business Review* article, GE CEO Jeff Immelt, along with co-authors Vijay Govindarajan and Chris Trimble state emphatically that the future of the company depends on becoming adept at what they call "reverse innovation": the ability to incubate low-cost innovations in the developing world and then migrate them up-market to the developed world.[15] As we will see later in this chapter, this idea is entirely consistent with the one that my colleague Clay Christensen and I have been arguing for nearly a decade. However, the fact that a global corporation like GE now recognizes publicly that this is the only way to avoid being pre-empted by the emerging innovators from the developing world is indeed an important tipping point.

With stagnation in the established markets of the world economy and rising antiglobalization sentiments, opportunities for serving the base of the pyramid are becoming increasingly attractive, given that the BoP space is largely decoupled from the vicissitudes of the "global economy." In fact, concealed below the surface of the purchasing power parity numbers is an immense and fast-growing economic system that includes a thriving community of small enterprises, barter exchanges, sustainable livelihoods activities, and subsistence farming.[16] Indeed, it is estimated that well over half of the total economic activity in the developing world takes place outside the formal economy, in the so-called informal or extralegal sector.[17]

The base of the pyramid is also rich in assets, although most are unregistered and, therefore, remain invisible. In his book *The Mystery of Capital*, Hernando de Soto estimates that there are well over $9 trillion in unregistered assets (houses, equipment, and so on) in the rural villages and urban slums of the world.[18] Because the poor typically do not hold legal title to these assets, they remain trapped and underleveraged, protected only by the informal property systems enforced by local strongmen.

Unlike the "underground" economy at the top of the pyramid, which is driven by the desire to avoid paying income taxes (just ask your waiter or carpenter), the informal sector at the base of the pyramid exists because of the difficulty and expense of becoming legally registered due to corruption and archaic rules. It has been estimated, for example, that it takes thousands of dollars, several hundred steps, and more than a year of effort to officially register a business in most developing countries today.[19] Small wonder, then, why the extralegal sector is thriving while the formal economies in many developing countries today show little or even negative growth. The challenge is to connect the informal and formal economies in a productive and mutually beneficial partnership.

In short, the emerging market opportunity may be much larger than previously thought. However, the new untapped source of promise is not the wealthy few in the developing world or even the rising middle-class consumers—it is the billions of aspiring poor who are seeking to join the market economy for the first time. Effectively reaching the base of the pyramid, however, calls for disruptive innovation on a massive scale and the creation of entirely new, more sustainable industries in the process.[20] And unlike Mao Zedung's Great Leap Forward in China, which ended up taking the country backward during the Cultural Revolution, the Great Leap Downward to the BoP may ultimately incubate more sustainable ways of living for people at the top of the pyramid.

Creative Creation

As Clay Christensen so eloquently explains in his path-breaking book, *The Innovator's Dilemma*, disruptive innovations involve products and services that initially aren't as good as those that historically have been used by customers in mainstream markets and that, therefore, can take root only in new or less-demanding applications among nontraditional customers.[21] Examples include transistor radios, small cars, personal computers, solar energy, and online investing; in each case, the initial offering was seen as different—even strange—from the standpoint of the mainstream market. Recall that transistor radios were initially adopted by teenagers, small cars by the cost-conscious, personal computers by artists and academics, solar energy by "greens," and online investing by the Internet-savvy.

Well-managed companies are pressured to invest in innovations that target markets large enough to sustain corporate growth rates and enhance overall profit margins. To them, pursuing disruptive innovations seems irrational. This allows disruptive innovators to incubate their businesses in the safety of markets that resource-rich competitors are motivated to ignore and then to grow up-market by attacking a sequence of market tiers that are the least attractive investment options facing the leaders.

Disruptive innovations typically enable a larger population of less-skilled or less-wealthy people to begin doing for themselves things that historically could be done only through skilled intermediaries or by the wealthy. Disruptions have thus been a fundamental mechanism for creating new growth businesses and improving our standard of living. Joseph Schumpeter's notion of creative destruction tells only half the story: In reality, before a disruptive innovation destroys industry leaders and incumbent technologies, a long and fruitful period of "creative creation" typically occurs. Indeed, the social good is well served through disruption, which has, over the decades, created millions of jobs, generated hundreds of billions of dollars in revenues and market capitalization, and raised standards of living by making available cheap, high-quality products and services. We have gained more through creative creation than we have lost through creative destruction.

For example, until the late 1970s, only employees of large companies and universities had access to computers—and that access could be had only by giving punched cards to the expert in the mainframe center who ran the job. Minicomputer makers such as Digital Equipment listened diligently to their customers, and their customers told them that the nascent technology of personal computing was a waste of time. It was a quirky new gadget only for artists, kids, and hippies, not something intended for the sophisticated technologists in large corporations and universities that controlled access to computing. Not surprisingly, the early market for PCs, led by upstarts such as Apple, was to be found among artists, academics, and other members of the counterculture.

But as PC technology evolved and developed, its performance improved, even on dimensions that were important to the mainstream market. Gradually, PCs began eating into the lower end of the minicomputer market. When companies such as IBM and Compaq entered the business, they were able to make computing accessible to a much larger population of average—and, ultimately, lower-income—non–computer scientists and nonprogrammers. Now that the masses could use computers without the level of training of experts, the technological progress and industry growth that followed enabled average people to do many more things than had been possible on mainframes run by experts.

Because computers and a host of other industries (such as automobiles, consumer electronics, and financial services) were disrupted, extraordinary waves of growth occurred. In each instance, we enjoyed higher quality, lower cost, and greater convenience. Those who are better off today include many more people than those few who could afford it before the disruptions. Disruptive innovators have generated hundreds of billions of dollars in revenue and market capitalization and created tens of millions of jobs in the process. And yet firms have achieved all this, as the left side of Exhibit 5.2 suggests, by dipping only slightly down from the peak of the population pyramid—by going from the wealthiest and highest skilled of those living in developed countries into the tiers of lower skills and income in those same developed countries.

Exhibit 5.2
The Upside of Disruptive Growth:
The Great Leap Downward

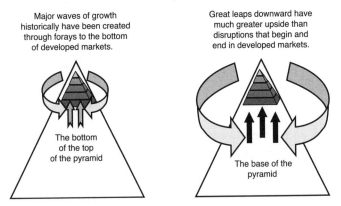

Source: Adapted from Hart, S. and Christensen, C. 2002. "The great leap: Driving innovation from the base of the pyramid." *Sloan Management Review*, 44(1): 51-56.

The disruptive technologies that were developed to reach just down to these tiers cannot be easily deployed toward even lower-income consumers—it is very difficult to remove cost from a business model aimed at higher-income customers without affecting its quality or integrity. But new waves of disruptive technology deployed by companies making a Great Leap to the BoP can have extraordinary potential to generate growth because they have even more upside once they have taken root. Indeed, the low-cost structure needed to serve the base of the pyramid presents the opportunity to later add cost and features to products and move up-market to tiers of higher income and affluence. In short, the farther down the income pyramid the technology begins, the more upside growth potential exists over the life of the innovation.

Driving Innovation from the Base of the Pyramid

As Clay Christensen and I have argued, the base of the pyramid is the ideal market for new disruptive technologies for at least two reasons.[22] The first is that business models forged in low-income markets can travel profitably to more places than can business models defined in high-income markets. Honda's success with motorcycles provides an example. In the 1950s, Honda began selling motorized bicycles to small distributors in the crowded and impoverished Japanese cities that were rebuilding from the ruin of World War II. The company developed a business model that could make money selling at very low price points. When Honda entered the United States market in the early 1960s with its disruptive Supercub, the product's simplicity and low price point enabled a much larger population—people who lacked the money or boldness to own Harleys—to buy and use motorcycles. Honda's base in impoverished Japan gave it a huge competitive advantage in disrupting the American motorcycle makers because it could make money at prices that were unattractive to the established leaders.

Toyota and Sony followed the same recipe and enjoyed decades of success while taking on the market leaders in developed countries. In fact, the industries that constituted the engine of Japan's economic miracle from the 1960s to the 1980s all followed the disruptive strategy of attacking markets that established competitors wanted to avoid because their likely revenue and profits seemed unattractive. Disruption was the nation's strategy for economic development. The reason Japan's economy suffered from no growth for most of the 1990s was that its institutions did not permit new waves of disruptive innovation to be launched against its multinational giants, the very companies that were yesterday's disrupters.[23]

In addition to having more adaptable business models, disruptive innovators compete against nonconsumption—that is, they offer a product or service to people who otherwise would be left out entirely or would remain poorly served by existing products. This is the second reason the base of the pyramid offers better markets for new growth businesses. When companies searching for growth fight against capable competitors to win the business of savvy customers in established markets, the barriers to success are formidable. But when they bring a disruptive product to customers who have been poorly served or even actively exploited, the customers are delighted to have simple products with modest functionality.

Consider a Chinese company called Galanz, which has achieved extraordinary growth through a Great Leap Downward.[24] In 1992, Galanz decided to enter the market for microwave ovens, even though the firm was a textile and garment manufacturer at the time. The global market for microwaves was mature and shrinking, and it was hard to differentiate products because most of them were good enough to do what people wanted them to do. Manufacturing had migrated to countries where labor costs were low and consumption was concentrated in developed countries. In China, only 2 percent of all households owned a microwave oven. Most families did not have kitchens large enough to accommodate the available models, which had been designed to fit into homes in the West.

Rather than pursue the obvious strategy of using inexpensive Chinese labor to make lower-cost ovens for export, Galanz's founder Qingde Liang chose to compete against nonconsumption in the domestic market. Galanz developed and introduced a simple, energy-efficient product at a price that was affordable to China's vast middle and lower-middle classes and small enough to fit in their kitchens. As sales steadily climbed, Liang stimulated demand by using the company's ever-declining cost per unit to reduce the product's price. Galanz's domestic market share rose from 2 percent in 1993 to 76 percent of a much larger market by 2000. Armed with a business model that could earn attractive profits at low price points, Galanz moved up-market to manufacture larger machines that had more features. It began to disrupt the microwave oven markets in developed countries by marketing its machines on a private-label basis to large MNC producers of home appliances. By 2002, it had become the largest producer of microwave ovens in the world, with a global market share of 35 percent.

Connecting the World

Galanz's success demonstrates the possibility for disruptive change to affect people in the middle of the pyramid. But the feasibility of disruptive business models has also been demonstrated in numerous experiments at the very bottom, where more than four billion people earn less than $1,500 in purchasing power parity annually. Perhaps the best-known such experiment occurred in the Grameen family of enterprises in Bangladesh, described in Chapter 3, "The Sustainable Value Portfolio." The original Grameen Bank, one of the originators of microcredit in the developing world more than 30 years ago, has since spawned several other ventures, including Grameen Telecom, launched in the late 1990s, which focused on bringing information and communication technology to rural Bangladesh in the form of "village phones."

Iqbal Quadir originally conceived of the idea of rural connectivity in 1993, after his New York firm's computer network went down. It reminded him of his childhood days in rural Bangladesh when he used to waste entire days walking long distances because there was virtually no phone service outside of the city.[25] More than half of humanity (three billion people) is still without reliable telecommunications service. Telephone service in rural areas has been slowed by the size of the capital investment required to extend the wireline infrastructure profitably from urban areas. Grameen Telecom's mission has therefore been to bring telecommunications service to the rural poor in Bangladesh (average per capita income of $286 per year). At this income level, the existing business model for telephone service would not be feasible—only disruption could do the job.

Accordingly, at the initiation of Professor Yunus, two independent companies were formed in 1997, one for profit (GrameenPhone), and another not for profit (Grameen Telecom). GrameenPhone is a consortium made up of four partners: Telenor of Norway (51 percent), Grameen Telecom (35 percent), Marubeni of Japan (9.5 percent), and Gonophone Development Company (4.5 percent). GrameenPhone was the recipient of the telecommunications license. It focused on serving all urban areas in Bangladesh by building a nationwide cellular network. Grameen Telecom buys bulk airtime from GrameenPhone and retails it through Grameen borrowers in the rural villages. Initially, few gave the venture much hope because only the richest city-dwellers in Bangladesh could afford their own mobile phones. But by changing its business model, Grameen Telecom was able to pilot-test and launch a venture that has proved to be highly profitable. Grameen Bank loaned the money to women in rural villages to establish them as independent entrepreneurs to sell mobile phone services. They received loans of up to $175 to purchase a mobile phone and a small solar recharger unit. The loan also included the necessary training needed to use and service the equipment. The pilot project started in 1997 with 950 villages, but in

Bangladesh alone, there was a potential market for tens of thousands of "village phones."

The results of the pilot test were impressive.[26] Village phone operators increased their income on average by about $300 per year, raising their status in their villages considerably. Most of these women spent their additional income on education and health care for their children, providing an additional development bonus. For users of the phone service, there was considerable consumer surplus. Rather than making the time-consuming and expensive trip to secure information about crop prices or to place orders with distributors through a slow, unreliable postal system, users could now simply place a call. Each call saved the average user $2.70 to $10—a whopping 2.5 to 10 percent of household monthly income. Significant reduction in travel, combined with the avoidance of a wireline infrastructure, provided significant environmental advantages as well.

The business model also proved to be very profitable for the company. The rural phones in the pilot project booked three times the revenue per phone as their urban counterparts ($100 per month in revenue for a village phone versus about $30 per month in the city). If extended to all of rural Bangladesh, it was estimated that the business could generate revenues in excess of $100 million per year. If a similar model were applied to rural India and China, tens of billions of dollars of revenue would be possible.

In fact, the performance of GrameenPhone has exceeded even the wildest dreams of those involved with the pilot project.[27] By 2006, net profits had grown to nearly $200 million. Demand for rural phone services was so strong that additional phone ladies were necessary in many villages. By the end of 2008, there were nearly 354,000 phone ladies spread across more than 70,000 villages. If you do the math, this means that GrameenPhone was now approaching one billion dollars in revenue in Bangladesh alone. This is all the more impressive when it is realized that until 2004, the government denied access to the wireline infrastructure, meaning that all calls had to be made from one

Grameen phone to another. Phone ladies were earning, on average, about $750 per year in 2006. While it may not sound like much in places like the United States or Western Europe, this level of income moved the phone ladies' families squarely into the middle class. Leveraging the success of the model, the Village Phone program was introduced in a handful of other countries by 2008, including Uganda and Rwanda.

By 2006, the company had invested $1 billion overall in Bangladesh (compare this figure to the $268 million in total foreign investment in Bangladesh in 2003). A study that year concluded that the mobile phone industry in Bangladesh created a total value add of $812 million, of which $256 million was retained by the operators and used to pay employee wages and taxes. The remaining $650 million, about 1 percent of GDP, went to dealers, suppliers, operators, and support services. In all, the report estimated that the mobile phone industry contributed, directly or indirectly, to more than 250,000 income opportunities (not including the work of the phone ladies themselves).[28] By 2008, the company had a subscriber base of 18 million and provided network coverage to nearly 98 percent of Bangladesh's population. Its employment base had also grown to a total of 5,000, with another 150,000 people directly dependent on GrameenPhone for their livelihood.[29]

Most recently, the incomes of phone ladies have begun to decrease as their numbers (as well as those of competitors) have swelled in what were previously the underserved villages of Bangladesh. Rural phone service has now become a competitive business! Accordingly, GrameenPhone began expanding its service to include rural Internet access, through the use of Internet kiosks. N-Logue, an emerging telecom player in India, adopted a similar business model but has developed new technology to dramatically lower connection costs in rural areas using wireless local loop (WLL) technology that separates voice and data traffic. The revenue and profit potential for this business is enormous.[30] Indeed, over the past few years, several new players have entered this space, including ITC's e-Choupal, and Drishtee.

Whereas fixed and mobile wireless technology is not performance- or cost-competitive with wireline access to the Internet in developed nations, it is vastly superior to the alternative in much of the developing world: nonconsumption. Telecommunications giants in developed countries have spent billions on 3G and 4G technology and spectrum licenses, hoping to provide enough bandwidth for current customers to do wirelessly the things for which they now use the wireline Internet. These investments have crippled many of these companies, and they are unlikely ever to produce adequate returns. Far better is to compete against nonconsumption at the base of the pyramid—and migrate from that profitable base toward successively more sophisticated customers and applications in global markets.

The case of Grameen Telecom illustrates how disruptive business model innovation can incubate sophisticated technologies at the base of the pyramid in ways that offer tremendous growth potential for businesses and positive social and environmental benefits for the rural poor. Innovating from the bottom up holds the potential to generate enormous growth and to address the root causes of antiglobalization sentiments, facilitating sustainable development.

Food, Health, and Hope?

A Great Leap Downward might also serve to reverse the present course of the agricultural biotechnology and genetically modified (GM) plant and animal industries, which continue to struggle for economic viability and social acceptance. Most early efforts to bring this technology to market were aimed at rapid penetration of the mainstream market. For example, despite its mantra of "Food, Health, and Hope," Monsanto focused virtually its entire strategy during the 1990s on designing genetically engineered seeds to lower costs for farmers growing commodity crops (such as corn, soybean, and cotton) in the developed world, especially the United States.

Reducing chemical and input usage through genes that made the plants pest-resistant (such as Bt Cotton) or resistant to the application of herbicides (such as Roundup Ready) made such seeds hard for farmers in the United States to resist because they were under intense margin pressure from food processors and manufacturers. The large-scale and centralized nature of the American agribusiness system meant that producers rapidly purchased GM seeds and planted crops. Indeed, the acreage dedicated to GM crops in the United States increased from virtually zero in 1995 to more than 60 million acres by the end of the 1990s.[31]

However, as we have seen, attempts to expand beyond the United States met with growing opposition. In Europe, environmentalists and consumers began to resist the importing and planting of such seeds. A backlash movement was set in motion and focused on several issues. First, consumers perceived no benefit from eating GM crops. Indeed, only farmers benefited from the first generation of seeds, and consumers were asked to take whatever risk there might be (such as allergic reaction), with no compensating health or nutrition bene-fit. Second, environmentalists grew more concerned that unforeseen ecological problems could be unleashed by the rapid rate of GM adoption by farmers, including the possibility of crossing with wild plants and the production of "super weeds." Third, critics from the developing world grew increasingly concerned that a few MNCs might come to control the world's seed supply, denying poor, small-shareholder farmers around the world the ability to save seed and engage in other age-old agricultural practices. Food manufacturers and retailers began to boycott GM crops, in some cases paying a pre-mium for conventionally grown foods. By the late 1990s, the backlash had become so severe that Monsanto and other agricultural biotech-nology producers were forced to scale back their business operations and reconsider the future of GM food.

The recent bioagricultural experience provides important lessons in technological innovation and commercialization. Disruptive innovation theory would predict that the attempt to pit GM foods against the established options in complex mainstream markets so soon would be fraught with difficulty. Reducing farmers' cost is not enough to guarantee acceptance of a radically new technology when customers already are well satisfied with the quality, quantity, and affordability of present food alternatives. Indeed, the greatest need for additional nutrition and agricultural productivity resides not with American agribusiness, but rather, at the base of the pyramid, where billions of small-shareholder farmers labor to produce crops, frequently for their own consumption, at very low levels of efficiency and productivity.

Properly designed and introduced, GM seeds might dramatically improve the lives of small farmers by lowering costs, enhancing pest resistance and productivity, conserving water and soil, and increasing nutritional value of foods made from such crops as rice, sweet potatoes, and cassava. Through microcredit and other forms of collaboration with small farmers, it might be possible to design a business model that results in a whole new approach to sustainable agriculture. Incubating such experiments from the ground up rather than introducing the technology on a massive scale from the top down also might encourage a more reasoned understanding of any significant environmental issues. Eventually, these approaches to agriculture might become so productive and successful that they could move up-market to out-compete the chemical- and energy-intensive agribusiness model prevalent in the United States. When we are building major new growth markets with new technology, the shortest distance between two points often is not a straight line. This is true even for the most sophisticated new clean technologies, such as solar energy, LED lighting, and biofuels. The base of the pyramid can be the best place to start, as we explore next.

Power to the People

Consider the case for distributed generation of power. The electric power infrastructure in the developed world is based upon large, centralized power facilities (fueled by coal, oil, gas, or nuclear technology) and an extensive grid system for the transmission and distribution of power. Incremental innovation has improved the efficiency of these power plants over the years, but significant inefficiencies still exist in generation and distribution. For example, nearly half the power generated is lost in distribution over an aging power grid. And despite calls for moving to a next-generation "smart grid," extending power lines to distant rural areas is capital intensive (costing, on average, $10,000–$20,000 per mile), and the pricing required to recoup those massive investments limits consumption. As a consequence, there are still more than two billion people in the world with no access to dependable electric power. These people instead burn dangerous and polluting fuels such as kerosene, diesel, candles, and dung.

At the same time, there is growing investment in the distributed generation of power (DG), including such technologies as solar photovoltaics, wind, fuel cells, and microturbines. In fact, venture capital investment in DG is now in the billions each year, up from only about $100 million in 1996. These technologies generate small quantities of electricity (less than 1mW) near the actual point of use, thereby avoiding the need for expensive distribution. DG technologies also lend themselves to the use of renewable fuels (such as the sun or wind, as well as biomass—crop and animal waste—in the case of fuel cells and microturbines). Biofuels made from non-food plants such as perennial grasses, jatropha, or jute, can also be produced for distributed use.

Engineers and marketers are struggling against a stringent standard, working to bring down the cost of these technologies to make them competitive with conventional sources of power in the developed world, where the existence of a sunk-cost grid system and subsidies for fossil fuels wipe away any cost advantage associated with distributed generation. In these markets, cost-accounting systems and rate structures tailored to the centralized generation of power using fossil fuels make it difficult for such technologies to gain a foothold in the mainstream markets because they have yet to achieve cost parity in the eyes of the consumer. Photovoltaic electricity, for example, still costs about $0.50 per kilowatt hour, compared to 7¢–15¢ per kilowatt hour for grid-connected electricity. Customers in the developed world are also understandably leery about taking on the additional risks and responsibilities of solar panels or fuel cells while the after-sale service infrastructure remains in its infancy.

But DG faces few of these obstacles among the rural poor in the developing world. It may be decades before the electrical grid system is extended to provide service to those who currently lack access to dependable electric power. As a consequence, the rural poor spend a significant portion of their income—as much as $10 per month—on candles, kerosene, and batteries to have access to lighting at night and periodic electrical service.[32] Furthermore, generating electricity using kerosene and batteries is expensive, costing $3–$5 or more per kilowatt hour. If offered a viable substitute, these people might abandon these dangerous, polluting, and expensive technologies in favor of clean, efficient, and renewable electric power. Yet few producers of DG have focused on the rural poor at the base of the pyramid as their early market for these technologies, despite the fact that the market is potentially huge and is populated by people who would be delighted with technologies that cannot compete along the metrics used in developed markets.

The crucial breakthrough for sustainable energy technologies, therefore, will not be in a laboratory. Instead, sustainable energy must be incubated and refined where the technology can be profitably deployed through disruptive strategies, in markets where it does not compete against established technologies. This means producers must tailor the technology for use in poor rural areas and develop production, sales, service, and microfinancing packages that enable nonconsumers to gain access.

Consider the innovative technology and business model created by the nonprofit Light Up the World (LUTW).[33] Dedicated to bringing a safe source of light at night to the billions of people without electric power around the world, LUTW teamed with Stanford University to develop an affordable rural (off-grid) lighting system that combines solar photovoltaics with light-emitting diode (LED) technology.

LED is an emerging lighting technology that is extremely energy-efficient (80–90 percent more efficient than incandescent light bulbs), long-lived (lasts 8–10 years), and durable (virtually unbreakable). Despite these advantages, however, to date, LEDs have been limited to niche applications in the developed world such as traffic signals, brake lights, and electronic displays, where vibrant color and durability are important. In recent years, however, white LED technology has been developed that holds the potential to replace light bulbs in the mainstream lighting market. Yet even though all the large lighting companies (including GE, Philips, and Osram-Sylvania) have growing LED businesses, there have been few commercial inroads into this vast market, despite the potential for massive energy and financial savings. We can explain this in part by the large installed base of light fixtures (which will not accommodate LEDs). It is also a result of the propensity for top-of-the-pyramid consumers to benchmark any substitute lighting technology against conventional incandescent bulbs, which cost less than a dollar but last only a matter of months (LEDs cost 10 times as much but last for nearly a decade). Indeed, the slow rate of compact fluorescent bulb adoption has already demonstrated the difficulty of changing consumer preferences to a substitute with a higher first cost but a lower life-cycle cost.

Of course, none of these problems exists if we focus instead on the billions of rural poor without access to electricity. There is no installed base of light bulb fixtures, nor are there any preconceived notions about how an electric lighting system should operate. And by combining the highly energy-efficient LED lighting arrays with solar power, we can dramatically reduce total system cost, downsizing the solar panel needed to power the system. Indeed, LUTW and Stanford have been able to design a system that includes the LED lighting arrays, the solar panel, the battery, wiring, and controls in a "rural lighting system" package that can be sold for as little as $50 retail.

For a poor family making less than $500 per year, this would be equivalent to the purchase of a car by a top of the pyramid family. Because the family is already spending as much as $5–10 each month on candles, kerosene, lanterns, and batteries, all that is required is a microfinancing package, along with a reliable local microentrepreneur to sell and service the equipment. This is precisely the approach that LUTW and Stanford have taken in launching a commercial venture to serve this market. Indeed, over the past few years, literally dozens of DG start-up companies have begun to spring up across the developing world, including players like SELCO, Cosmos Ignite, Duron Energy, D.Light, Barefoot Solar, Shanghai Roy Solar Company, and Tata BP Solar, to name a few.

A distributed business model like this could tap into a potential market of more than two billion people. With the volume and experience from the sale and service of solar and LED at the base of the pyramid, it would be only a matter of time before this technology became so efficient—and affordable—that it began to eat its way into the low-end markets in urban areas, perhaps starting with shantytowns, where grid-based electric power is expensive and unreliable. For example, the Solar Electric Light Company (SELCO), a for-profit enterprise that serves the middle-of-the-pyramid market with full-scale solar home electric lighting systems that sell for as much as $500 each, has a growing business in India and Southeast Asia. Ultimately, such systems could become so attractive and affordable that even the wealthy at the top of the pyramid would find them difficult to resist.

Given the enormous growth potential of this business model, it comes as no surprise that electronics giant Philips launched such a commercial venture in rural India during 2005. Philips (along with British Petroleum) is also pilot testing a smokeless stove for use in rural areas that dramatically reduces fuelwood requirements (and hence deforestation). Use of the stove also saves rural women significant amounts of time otherwise spent hunting for and collecting firewood. As with DG, there are now dozens of smokeless stove start-up companies, each with its own particular twist on technology and business model.

Sustainable energy pioneers who focus on the base of the pyramid could set the stage for one of the biggest business bonanzas in the history of commerce because extensive adoption and experience there would almost certainly lead to dramatic improvements in cost and quality. If firms such as Philips create a business model that can be profitable in these markets, solar energy has a chance. But this is the only strategy by which this technology can succeed without massive and ongoing government subsidy. Could we now be witnessing the start of the real clean-tech revolution, driven by bottom-up innovation on a massive scale? Or will change on the necessary scale still require us to jettison some mental baggage when it comes to driving clean-tech innovation from the base of the pyramid?

The Great Convergence

I would argue that the examples of bottom-up innovation offered here represent more the exception rather than the rule to date. More commonly, clean-tech entrepreneurs and BoP business innovators operate in isolation from one another. Each has evolved with its own particular dominant logic and core assumptions. In some respects, each represents a separate "world" with its own set of beliefs, priorities, and culture (see Exhibit 5.3).

Exhibit 5.3
Two Different Worlds

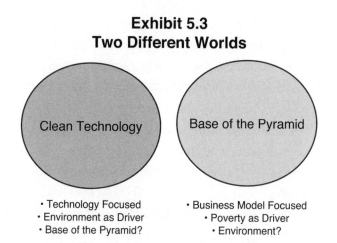

Clean Technology	Base of the Pyramid
• Technology Focused	• Business Model Focused
• Environment as Driver	• Poverty as Driver
• Base of the Pyramid?	• Environment?

At the risk of over-simplification, Clean Technologists typically see the road to success as paved by new, "sustainable" technologies that dramatically reduce or eliminate the human footprint on the planet. The focus is on technology development and early penetration of high-end "green" markets at the top of the pyramid, with the promise of eventual "trickle down." BoP advocates, in contrast, focus on new business models for reaching and serving the poor. Confronting poverty and finding new avenues for growth are the primary foci, and there is often little attention paid to the environmental implications of such strategies.[34]

The crucial next step is, therefore, to consciously merge these two mindsets in a *Great Convergence*. This convergence of thinking recognizes that clean technologies (especially the distributed "Green Sprout" variety) are almost always "disruptive" in character—they threaten incumbents in current served markets at the top of the pyramid. As a result, the base of the pyramid is often the best place to focus initial commercialization attention. At the same time, the Great Convergence also recognizes that successful BoP strategies must be environmentally sustainable to avoid taking all of humanity over the proverbial environmental cliff.

Unlike the traditional model of industrialization, which relies heavily on conventional (unsustainable) technology, the Great Convergence seeks instead to fuel growth through the incubation and rapid commercialization of distributed green technologies from the bottom-up. The challenge is to combine the advanced technology of the Rich World with the entrepreneurial bent and community focus of the BoP. Learning how to build upon, and not over, ancient foundations and local knowledge is key. Through such a strategy, the villages and slums of the developing world could become the breeding ground for the Clean-Tech Revolution. However, declining industrial cities in the developed world also offer the opportunity to "start again" with thousands of acres of vacant and abandoned land in places like Detroit, Michigan, and a population hungry for new opportunities.

Unfortunately, most effort to date has been focused on driving clean technologies into the "developed" markets at the top of the income pyramid, often with little result. Given the perverse incentives and incumbent inertia that exists, this should come as little surprise—just witness what happened at Copenhagen with the climate change negotiations. As Van Jones, Tom Friedman, and others have pointed out, as long as "green" remains synonymous with "rich," it will never change the world. Because the BoP provides the best early opportunity for innovators seeking to stake out the future in the full range of emerging clean technologies, governments would be wise to construct policies that encourage their technologists and entrepreneurs to immerse themselves in this space: Just as companies that ignore this enormous opportunity do so at their peril, so too do countries and states that place all of their focus on eco-efficiency or rebuilding centralized infrastructures in existing settlements—they risk missing what comes next.

A New Development Paradigm

The theory of disruptive innovation suggests that existing main-stream markets are the wrong place to look for major new waves of growth. Indeed, forcing a potentially disruptive innovation into a conventional business model, thereby moving it into head-on competition with incumbents, may only ensure its early demise. Instead, we argue that the vast, underserved market at the "base of the pyramid" is an ideal place for the incubation of new, sustainable technologies through a bottom-up form of innovation.

Our thinking about the potential rewards resulting from a great leap to the base of the pyramid extends this strategy as a framework not just for corporate growth, but also for more balanced and sustainable macroeconomic development in poor countries. Such an approach is potentially significant because existing strategies for economic development now appear to be all but bankrupt.[35] Import substitution, for example, which emphasized the development of domestic capacity to serve established home markets, was discredited more than 20 years ago; its protectionist stance failed to produce competitive or efficient national producers.[36]

More recently, the export-led growth strategies advocated by the so-called Washington Consensus have come under increasing fire as well.[37] By asserting that developing countries can generate growth by producing commodities and goods for export to the top of the pyramid, the doctrine of export-led growth has resulted in excess capacity and global deflation. Indeed, after a decade of international financial crises, mounting Third World debt, environmental devastation, and rising inequity, the Washington Consensus is crumbling. It now appears clear that the only way to spur sustainable growth for the long term is to design a development strategy that focuses on the unmet needs in the developing world itself, the base of the pyramid. Indeed, bottom-up innovation holds the prospect of lifting the poor out of poverty, averting environmental meltdown, and opening the way to sustainable growth for the global economy.

Consider the case of Mexico. Since signing on to the North American Free Trade Agreement (NAFTA) more than a decade ago, the country has been caught in a no-win situation. By opening its borders to foreign investment, Mexico became a haven for Maquiladora plants near the U.S. border and new export-oriented MNC assembly facilities in search of low labor costs or lax environmental enforcement. There can be no doubt that these foreign direct investments created factory wage jobs in the short term. Unfortunately, few of these investments provide any long-term development payoff for Mexico.

There are two reasons for this conundrum. First, as even lower-cost locations (such as China) became more attractive, many of the plants and assembly facilities closed their doors and moved overseas, leaving Mexico's workers high and dry. Like unemployed factory workers in the U.S., they are victims of the global "race to the bottom" for the lowest wages and operating costs. Second, the export-oriented investments in Mexico have provided few of the skills or capabilities needed to compete more effectively in the game of global capitalism. Indeed, few Mexican companies are now better able to compete against the highly sophisticated U.S., European, and Japanese multinationals for the top of the pyramid markets as a result of these investments. In short, low factor costs alone do not translate into knowledge or skills that have value in the highly competitive marketplace of today's global capitalism.

The combination of NAFTA and the draconian structural adjustment policies imposed on Mexico by the International Monetary Fund have served only to hasten the country's slide into rising inequity, social rebellion, and financial meltdown—witness the recent spike in drug-related violence that threatens the country's stability. It should come as no surprise, then, that some enlightened business leaders and government officials in Mexico have become increasingly interested in the base of the pyramid as a potential way out of this trap: By using the power of commerce as a vehicle for serving the needs of the country's massive underclass, Mexico can incubate entirely new enterprises with the unique capabilities needed to become the globally competitive companies of the future.[38] Just like China, India, and Bangladesh, Mexico could become a wellspring for the truly disruptive—and sustainable—enterprises of the twenty-first century.

Taking the Great Leap

If history is any guide, most of the growth opportunities in the vast, underserved space at the base of the pyramid will be seized by entrepreneurs (such as Grameen, Tata, and Galanz) in developing countries, just as the opportunities in impoverished postwar Japan were captured by innovators such as Sony, Matsushita, Honda, and Toyota. In addition, countries such as China, India, Brazil, and Mexico may well make the Great Leap to the BoP their primary strategy for national economic development. Indeed, we may be witnessing the birth of the next generation of multinational corporations, nurtured in the base of the pyramid through bottom-up innovation and ready to take on the high-cost structures and rigid management models of the existing MNC incumbents.

Today's global corporations, however, should not assume that such an outcome is inevitable; they, too, can seize these growth opportunities before they become threats. As is always the case in pursuing disruptive innovation, however, such companies will need to manage these new opportunities independently from their mainstream incumbent businesses. Even more importantly, they will have to build new business models that include strategies, organizational structures, and management processes actually suited to conditions at the base of the pyramid. Reaching the base of the pyramid requires radical business model innovation. However, actually *raising* the BoP through enterprise requires that managers and entrepreneurs think about the full range of social and environmental benefits (and costs) resulting from their strategies. It is to this objective that we turn our attention in the next chapter.

Notes

1. Tom Friedman, *Hot, Flat, and Crowded* (New York: Farrar, Straus, and Giroux, 2008), 5–6.

2. Van Jones, *The Green Collar Economy* (New York: HarperOne, 2008), 6.

3. This section is adapted from Stuart Hart, "Taking the Green Leap," Cornell University, Working Paper, 2009.

4. Parts of this chapter are excerpted from Stuart Hart and Clayton Christensen, "The Great Leap: Driving Innovation from the Base of the Pyramid," *Sloan Management Review* 44(1) (2002): 51–56.

5. C.K. Prahalad and Ken Lieberthal, "The End of Corporate Imperialism," *Harvard Business Review* July–August (1998), www.hbsp.harvard.edu/hbr/index.html.

6. C.K. Prahalad and Stuart Hart, "The Fortune at the Bottom of the Pyramid," *Strategy+Business* January (2002): 54–67.

7. Including C.K. Prahalad, Michael Gordon, Bob Kennedy, and Ted London (University of Michigan), Clayton Christensen (Harvard Business School), Miguel Angel Rodríguez and Joan Enric Ricart (IESE Business School), Sanjay Sharma (Concordia University), Allen Hammond (Ashoka), Nicholas Guttierez (Tec Monterrey), Jim Johnson and Lisa Jones (University of North Carolina), Miguel Angel Gardetti (IEEC-Argentina), Oana Branzei (Western Ontario University), Stef Coetzee (Stellenbosch University), Jac Geurts and Erik van Dam (Tilburg University), Reuben Abraham and V. Chandrasekar (Indian School of Business), and Professors Yunhuan Tong and Xudong Gao (Tsinghua University).

8. At the suggestion of my UNC colleague, Ted London, we changed the name from "bottom" to "base" of the pyramid to remove any hint that those on the lower end of the income scale are in any way inferior to those at the high end of the income scale.

9. The BoP Learning Lab's contributing members have included DuPont, HP, J&J, P&G, Nike, IBM, SC Johnson, Ford, Dow, Coke, and Tetrapak. Nonprofit organizations such as the Grameen Foundation, ApproTEC, Tata Energy and Resources Institute, and the World Resources Institute are also actively involved.

10. See www.bopnetwork.org.

11. Portions of this section are excerpted from Prahalad and Hart, "The Fortune at the Bottom of the Pyramid."

12. Tom Friedman, *The World Is Flat* (New York: Farrar, Straus, and Giroux, 2005).

13. For an extended discussion of this issue, see Ted London and Stuart Hart, "Reinventing Strategies for Emerging Markets: Beyond the Transnational Model," *Journal of International Business Studies* 35 (2004): 350–370.

14. C.K. Prahalad and Allen Hammond, "Serving the World's Poor, Profitably," *Harvard Business Review* 80(9) (2002): 48–57.

15. Jeffrey Immelt, Vijay Govindarajan, and Chris Trimble, "How GE is Disrupting Itself," *Harvard Business Review* October (2009): 3-11.

16. Ted London and Stuart Hart, "Reinventing Strategies."

17. Hernando de Soto, *The Mystery of Capital: Why Capitalism Triumphs in the West and Fails Everywhere Else* (New York: Basic Books, 2000).

18. Ibid.

19. Ibid.

20. Parts of the following section are excerpted from Stuart Hart and Clayton Christensen, "The Great Leap."

21. See Clayton Christensen, *The Innovator's Dilemma: When New Technologies Cause Great Firms to Fail* (Boston: Harvard Business School Press, 1997).

22. Stuart Hart and Clayton Christensen, "The Great Leap."

23. Clayton Christensen, Thomas Craig, and Stuart Hart, "The Great Disruption," *Foreign Affairs* 80(2) (2001): 80–95.

24. My thanks to Clay Christensen for this example.

25. Iqbal Quadir, presentation at the Wharton Global Compact Conference, University of Pennsylvania, 17 September 2004.

26. For details, see Muhammad Yunus, *Banker to the Poor* (Dhaka: The University Press Limited, 1998); D. Richardson, R. Ramirez, and M. Haq, *Grameen Telecom's Village Phone Programme in Rural Bangladesh: A Multi-Media Study* (Guelph, Ontario: TeleCommons Development Group, 2000).

27. Nicholas Sullivan, *You Can Hear Me Now* (San Francisco: Jossey-Bass, 2007). Thanks also to Muhammad Yunus and Iqbal Quadir for personal conversations regarding GrameenPhone and Grameen Telecom.

28. Ibid.

29. "GrameenPhone 2007 Annual Report."

30. J. Howard, C. Simms, and E. Simanis, *Sustainable Deployment for Rural Connectivity: the N-Logue Model* (Washington, D.C.: World Resources Institute, 2001).

31. Erik Simanis and Stuart Hart, *The Monsanto Company (A): Quest for Sustainability,* www.globalens.com, 2009.

32. Light Up the World Foundation, LUTW_factsheetdec23.pdf, p. 5.

33. Light Up the World, www.lightuptheworld.org.

34. This section is adapted from Stuart Hart, "Taking the Green Leap."

35. Thomas Palley, "A New Development Paradigm: Domestic Demand Led Growth," *Foreign Policy Focus* September (2002): 1–8.

36. See Jagdish Bhagwati, *In Defense of Globalization* (New York: Oxford University Press, 2004).

37. See, for example, Joseph Stiglitz, *Globalization and Its Discontents* (New York: W. W. Norton & Company, 2002).

38. The BoP Learning Lab in Mexico, based at EGADE-Tec Monterrey is actively engaging several Mexican companies, including Cemex, Bimbo, and Amanco, in developing such strategies.

6

Raising the Base of the Pyramid

The poorest populations present a prodigious new managerial challenge for the world's wealthiest companies. Indeed, over the past few years, it has become apparent that there is a large prospective market to be served in the BoP. It has also become clear that the prospect transcends mere market potential: The opportunity is to use commerce as a driving force for human betterment and environmental restoration—to literally *raise the base of the pyramid.* Attempts to adapt the top of the pyramid model for use at the base, however, appear destined to fail. Only through a concerted focus on the base of the pyramid will it be possible for large corporations to combine a humanitarian, even activist, orientation with the conventional motivations of growth and profitability.

Indeed, now is the time for the leaders of corporations to expand their conception of globalization and strategy.[1] For boards, senior executives, and business leaders with the audacity and desire to compete at the base of the world economic pyramid, the prospective rewards include growth, profits, and incalculable contributions to humankind. As we have seen, countries that are not encumbered by billions of dollars of sunk costs in centralized infrastructure are ideal incubators for environmentally sustainable technologies and products that might one day benefit the entire world. Furthermore, MNC investment at the base of the pyramid means lifting billions of people out of poverty and desperation—and averting the social decay, political chaos, terrorism, and environmental meltdown that is certain to result if the gap between rich and poor continues to widen.

As C.K. Prahalad and I have argued, doing business with the world's four billion poorest people—two-thirds of the total population—will require radical innovations in both strategy and business models. It will require companies to re-evaluate price-performance relationships for products and services. Companies will also be forced to transform their understanding of scale from "bigger is better" to highly distributed small-scale operations married to world-scale capabilities. And it will demand new and expanded ways of measuring success and effectiveness.

BoP Pioneers

Hindustan Lever, Ltd. (HLL), a subsidiary of Great Britain's Unilever PLC, has been a pioneer among MNCs exploring markets at the base of the pyramid. For more than 50 years, HLL (recently renamed Hindustan Unilever) served the small elite in India with the income to buy the company's products. Then in the 1990s, HLL noted that an Indian firm, Nirma, Ltd., was offering detergent products for poor consumers; in fact, Nirma had created an entirely new business system designed to meet the needs of underserved consumers, mostly from poor, rural areas. This included a new product formulation, a low-cost manufacturing process, a wide distribution network, special packaging for daily purchasing, and pricing for consumers with limited means.

In typical MNC fashion, HLL initially dismissed Nirma's strategy—it appeared, on the surface, to have no implications for HLL's served market at the top of the pyramid. However, as Nirma rapidly grew, HLL could see that its local competitor was winning in a market it had foolishly disregarded. Furthermore, as Nirma grew, it began to migrate up-market from the strong base in the BoP; HLL finally saw its vulnerability—and its opportunity. In 1995, the company responded with its own offering for the BoP market, drastically altering its traditional business model.[2]

HLL's new detergent product, Wheel, was reformulated to substantially reduce the ratio of oil to water, responding to the fact that the poor often wash clothes in rivers and other public water systems. Most raw materials were sourced from local suppliers. Production, marketing, and distribution were all decentralized to leverage the large labor pool in rural India, quickly creating selling channels through the thousands of small outlets where people at the base of the pyramid shop. HLL also changed the cost structure of its detergent business so it could introduce Wheel at a low price point.

Today Nirma and HLL are close competitors in the detergent market, with about 40 percent market share each, according to India Infoline.com, a business intelligence and market research service covering the Indian market. And the BoP accounts for more than half of HLL's total revenues—and profits. Unilever's own analysis of competition in the detergent business, however, reveals even more about the profit potential in the BoP marketplace (see Exhibit 6.1). Contrary to popular assumptions, the BoP can be a very profitable market, especially if MNCs change their business models.

It's the Business Model, Stupid

As Exhibit 6.1 makes clear, in the consumer goods industry, the BoP is not a market that allows for the traditional pursuit of high margins; instead, volume and capital efficiency are the name of this game. In this business, margins are likely to be low (by current norms), but unit sales extremely high. Managers who focus on gross margins will miss the opportunity; managers who innovate and focus on economic profit will be rewarded.[3]

Thus, getting the metrics right is critically important to success in the BoP: Imposing the established performance criteria from the top of the pyramid will almost certainly kill the opportunity. The decentralized nature of Unilever's corporate structure enabled HLL to "fly under the radar" long enough to establish a successful new business model for the BoP. More centralized MNCs might not allow such latitude to experiment; yet without it, the BoP will almost certainly remain elusive.

Exhibit 6.1
Nirma Versus HLL in
India's Detergent Market (1999)

	Nirma	HLL (Wheel)	HLL (High-End)
Total sales ($ million)	150	100	180
Gross margin (%)	18	18	25
Return on capital (%)	121	93	22

Source: Presentation by John Ripley, Senior Vice President, Unilever, at the Academy of Management Meeting, 10 August 1999.

Yet despite its early success in the market, Wheel's introduction was far from perfect. Although it represented a considerable improvement over the low-cost but harsh formulation offered by Nirma, HLL's detergent was phosphate-based, which meant that it still polluted public waterways. Wheel also introduced a new solid waste problem in the form of millions of spent sachet (single-use) packets. Only after HLL's experiment in serving the poor was validated and supported by the parent company was it possible to connect Unilever's corporate capability in environmental management and sustainability to HLL's innovative approach to reaching the BoP market. Solving these environmental challenges in the BoP will clearly require the combination of corporate know-how and local knowledge.

As a direct result of business model innovation, first-mover Nirma is today one of the largest branded detergent makers in the world. Meanwhile, HLL, stimulated by its emergent rival and its changed business model, registered a 20 percent growth in revenues per year and a 25 percent growth in profits per year for 1993–1999. Over the same period, HLL's market capitalization grew to $12 billion, a growth rate of 40 percent per year. HLL's parent company, Unilever, also benefited from its subsidiary's experience in India. Unilever transported HLL's business principles (not the product or the brand) to create a new detergent market among the poor in Brazil. The brand Ala has been a runaway success. Even more important, Unilever has adopted the base of the pyramid as a corporate strategic priority. Indeed, by the early 2000s, the BoP accounted for more than 20 percent of Unilever's sales on a global basis.[4]

However, soon thereafter, HLL's rapid growth in the BoP began to stagnate. In fact, the company seemingly stopped growing after 1999. The business model that had fueled the growth in the 1990's— single-serve packaging, low-cost production, and "mom and pop" distribution—was reaching its limits. Indeed, as radical as the initial HLL BoP strategy was, it still failed to serve more than 500,000 rural villages, meaning the company was ignoring over 500 million potential customers living in these smaller, more remote settlements (half of the country's population). By 2004, HLL's share price on the Bombay Stock Exchange sank to a new low. As part of a new growth strategy dubbed the Millennium Plan, HLL launched a new BoP initiative called Project Shakti, which aimed to reach the 500 million plus rural people currently unserved by the company's business model.[5]

Through "Project Shakti," the company has taken a page out of Grameen Telecom's book by seeking to develop a cadre of women microentrepreneurs at the village level.[6] Project Shakti is built around women's self-help groups that have been in existence in India for decades. HLL recognized the opportunity to create a new type of profitable venture for these women by applying micro-finance to help them build a local HLL micro-franchise. By 2008, HLL had already trained more than 45,000 Shakti Entrepreneurs (SEs) serving 135,000 villages, and they were adding more than a thousand every month.

Ultimately, the company might build a network of a million or more SEs located throughout the rural villages of India. SEs are imparted basic selling and accounting skills to enable them to operate as micro-entrepreneurs earning a steady income from the sales of HLL's products. In addition, the women are trained to be health and hygiene communicators in a bid to improve the well-being of their communities. If successful, Project Shakti's unique win-win direct-distribution model may supplant the current complex and unwieldy approach to BoP distribution through thousands of small-scale distributors and small "mom and pop" shops. However, as we will see in Chapter 8, Project Shakti is not without its problems and challenges: Despite the rapid scale-out of SEs, there remains a high turnover rate among SEs, and the initiative has yet to break even financially.

Clearly, the base of the pyramid presents unique challenges for MNCs: Serving it violates nearly every assumption associated with successfully serving the top of the pyramid. In point of fact, the biggest challenge for corporations may have less to do with technology, intellectual property, or rule of law, even though these issues have dominated most of the work to date relating to emerging markets.[7] Instead, the fundamental challenge may be one of business model innovation—breaking free of the established mindsets, systems, and metrics that constrain the imagination of incumbent firms.

As the Unilever case demonstrates, to effectively reach the BoP, managers must learn to expand their vision beyond narrow product-centric or financial metrics for success. This can be done in several ways. First, MNCs can seek to identify and remove constraints that prevent the poor from taking control of their own futures. Second, through their business models, MNCs can seek to increase the earning power of the poor. Finally, MNCs can consciously look to create new economic and social potential at the base of the pyramid. We explore each of these in greater detail in the following sections.

Removing Constraints

Business exists to solve problems. Most material needs have already been provided for people at the top of the pyramid, which is why it is so difficult to identify successful new business strategies—customers are already quite well-served. The reverse logic applies at the base of the pyramid—major needs remain unmet for massive numbers of people. Barriers, constraints, gaps, and snafus abound for the poor. What we need to realize as businesspeople is that learning to see these constraints from the point of view of the poor is the best way to identify new breakthrough business strategies that offer both profit and growth potential for the firm—and a significantly better life for those in the BoP.

As C.K. Prahalad and Al Hammond point out, the poor—especially those in urban slums and shantytowns—live in high-cost economies.[8] Their needs are typically not well met by local vendors. In fact, quite frequently, the poor are victims of active exploitation by local moneylenders, corrupt officials, and low-quality service providers. Prahalad and Hammond present data showing that the poor often pay anywhere from twice to 20 times as much as consumers at the top of the pyramid for basic goods and services such as water, food, medicine, phone service, and, as we have seen, access to credit. If we adjust for income level, these differentials become downright obscene. Thus, there is an enormous opportunity to create consumer surplus in the BoP, if we could only open our eyes to the reality on the ground.

We must learn to identify and remove the constraints—"unfreedoms," according to Nobel Prize–winning economist, Amartya Sen[9]—that prevent those in the BoP from realizing their full potential. Unfreedoms mean that the poor often suffer from a systematic lack of opportunity, poor health, and even premature death. These constraints can come in many shapes and sizes: usurious interest rates for credit, poor-quality products, exorbitant prices, exploitive business models, or a total lack of problem recognition.

Cemex, Mexico's largest cement company, provides a glimpse into how to go about constraint identification as a vehicle for reaching the BoP.[10] The 1994 financial crisis in Mexico was a major blow to the company's domestic business, which constituted nearly half of Cemex's cement sales at the time. The construction sector, in particular, was one of the hardest hit in Mexico. However, Cemex executives noted that whereas revenues from upper- and middle-class customers dropped by half, cement sales to the poorest tier of the population were hardly affected. In fact, sales to the poor seemed to follow a completely different logic than those in the affluent market. (It would later be recognized that the formal and informal economies do, indeed, follow completely different logics.) Given that cement sales to the poor constituted 40 percent of Cemex's Mexican business and that the company knew little about this customer segment, corporate leadership decided that it was worthy of further investigation.

In 1998, a team of Cemex employees began to explore this issue in greater depth. They began by issuing a "Declaration of Ignorance," an open admission that the company knew virtually nothing about 40 percent of its Mexican market. They then resolved to learn all they could about the needs and problems of the people in the urban slums and shantytowns where demand for the company's cement was the strongest. To accomplish this, the team lived in the shantytowns for six months. Their mission was to better understand the context in the BoP, not to sell more cement.

Initially the team, led by Hector Ureta, had a difficult time appreciating the situation.[11] At first glance, the shantytowns appeared to be chaotic assemblages of half-built squatter homes stretching as far as the eye could see. Building materials lay around exposed to the elements—and theft. Partially constructed rooms with steel rebar rods reaching skyward formed the streetscape. It was easy to assume that the people must be ignorant or stupid to engage in such poorly planned and executed construction activity. But after spending several months living in this context, the team came to realize that the people were doing the best possible job that could be done, given the constraints and the circumstances.

Poor, do-it-yourself homebuilders in the shantytowns, they learned, often take four years to complete just one room and 13 years to finish a small four-room house. The reason is that banks and other businesses will not engage with poor residents in informal settlements where the legal status of their property ownership is murky. Haphazard design, combined with material theft and spoilage, conspire to make home construction a costly and risky proposition. Vendors prey upon the poor, selling them off-quality goods in quantities that are inappropriate because they have little bargaining power or ability to complain. The Cemex team came to realize that if these constraints could be removed, it might be possible for the poor to build much better-quality homes in less time, while also saving money on materials in the process. And, yes, they might also grow the cement business as well.[12]

To accomplish this end, the team created a new business model. Through its program called Patrimonio Hoy, which, roughly translated, means "Equity Today," Cemex formed savings clubs that allowed aspiring homebuilders to make weekly savings payments. These savings clubs built upon the already prevalent Tandas, community savings plans that had been common in the marginalized sectors in Mexico for decades. In exchange, Cemex provided material storage and architectural support so that homes could be well-designed and built in sensible stages. Given its clout as a major buyer, Cemex could negotiate with material suppliers for the best possible prices and quality, something that the shantytown dwellers themselves were unable to do. Participants in the program built their houses three times faster, with higher-quality materials and designs, and at two-thirds the cost. To date, the program has reached over 200,000 families in 22 Mexican states and is also operating in other Latin American countries such as Colombia, Venezuela, Nicaragua, and Costa Rica.[13]

The Patrimonio Hoy experience demonstrates how important it is to view the BoP through a new set of lenses to see opportunity. Rather than assuming that poor people are irrational, stupid, or lazy, it behooves companies to instead assume that people in the BoP are doing the best they can under the circumstances. The key is to ask the question, "Why are they doing things this way?" If we can gain a better understanding of the constraints that cause this behavior, we can construct new business models designed to remove these constraints—and profit in the process.

Increasing Earning Power

According to the International Labor Organization (ILO)'s *World Employment Report 2001*, nearly a billion people—roughly one-third of the world's work force—either are underemployed or have such menial jobs that it is not possible to support themselves or their families. Compounding this problem is the growing global income gap—a trend the ILO's 2008 *World of Work* report (the most comprehensive study of income inequity to date) shows conclusively: Between the early 1990s and 2007, global unemployment rose by 30 percent, and the income gap between richer and poorer households increased, affecting low-income groups disproportionately. This trend "reflects the impact of financial globalization and a weaker ability of domestic policies to enhance the income position of the middle class and low-income groups," said the ILO's International Institute for Labour Studies Director, Raymond Torres. "The present global financial crisis is bound to make matters worse unless long-term structural reforms are adopted."[14]

Indeed, the harsh realities of structural adjustment in many of the world's poorest countries have made it all but impossible for those in the BoP to survive exclusively through self-provisioning, barter, and community exchange. Helping the world's poor to elevate themselves above this desperation line by increasing earning power is thus a business opportunity to do well and do good simultaneously. Creating consumer surplus and generating income are crucial here. A few farsighted organizations have already begun to blaze this trail, with startlingly positive results.

As we saw in the case of Cemex's Patrimonio Hoy program, it is possible, through business model innovation, to create significant consumer surplus for BoP customers while simultaneously making a healthy profit. Indeed, do-it-yourself homebuilders in Mexico's shantytowns saved considerable time and money through the program, while Cemex realized significant incremental cement sales and profits. The creation of consumer surplus in the BoP is possible because, more often than not, the poor are badly served by local vendors. In some instances, particularly in rural areas, however, there are actual service vacuums.

This was the situation faced by Grameen Telecom, as discussed in detail in the last chapter. Because phone service was nonexistent in rural Bangladesh before the introduction of Grameen's service, the relevant point of comparison was how much time and money villagers were spending to gain access to information such as crop prices and currency exchange rates. Although the phone service offered by Grameen was considered expensive by developed world standards, users still saved between 2.5 and 10 percent of household monthly income ($2.70–$10) with each call because the alternative to making the call was spending days traveling to secure the necessary information—an expensive and risky proposition.

Providing consumer surplus through innovative new products and services is important to increased earning power; saving the poor time and/or money frees up resources to be used more productively for other purposes. Procter & Gamble's new clothes rinse product for the rural poor, for example, reduces by two-thirds the amount of water needed to rinse clothes after washing with detergent. It saves an enormous amount of time as well because, instead of finding and hauling as much water as before, people can engage in more productive activities.

Even more important than the provision of consumer surplus, however, is the actual generation of income in the BoP. Businesses that lead to income generation are therefore of special importance. Perhaps the quintessential example of such a business is the micro-credit model introduced by Muhammad Yunus and the Grameen Bank. The loans made to the poor through the bank lead directly to income generation through microentrepreneurship and other forms of local enterprise development. In addition to providing credit, companies can develop new technologies to raise BoP incomes and start businesses.

One example of such a venture is Appropriate Technologies for Enterprise Creation (now KickStart), founded by Dr. Martin Fisher in 1991.[15] Begun as a non-profit, KickStart has helped to create thousands of jobs in Kenya and other parts of East Africa, where more than half the population lives on less than $1 per day, by developing enabling technologies and working with local entrepreneurs to launch businesses using those technologies. Profits from the new small-scale businesses enable thousands of poor families to escape poverty, educate their children, afford health care, and plan their futures.

KickStart's best-selling technology is the leg-operated Money-maker Micro-irrigation Pump. These simple but effective water pumps, which retail for less than $100, enable poor farmers to grow high-value fruits and vegetables year-round by supplying their crops with much-needed water. Customers have also been very creative in finding other ways to use the pump to generate income, including car washing, plant nurseries, and provision of drinking water. On average, users earn an additional $1,200 profit per year, recovering their investment in three months, and increasing overall farm income by a factor of 10. Since its inception in the early 1990s, KickStart has helped to create 35,000 new microenterprises in East Africa, with a total of $36 million per year in new profits. Revenues generated by these enterprises equal more than 0.5 percent of Kenya's GDP.

Today, more than 800 new businesses are being started every month using KickStart technology.

In the early 2000s, KickStart teamed up with SC Johnson Company in Kenya to create more sustainable livelihoods for thousands of poor farmers dependent on growing pyrethrum for a living.[16] When SC Johnson launched its best-selling brand Raid® in 1956 as the world's first commercial aerosol insecticide, the company chose to use environmentally benign pyrethrum as the active ingredient. Pyrethrum is the fourth-largest export crop in Kenya, after tea, coffee, and horticultural plants. The Pyrethrum Board of Kenya (PBK) is a parastatal agency reporting to the Ministry of Agriculture that operates as a monopoly, controlling all aspects of Kenya's pyrethrum production, processing, marketing, and export. PBK produces nearly 70 percent of the world's supply of pyrethrum through a network of 200,000 subsistence farmers and their families (nearly 1 million people) organized into cooperatives and self-help groups throughout Kenya's central highlands. SC Johnson has been its biggest customer by far since 1956.

Unfortunately, droughts in Kenya during the 1990s threatened the quality and stability of the natural pyrethrum supply. When Japanese giant Sumitomo developed a lower-cost synthetic alternative, SC Johnson was presented with a difficult choice: Either switch totally to the synthetic or work with the Kenyan producers to lower the cost, improve the quality, and ensure the long-term availability of the natural product. The company chose the latter strategy.

In a partnership with SC Johnson and KickStart, PBK monitored pyrethrum quality and quantity, and provided ongoing assistance to farmers in the form of access to higher-quality seed. A 2005 pilot project involving 600 farmers sought to increase net household incomes on average from $100 to $750–$1,000 per year. Such a boost in income would enable poor farmers to dramatically improve food security, health, and nutrition. It was expected that pyrethrum production per acre would increase substantially, and quality would also improve, enabling the company to continue to source the natural botanical at a competitive price rather than switching to the synthetic chemical.

Unfortunately, the results of the pilot project have been mixed: Given PBK's penchant to defer payments to the farmers, most used the micro-irrigation to raise crops other than pyrethrum (e.g., vegetables, cut flowers). So while the farmers raised their incomes, as expected, and KickStart was able to reach an entirely new, largely rural, population with their pumps, SC Johnson was unable to have a significant impact on either the quantity or quality of botanical pyrethrum. The company has since initiated a similar effort in Rwanda, where the government is more transparent and takes a more entrepreneurial approach to the growth of the pyrethrum industry.

Nonetheless, KickStart's ability to generate income for the users of its money-maker pump is beyond question. However, KickStart now faces the challenge of sustaining its own growth and development. It is clear that it cannot continue to rely exclusively on donor capital to fund the technology development work. Indeed, fundraising has now become the primary activity for the organization's leaders. Accordingly, KickStart has embarked on a strategy to move a part of its operation toward a for-profit model, through direct distribution of its technology to end users. Indeed, the partnership with SC Johnson represents one way for it to achieve this end. Only by generating a surplus itself can KickStart continue to generate income for others.

Increasing earning power is of vital importance in the BoP, especially in a post-structural adjustment world where poor countries are increasingly dependent upon the cash economy and the generation of foreign currency to survive. MNCs can therefore identify opportunities to both create consumer surplus and generate income through innovative products and business models. As with removing constraints, opportunities to increase earning power provide a useful lens for identifying the best opportunities to reach the base of the pyramid.

Creating New Potential

Because BoP communities are often physically or economically isolated, better distribution systems and communication links are essential to sustainable development. Few poor countries have distribution systems that reach more than half the population—hence the continued dependence of the poorest consumers on often low-quality local products and services and exploitative moneylenders. MNCs can therefore create new potential in the BoP by enabling outreach (providing distribution channels for local products and more inclusive supply chains) and in-reach (providing access to affordable products, services, and information).

With regard to outreach, MNCs can play a key role in sourcing or distributing the products of BoP enterprises for use in top of the pyramid markets, giving BoP enterprises their first links to international markets. Indeed, it is possible through partnerships to leverage traditional knowledge bases to produce more sustainable—and, in some cases—superior products for consumption by affluent customers. Anita Roddick, CEO of the Body Shop International PLC, demonstrated the power of this strategy in the early 1990s through her company's "trade, not aid" program of sourcing local raw material and products from indigenous people.

More recently, the Starbucks Corporation, in cooperation with Conservation International, has pioneered a program to source coffee directly from farmers in the Chiapas region of Mexico. These farms grow coffee organically using shade-grown practices, which preserve songbird habitat and prevent soil loss. Starbucks markets the product to U.S. consumers as a high-quality, premium coffee; the Mexican farmers benefit economically from the sourcing arrangement, which eliminates middlemen from the business model. This direct relationship also improves the local farmers' understanding and knowledge of the market at the top of the pyramid and its customer expectations, making a steady transition from the informal to the formal economy possible.

Daimler-Chrysler has also been instrumental in the launch of an outreach-oriented alliance in Brazil called POEMA (Poverty and Environment in Amazonia Research and Development).[17] This alliance is focused on the development of natural fibers for use in the production of interior car parts. With financial and technical assistance from Daimler-Chrysler, POEMA pioneered the use of coconut fibers and latex sourced from the Amazon in the production of headrests, sun visors, and seat cushions in the Class A Mercedes-Benz model. After a successful pilot project, a for-profit enterprise, POEMAtec Amazon Natural Fibers, was created near the city of Belem in northeastern Brazil. Daimler-Chrysler has since signed a 10-year supply contract with the new company.

Before POEMAtec, coconut fibers were considered waste. Now they are a source of income. POEMAtec worked with the small landholders in the region to help them switch from slash-and-burn agriculture of single crops to a multicrop system that includes coconut palms, rubber, cacao, bananas, and Brazilian chestnut trees. Sourcing communities were set up with processing centers to extract the coconut fibers and produce the latex. These raw materials were then sold to POEMAtec for the manufacture of the final product. The parts produced by the alliance meet all Daimler-Chrysler's stringent quality requirements and are also about 5 percent cheaper to produce than conventional plastic components. Approximately 4,000 new jobs have been created, including agricultural producers, processing plant workers, and POEMAtec employees. Average family income in the community has increased from about $36 per month to nearly $300 per month since the beginning of the alliance. The results of this BoP marketing outreach alliance in Brazil have also been transferred to South Africa and the Philippines.

With regard to in-reach, information technologies such as phones and Internet connections hold the potential to literally transform the way BoP communities view the world. Indeed, information poverty may be the single biggest roadblock to sustainable development.

Through in-reach, it is possible to imagine, for the first time in history, a single, interconnected market uniting the world in the quest for a truly sustainable form of economic development. This process could transform the "digital divide" into a "digital dividend" for the companies willing to take the initiative.

New ventures such as N-Logue and Drishtee in India are developing information technology platforms and business models suited to the particular requirements of the rural poor at the base of the pyramid. Through shared-access models (for example, Internet kiosks) and focused technology development, companies are dramatically reducing the cost of being connected. For example, IT connectivity typically costs $850–$2,800 per line in the developed world; the CorDECT (wireless local loop) technology employed by N-Logue has reduced this cost to less than $400 per line, with a goal of $100 per line, which would bring telecommunications within reach of virtually everyone in India.[18]

Drishtee founder Satan Mishra's audacious vision is to establish a network of tele-kiosks in each of India's 650,000 villages—enabling local entrepreneurs to sell a range of services, from computer training classes, to international calls, to sending family photos over the Internet. The venture began in 2005 in 500 villages. In 2008, with financing from the Acumen Fund, Drishtee began expanding more rapidly than Starbucks did in its early years, opening four kiosks per day. By late 2008, the company was operating in more than 4,000 villages and serving 7.5 million people.[19]

Recognizing the opportunity to create new economic potential, ITC, an Indian conglomerate, has spawned a network of electronic meeting places in more than 40,000 rural villages in India dubbed *e-choupals*.[20] To address the obvious shortages—phone lines, electricity, and literate farmers—the company has provided satellite links, solar batteries, and carefully chosen microentrepreneurs (Sanchalaks) to run the meeting places. As part of a diversification strategy into a broader range of agribusinesses, ITC has made the e-choupal initiative an integral part of its rural development business strategy. The company intends to reach 100,000 villages with its network by 2015.

The traditional agricultural system in India was centered on mandis, the markets where farmers brought their produce to be auctioned. Given the obvious power asymmetries (that is, the auctioneers had better information about commodity prices than the farmers), small farmers were often paid far less than they deserved for their produce. To facilitate better information access, ITC created websites for the various crops covered: soya, wheat, coffee, and shrimp. This enabled farmers to level the playing field by gaining better access to market conditions, prices, and even other potential buyers. By eliminating the stranglehold of the mandis, ITC has been able to source agricultural commodities at more favorable prices, while at the same time increasing the bargaining power—and incomes—of the small farmers.[21] Thus, two of the big roadblocks faced by rural economies are mitigated by e-choupals: Virtual aggregation provides bargaining power for even the smallest producers, and better information helps overcome uncertainty and isolation.

Once a virtual meeting place is established in a village, there is no shortage of other potential users: governments putting their services online, companies that are otherwise unable to reach rural villages, microcredit providers, and so on. The possibilities are virtually limitless. Recently, for example, ITC (in alliance with Monster India) added an online employment service, enabling rural job seekers to apply to jobs through e-choupals. e-choupals also leverage the power of the internet to empower small and marginal farmers with a host of services which allow for a virtual integration of the supply chain and create significant efficiencies in the traditional system. ITC itself has begun to utilize the e-choupal as a vehicle for bringing appropriate and affordable products and services to rural areas in addition to purchasing agricultural produce. Thus, e-choupals are now coming to serve as "digital rural highways," creating the potential for many new, perhaps unanticipated, economic activities to blossom, driven by local needs and capabilities. In return, ITC charges a margin for each good or service sold. The presence of this digital rural highway also enables locally-based businesses to gain better access to markets (e.g., horticultural growers, fruit and vegetable producers).[22]

Based in part on the e-choupal experience, the Multi-Commodity Exchange of India (MCX) launched in 2005 a National Spot Exchange for Agricultural Produce (NSEAP). When fully implemented, this initiative will establish rural commodity trading platforms for all forms of agricultural produce throughout all of India.[23] The rural connectivity brought by initiatives such as N-Logue, Drishtee, e-choupals, and NSEAP could literally transform the countryside in India. Ventures like these, which provide both in-reach and outreach, constitute the ultimate in creation of potential. For corporations, therefore, identifying opportunities to create new potential constitutes another important vehicle for effectively reaching—and raising—the base of the pyramid.

Assessing Sustainability Impact

Effectively serving the BoP means more than simply selling affordable products to the poor: It means engaging with the poor as producers, agents, and partners to create entirely new business ecosystems. Tracking the economic and development impact of BoP business initiatives throughout their entire value chains—from raw material sourcing and production all the way to distribution and product use—is therefore crucial. In a recent research project, Unilever and Oxfam teamed up to do exactly that, focusing on Unilever's Indonesia business as a case study.[24] The findings were quite interesting—and provocative: Unilever Indonesia (UI) is heavily embedded in the local economy, with significant forward and backward linkages. The majority of revenues generated by UI remain in Indonesia, through its local sourcing, wages, margins, taxes, and dividends to local shareholders.

Overall, the research estimates that the full-time equivalent (FTE) of about 300,000 people make their livelihoods from UI's value chain (for comparison, UI has a core workforce of only 5,000 in Indonesia). Strikingly, more than half of this employment is found in UI's distribution and retail chain with about one third in the supply chain. The total value generated along the entire UI value chain is estimated conservatively at US$ 633 million. Of this UI earns about US$ 212 million; the remaining US$ 421 million is distributed among the other actors in the chain. Thus, Unilever's presence in Indonesia creates significant wealth in the larger community, particularly in the distribution end of the value chain.

Importantly, the study also noted some concerns: The value captured by poorer people working at either end of the value chain, especially primary producers at the supply end, is much lower than the value captured by those who are in direct interaction with UI and closer to the center of the chain. And while 95 percent of Indonesians use at least one UI product (e.g., single-serve hand soap, laundry products, and tea), it was not possible to determine the impacts on poor consumers through their purchase of UI products. Finally, UI's success and expansion as a company raised questions about whether UI is displacing smaller-scale local producers, ultimately constraining competition in the marketplace. While none of these concerns should come as a surprise, they clearly point to areas of opportunity for Unilever's BoP strategies looking forward: In addition to tracking the direct economic impacts, it is also imperative to gain a wider understanding of the social, cultural, and environmental affects—the "triple bottom line" sustainability impact on both customers and the ecosystem of partners making up the supply chain.

In 2009, my colleague Ted London pioneered the development of a Base of the Pyramid Impact Assessment Framework, which offers managers of ventures serving the poor a systematic process for measuring and enhancing the effects their activities are having on the ground.[25] The framework provides a systematic process for examining the positive and negative impacts those activities have on the well-being of three constituencies: sellers (local distributors or producers), buyers (local customers or agents), and communities. For each of these constituencies, the framework assesses potential changes in economics, capabilities, and relationships, including how the venture affects the natural environment.

Identifying the opportunity is thus only the first step in success-fully reaching the base of the pyramid. While serving a real need through the firm's product or service is necessary for a successful strategy, it is not sufficient. It is equally important to evaluate the effect of the entire business system on the communities and environments where it is to be introduced. That means monitoring and assessing the triple bottom line (social, environmental, and economic) impact of the business system. This step is necessary because often the biggest impacts—positive and negative—are felt through the upstream (supply chain) or downstream (end use) effects of the company's activities rather than directly through its immediate products or services. Provision of credit, for instance, may not appear to have much impact in itself; the activities enabled by credit, however, may have wide-scale impacts. Furthermore, a company's entry into the BoP may have implications for existing organizations and institutions that play an important role in the community. Understanding these total system impacts is thus crucial to assessing whether a company's activities enhance or inhibit sustainable development.

In assessing sustainability impact, managers need to recognize that any new business intervention has both positive and negative effects. The problems that a sustainable global enterprise solves should, of course, be more significant than the new ones it creates. Unfortunately, from a societal perspective, many new technologies and businesses do not pass this test; the problems they create are more significant than the problems they solve. Take, for example, the nuclear power industry. In its beginning stages, the industry was seen as the source of pollution-free electricity that was too cheap to meter. It was heralded as the salvation of the world: It would rescue us from dependence upon nonrenewable and polluting fuels such as coal, oil, and gas. However, as it turned out, the nuclear power industry created massive new problems: We had not fully thought through how to deal with the expensive process of decommissioning old nuclear facilities, nor had the disposal of high-level radioactive waste been adequately addressed.

The operation of the facilities themselves also proved to be problematic, with accidents raising public fears—and operating costs—to astronomical levels. In the end, new nuclear facilities became so expensive to build and engendered so much public resistance that it no longer made sense to construct them, at least in the United States. Today nuclear power is viable only where massive government subsidies make it so: France and Japan, and perhaps soon, the U.S. once again. Therefore, in evaluating the sustainability impact of a BoP business initiative, a comprehensive and continuous assessment of both the upside and the downside of the total business system is critical.

Village Phones: The Triple Bottom Line

Let us return to the case of Grameen Telecom, described in detail in Chapter 5, "Innovation from the Bottom-Up," for an in-depth assessment of sustainability impacts. As you may recall, the venture was established as a nonprofit experiment in a few hundred villages before it was introduced on a widespread basis. This was done intentionally to allow time to test the model, identify problems, and make mid-course corrections prior to scale-up. Grameen enlisted the aid of local universities and NGOs in conducting the impact assessment, both to facilitate the work and to ensure the independence and legitimacy of the results.[26]

The results of the sustainability assessment for the village phones are summarized in Exhibit 6.2.[27] The diagram displays the triple bottom line (economic, social, and environmental) impacts associated with the introduction of mobile phone service in the 950 villages that constituted the pilot test in rural Bangladesh. Economically, the introduction of phone service was clearly a net positive. As we have seen, not only did the "phone ladies" themselves realize a significant increase in their income, but, more importantly, users of the service realized significant consumer surplus (a trip to Dhaka was 2–8 times the cost of a phone call, meaning that each call saved $2.70–$10, the equivalent of 2.5–10 percent of household monthly income). In some cases, the phone service produced dramatic increases in income for users. For example, with better access to competitive agricultural prices, local farmers were able to get substantially better prices for their crops. Indeed, the efficiency of the village economies was significantly enhanced through more rapid and accurate information flow. In the words of Iqbal Quadir, "Connectivity is productivity." Phone ladies and other local businesspeople also became more aware of and capable in the ways of the formal economy, increasing the prospects for further growth and development in the future.

Exhibit 6.2
Sustainability Assessment: Village Phones

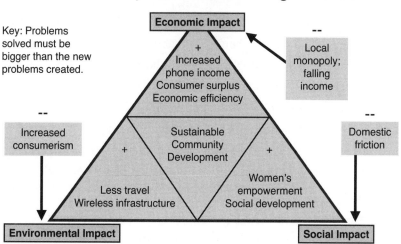

Socially, the introduction of the village phone gave the phone ladies status and visibility within their villages (if you wanted to make a phone call, you had to seek them out or come to their home). The incremental income these women contributed to their households also gave them a bigger voice in family decision making. They spent most of the new income from the village phone on their children, in the form of tuition for schooling, clothes, and health care. This raised their standard of living and opened up opportunities for their children that would not have otherwise existed.

Environmentally, the availability of phone service meant that fewer trips to the city in inefficient and polluting buses and cars were necessary. Furthermore, by moving directly to wireless telecommunications, Grameen Telecom enabled poor villages to avoid the expensive, material-intensive, and environmentally destructive step of installing cables and phone lines. The village phone, in other words, enabled the poorest communities in rural Bangladesh to leap directly to the most modern and least-polluting technology available.

Although Grameen Telecom's sustainability impact has been overwhelmingly positive, it has, predictably, created some new problems on each of the three dimensions. From the social perspective, in some cases, phone ladies' newfound earning power introduced friction and even conflict within households that were previously dominated by the husbands. Some have even experienced increased physical abuse and violence. Not surprisingly, there are those who view this as being disruptive to local communities and cultural traditions. Others, however, including most of the phone ladies themselves, view it as a necessary step toward the emancipation of women throughout the world. It may also hold the key to stabilizing population growth because raising the status of poor women is now recognized as being one of the most effective ways of lowering fertility rates.

From the environmental perspective, the rapid spread of cellular phones in the BoP has produced a burgeoning electronic waste problem, with spent batteries presenting the biggest toxic threat. Other observers are concerned that the introduction of phone service into rural areas, with its attendant rise in income and economic activity, will lead to increased consumerism and environmental degradation. Although this is a legitimate concern, it would appear that the alternative—keeping the majority of people in the world isolated and without access to information—has even larger negative consequences. Indeed, through the Great Leap to the BoP, discussed in the previous chapter, we may be able to successfully incubate and launch the renewable and inherently clean technologies of tomorrow in the BoP.

Perhaps the most significant problems that have arisen have been economic in nature. In the early going of the initiative, monopolistic practices emerged by some of the phone ladies.[28] As demand for rural phone services grew, the initial business model of having a single phone operator in each village proved to be problematic: With demand exceeding supply in many villages, prices rose, and phone ladies' incomes soared. Some phone ladies were becoming "rich" by village standards, with incomes grossly out of proportion to what they once were. To address this problem, the company removed its limit of one phone lady per village, creating a "free market" for phone service in the villages of Bangladesh. In short order, the number of phone ladies virtually doubled. With competition, prices came down, and the new incomes returned to a more reasonable level.

As noted in the previous chapter, by 2008, there were 354,000 phone ladies in Bangladesh, each averaging $1,500–$2,000 in revenue (and roughly $500–$750 in profits) each year. The new problem has been translated into yet another opportunity. In fact, recently, competition among phone ladies and other mobile phone service providers has become so intense that some complain that their annual profits have fallen below $100 per year. Mobile phone service in rural Bangladesh has now become a highly competitive industry—much to the benefit of the villagers.

The case of Grameen Telecom underscores the importance of tracking the sustainability impact of the entire business system. By starting with a nonprofit pilot experiment, Grameen was able to understand and document the economic, social, and environmental impacts of its business system from the beginning. It was also able to create a mechanism for continuously monitoring the triple bottom line performance of its business. By recognizing that any intervention will not only solve problems but also create new ones, Grameen Telecom has been able to identify and address new problems as they emerge through the continuous and creative adjustment of the business model.

The MNC Advantage

Multinationals have much to learn from the approach Grameen took in introducing its rural mobile phone service. Even if multinational managers are intellectually persuaded, however, it is not obvious that large corporations have real advantages over locally oriented firms and nonprofits such as Grameen Telecom. Indeed, the inflexible nature of corporate systems and processes may make experimenting with such business models appear beyond reach. In addition, MNCs must overcome significant negative reputational equity, given the extractive nature of much of their past behavior in the traditional economy. However, there are several compelling reasons for MNCs to embark on this journey:

- **Resources.** Building a commercial infrastructure for the base of the pyramid is a resource- and management-intensive task. Developing environmentally sustainable products and services requires significant research. Distribution channels and communication networks require extensive effort to develop and sustain. Few local entrepreneurs have the managerial or technological resources to create this infrastructure.

- **Convening of power.** MNCs can be nodes for building the commercial infrastructure, providing access to knowledge, managerial imagination, and financial resources. Without MNCs as partners, well-intentioned NGOs, communities, local

governments, entrepreneurs, and even multilateral development agencies will continue to flounder in their attempts to
bring development to the base. MNCs are well positioned to
unite the range of actors required to reach the BoP.

- **Knowledge transfer.** MNCs are able to transfer knowledge
  from one BoP market to another, such as from China to Brazil
  or India, as Unilever and others have demonstrated. Although
  practices and products have to be customized to serve local
  needs, MNCs, with their unique global knowledge base, have
  an advantage that is not easily accessible by local entrepreneurs.

- **Upmarket migration.** Not only can MNCs leverage learning
  across the base of the pyramid, but they also have the capacity
  to move innovations up-market all the way to the top of the
  pyramid. As we have seen, the BoP is a testing ground for disruptive innovations that enable a more sustainable way of living. Many of the innovations for the base can be adapted for
  use in the resource- and energy-intensive markets of the developed world.

A Common Cause

The four billion people who comprise the base of the pyramid
represent a great opportunity for corporations. Indeed, the BoP represents a chance for business, government, and civil society to join
together in a common cause. Pursuing strategies for the base of the
pyramid may hold the potential to dissolve the conflict between proponents of free trade and global capitalism on the one hand, and
adherents of environmental and social sustainability on the other.

However, the products and services currently offered at the top of
the pyramid are not appropriate for the BoP, and reaching out to the
base will require fundamentally different approaches than those even
in the emerging markets of the developing world. Changes in technology, production, credit, cost, and distribution are critical prerequisites.
Only large firms with global reach have the technological, managerial,
and financial resources needed to fully realize this opportunity.

New commerce in the BoP will not be restricted to businesses serving such basic needs as food, water, energy, and housing. The base of the pyramid is waiting for high-tech businesses such as financial services, cellular telecommunications, and affordable computers. In fact, as we have seen, for many emerging disruptive technologies (such as fuel cells, photovoltaics, satellite-based telecommunications, biotechnology, and nanotechnology), the base of the pyramid may prove to be the most attractive early market.

To date, however, NGOs, social entrepreneurs, and local businesses with far fewer resources than the MNCs have been more innovative and made more progress in developing these markets. It is tragic that as Western capitalists we have implicitly assumed that the rich will be served by the corporate sector (MNCs), while governments, NGOs, and social entrepreneurs will focus on the poor and the environment. This division of labor is stronger than most realize. Managers in MNCs, public policymakers, and NGO activists all suffer from this historical divide. A huge opportunity lies in breaking this code, linking the entire human community in a seamless market organized around the concept of sustainable growth and development.

Collectively, MNCs have only begun to scratch the surface of this massive opportunity. Those in the private sector who commit their companies to strategies for the base of the pyramid can lead the movement toward a more inclusive capitalism. It is imperative, however, that managers recognize the nature of business leadership required in the BoP arena. Imagination, tolerance for ambiguity, stamina, passion, empathy, self-reflection, and courage may be as important as intelligence, analytical skill, and technical expertise. And as the final section of the book shows, leaders need to develop a deeper understanding of the complexities and subtleties of sustainable development in the context of the BoP if they are to become truly indigenous—and successful.

Notes

1. This introduction and other parts of this chapter are adapted from C.K. Prahalad and Stuart Hart, "The Fortune at the Bottom of the Pyramid," *Strategy+Business* 26 (2002): 2–14.

2. Brian Ellison, Dasha Moller, and Miguel Angel Rodriguez, *Hindustan Lever: Reinventing the Wheel* (Barcelona, Spain: IESE Business School, 2003).

3. Low margins are not the rule in all BoP businesses or industries. Indeed, in the IT sector, rural mobile telephony can have higher margins than the established urban business due to the high utilization rate of shared-use phones.

4. Ellison, *Reinventing the Wheel*.

5. This description was adapted from Maulin Vakil and Ted London, "Hindustan Lever at the Base of the Pyramid: Growth for the 21st Century," www.globalens.com, 2006.

6. My thanks to Vijay Sharma, head of Project Shakti at HLL, for this information.

7. See, for example, R. Hoskisson, L. Eden, C. Lau, and M. Wright, "Strategy in Emerging Economies," *Academy of Management Journal* 43(3) (2000): 249–267; and D. Arnold and J. Quelch, "New Strategies in Emerging Economies," *Sloan Management Review* 40(1) (1998): 7–20.

8. C.K. Prahalad and Alan Hammond, "Serving the World's Poor, Profitably," *Harvard Business Review* 80(9) (2002): 48–57.

9. Amartya Sen, *Development as Freedom* (New York: Anchor Books, 1999).

10. Ruth Romo and Francisco Ballester, *Cemex: Patrimonio Hoy and Contrumex* (Mexico City: IPADE [English translation], 2004).

11. My thanks to Hector Ureta for his visit to Chapel Hill in April 2004 to tell the story of Patrimonio Hoy to the students in a class jointly taught by Ted London and me, called "Business Strategy for the Base of the Pyramid."

12. Ted London and Magdalena Kotek, "CEMEX's Patrimonio Hoy: At the Tipping Point?" William Davidson Institute, www.globalens.com, 2006.

13. http://www.cemexmexico.com/se/se_ph.html.

14. http://www.ilo.org/public/english/region/ampro/cinterfor/news/world_r.htm.

15. Martin Fisher, *ApproTEC: Kick Starting Economic Growth in Africa* (San Francisco: ApproTEC report, 2004).

16. My thanks to Scott Johnson at SC Johnson for this example.

17. The description of this alliance is excerpted from Yerina Mugica and Ted London, *Partnering for Mutual Success: Daimler-Chrysler-POEMAtec Alliance* (Chapel Hill, NC: Kenan-Flagler Business School, 2004).

18. Joy Howard, Charis Simms, and Erik Simanis, *Sustainable Deployment for Rural Conductivity: The N-Logue Model* (Washington, D.C.: World Resources Institute, 2001).

19. Jacqueline Novogratz, *The Blue Sweater* (New York: Rodale, 2009).

20. For a full description of e-choupals, see "Yogeth Deveshwar, The Boss of India's Biggest Tobacco Firm, Is Putting Rural India Online," *The Economist* (June 5, 2004).

21. For more information on the e-choupals, see C.K. Prahalad, *The Fortune at the Bottom of the Pyramid* (Upper Saddle River, NJ: Wharton School Publishing, 2005).

22. My thanks to Mr. Nazeeb Arif, Vice President for Corporate Communications at ITC for the latest data on the initiative.

23. I would like to recognize Vipul Arora, founder of NSEAP, for providing me with the information about this exciting initiative.

24. For details, see Jason Clay, *Exploring the Links Between International Business and Poverty Reduction: A Case Study of Unilever in Indonesia* (Oxford: Oxfam House, 2005).

25. Ted London, "Making Better Investments at the Base of the Pyramid," *Harvard Business Review* (May 2009): 3–11.

26. See D. Richardson, R. Ramirez, and M. Haq, *Grameen Telecom's Village Phone Programme in Rural Bangladesh* (Geulph, Ontario: International Telecommunications Union, 2000).

27. This is my interpretation of the results, placed in the framework of the triple bottom line. My thanks to John Elkington for letting me borrow this concept. For details on this framework, see John Elkington, *Cannibals with Forks: The Triple Bottom Line of 21st Century Business* (Oxford: Capstone Publishing Ltd., 1997). For full text of the pilot study, see D. Richardson, R. Ramirez, and M. Haq, *Grameen Telecom's Village Phone Programme*.

28. Personal communication with Muhammad Yunus, April 2004.

Part Three

Becoming Indigenous

7

Broadening the Corporate Bandwidth

When we set our sights on the world's "poor countries," we tend not to see complex societies with unique histories and economies. Instead, we see societies with economies that are "underdeveloped" versions of our own.[1] Indeed, my colleague Erik Simanis at Cornell University has made it very clear to me that our conceptual categories, which seem as though they were decreed by God, are only one way of looking at the world.[2] Whether we speak of industry boundaries—automobiles, computers, energy, telecommunications—or societal subsystems—economy, government, education, church, family, community—all serve to blind us to the actual conditions and constraints that exist for those beyond our realm, particularly at the base of the pyramid.

Because we tend to impose our preexisting categories on the BoP, we often fail to see business opportunities of potentially vast proportion. Existing core competencies and strategies within companies further constrain our thinking. The BoP thus presents MNCs with a unique opportunity, a "license to imagine," to reconceptualize the corporation in a manner that can recognize and serve the diversity of needs and values of all people in the world.[3] This does not mean selling extractive products and services to the poor; it means learning how to codevelop a commercial model aimed at improving the lives of those who have been bypassed or actively exploited by globalization. Cultural sensitivity, environmental sustainability, and mutual learning hold the keys to this process.

Unfortunately, most managers in MNCs have little knowledge or understanding of those in the BoP, let alone poor peoples' views about social equity, environmental quality, or what represents a "good life." Indeed, it has been strongly argued that the dominant conceptualizations of "development" and "modernization" reflect a Western cultural bias and a preoccupation with simply raising GDP per capita.[4] Together, these shortcomings significantly hinder efforts to imagine and build BoP communities and markets.[5] Successfully serving the needs of the entire human community therefore requires that corporations broaden their bandwidth to include the true voices of those on the periphery of the global economy.

Learning from Ladakh

In her book *Ancient Futures: Learning from Ladakh*, Helena Norberg-Hodge provides a bird's-eye view of both the problem—and the opportunity—confronting global capitalism.[6] Trained as a linguist, Norberg-Hodge in the mid-1970s set about the task of documenting the language of the Ladakhi people, an ancient tribal society of the Himalayan region who had lived a self-contained existence, due to their remote location. Having mastered the language in the first year, she became increasingly fascinated by the way of life of the people of Ladakh.

Despite the rigorous climate, short growing season, and arid environment, the people had learned how to grow crops and utilize water for irrigation on a sustainable basis. They had evolved a society in which nothing was wasted or thrown away—a use was found for everything. The concept of crime was virtually nonexistent. The Ladakhis had developed a natural sense of responsibility toward each other and their environment, and were, by and large, happy, healthy, and fulfilled. They led a rich artistic, symbolic, and ceremonial life, "working" no more than about four months out of the year, during the short growing season. Norberg-Hodge was utterly struck by what she described as their joie de vivre, true joy and contentment. She set about documenting their way of life and committed to spending roughly six months in Ladakh annually, a practice she continues to this day.

However, things began to change rather abruptly in the late 1970s and '80s. Given the growing conflict with Pakistan over the contested region of Kashmir, of which Ladakh was a part, the Indian government threw the area open to tourism, and concerted efforts were initiated to "develop" the region. This process, as usual, consisted primarily of building up the infrastructure, especially roads and utilities. Western-style health centers and schools were also established in even the most remote villages. Other fundamental changes included a growing police force, courts, banks, and radio and television. Spurred on by the development efforts, the formal sector grew rapidly. Traffic increased exponentially, with hundreds of trucks a day making the long journey to the Himalayan plateau. Jeeps and buses, crammed with thousands of tourists, added to the congestion and air pollution in the provincial capital of Leh.

The sudden influx of Western influence caused growing numbers of Ladakhis—the young men, in particular—to develop feelings of inferiority. Tourists would spend more money in one day than a typical Ladakhi family would earn in a year. Ladakhis did not realize that money played a completely different role for the foreigners; that back home, they needed it to survive, whereas in their traditional culture, villagers provided for their own basic needs without money. Western media provided overwhelming images of wealth, luxury, ease, and glamour (the side effects of pollution, stress, drug addiction, and homelessness were never shown). By contrast, the Ladakhis' own lives seemed primitive and trivial. As local people became more focused on earning money, the age-old practices of communal farming and local self-reliance began to erode. Cash cropping became the norm. More young people left for the city to find paid work, leading to a building boom in and around Leh, where urban sprawl began to resemble the slums that characterize cities throughout the Third World.

With the breakdown of the Ladakhi traditional extended family and the practice of polyandry,[7] the population, which had been virtually stable for centuries, began to grow at a rate higher than the Indian average. For the first time, a noticeable gap between rich and poor developed. With unemployment on the rise, crime became a growing problem. Children no longer greeted strangers with wonder and laughter, but rather as beggars or worse. Modern education ignored the old ways and made the children think of themselves as inferior. As mutual aid gave way to dependence on faraway forces, people began to feel powerless to make decisions concerning their own lives. Striving for the modern ideal required that Ladahkis, in effect, reject their own culture. The resulting alienation gave rise to a growing resentment and anger, which lay behind much of the violence and religious fundamentalism that has come to plague the region.

In effect, the "development" of the region led to the systematic dismantling of Ladakhi culture and a growing economic dependence, cultural rejection, and environmental degradation. Although per-capita incomes definitely rose, it is quite clear that happiness, security, and contentment did not. That is not to say that there have been no benefits from development. Many aspects of the traditional culture were far from ideal: Communication with the outside world was limited, illiteracy rates were high (although this had little impact on the functioning of the traditional culture), and infant mortality was higher and life expectancy shorter than in the developed world. The introduction of money and technology and the advent of modern medicine did bring with them certain benefits. However, on balance, the traditional nature-based society, with all its flaws and limitations, was probably more sustainable, both socially and environmentally, for the Ladakhis.

The Post-Development Challenge

The Ladakh situation is a microcosm of what has played out across the Third World over the past 50 years under the banner of development. As one of the last subsistence societies to survive virtually intact into the 1970s, it provided a unique vantage point from which to observe the process of development unfold. Throughout most of the Third World, the process began much earlier, in colonial times, and at an accelerated pace in the 1950s, following the creation of the post-war Bretton Woods Institutions of the World Bank, International Monetary Fund (IMF), and the GATT.

As many have pointed out, the modern concepts of poverty and development were constructed only following World War II.[8] For the United States, the dominant concern at that time was the reconstruction of Europe. Addressing the collapse of the colonial system was a key component of reconstruction because continued access to raw materials was seen as crucial not only for European recovery, but also for U.S. growth. However, by the late 1940s, many of the former colonies had achieved independence. The consolidation of the communist block had created three worlds: the free industrialized nations (First World), the communist industrialized nations (Second World), and the poor, nonindustrialized nations (Third World). There was a need, therefore, to define a new world order based not on subjugation, but rather on development.

In 1949, U.S. President Harry Truman announced in his inaugural address the concept of a "fair deal" for the entire world. An essential component of this was his appeal to the U.S. and the world to solve the problems of the "underdeveloped areas" of the globe. The intent was quite ambitious: to replicate the features that characterized the "advanced" societies of the time—industrialization, urbanization, and rapid growth of production and living standards, along with the adoption of modern education and cultural values—

throughout the world. Greater production was seen as the key to prosperity and peace.

This was an audacious and visionary goal, to be sure. Within a few years, it was universally embraced by the First World and many Third World countries as well. Unfortunately, this framing ignored the immense cultural diversity, unique historical circumstances, and varied skills and capabilities of the Third World by focusing attention primarily on increasing production and standard of living. In short, poverty came to be defined across the world through a single metric—income poverty—and the solution to poverty was economic growth.

The reality, we now realize, is that "standard of living" can actually be quite high in places where GDP per capita is quite low. Bhutan, for example, where people still provide for many of their own needs and produce beautiful art and music, is considered to be one of the poorest countries of the world because its gross domestic product is virtually zero.[9] With GDP as the metric, no distinction is made between homeless beggars who live on the street and the Bhutanese or Ladakhi farmers. In both cases, there may be no money income, but the life behind the statistics is entirely different. In fact, Bhutan is pioneering the development of an alternative to GDP as an indicator of standard of living, called the Index of Gross Domestic Happiness.[10]

In this way, poverty has been used to define whole peoples not according to who they are or what they want to be, but according to what they lack (income). This, it turns out, is development's fatal flaw. It has systematically failed to recognize the wealth of indigenous resources and alternatives. We have projected on the rest of the world our own Western post-war fixation with industrial production as the only path to prosperity and well-being. As a consequence, we have committed the better part of 50 years to using one-size-fits-all solutions to what are really complex, diverse, and unique problems.

Paradoxically, the development era, quite unintentionally, has created the base of the pyramid as we know it today. Traditional societies such as the Ladakh have been systematically disrupted by the development process. As peasants, nomads, and tribal peoples have been either lured away or driven from their land to urban slums in search of wage labor, poverty is often the result, not the cause. Populations that were once stable ballooned out of control as the old social norms and extended family structures that once kept them in check steadily eroded. (Why do we think that the human population has exploded from 2 billion to 6.5 billion since the end of World War II?) Increasing dependence on the money economy means that income eventually does become the most critical factor; unfortunately, job opportunities in the money economy have not been adequate to match the tens of millions of poor people flooding into the job market. Thus, massive poverty in the modern sense appeared only when development broke down community ties and cut off millions of people from access to land, water, and other resources.

The postwar development paradigm has come under increasing criticism in recent years not only from post-colonialists and antiglobalizers such as Wolfgang Sachs, David Korten, and Arturo Escobar, but also from development insiders such as Joe Stiglitz, George Soros, Jeff Sachs, and William Easterly.[11] All condemn the one-size-fits-all prescriptions of the International Monetary Fund and other Bretton Woods institutions. Most recognize that government-to-government aid programs, despite the best of intentions, have been plagued by waste, corruption, and mismanagement. Many, including George Soros, call for more reliance on civil society and other important "on-the-ground" actors (e.g., humanitarian organizations, private foundations, and NGOs) working directly with those in the BoP.

Easterly has been especially critical: In his recent book, *The White Man's Burden*, he contends that development's preoccupation with lofty goals, large-scale intervention, and top-down prescription has all but squelched the ability of local people to solve their own problems. He notes that the West has spent $2.3 trillion on foreign aid over the past five decades with shockingly little to show for it. At this point in history, then, it is probably safe to say that the development era as articulated after World War II is officially dead.

Clearly, there need not be a dichotomous choice between full-scale modernization and returning to the old ways: Neither Old Ladakh nor New Ladakh is viable any longer. As we have seen, a sustainable enterprise-led strategy has the potential to avoid the pitfalls of one-size-fits-all policies (such as structural adjustment), with development experts dictating the way people should live. Through decentralized business models and disruptive innovation, it is possible to foment a bottom-up revolution of wealth creation and life enhancement. As Norberg-Hodge observed, the real lesson of Ladakh is the realization that plateau-dwelling farmers in the Himalayas have as much to teach us about how to live as we have to teach them. They need not sacrifice the sort of social and ecological balance that they have enjoyed for centuries. To do so, however, they will need to build upon their own ancient foundations rather than tear them down, as is the way of conventional development. It is time that we get on with this enterprise in a spirit of mutual respect and learning, rather than implied or explicit superiority.

As businesspeople, therefore, we cannot know in advance what is required to serve the real needs of those who have been bypassed or damaged by the globalization process. A new capability is needed, focused on hearing these voices for the first time. In his book, *A Whole New Mind*, Daniel Pink explains why the future will belong to the creative and empathetic "right-brain" thinkers rather than the reductionist "left-brain" analysts who have dominated the corporate world for the past half-century. Indeed, in the coming "conceptual age," the abilities to detect patterns and new opportunities, to understand the subtleties of human interaction, and to combine seemingly unrelated ideas into novel combinations will take on increasing importance.[12] These are precisely the skills needed to broaden the corporate bandwidth and effectively address the challenges of global sustainability.

In fact, rather than engaging only known or powerful stakeholders of existing businesses, we need to systematically identify, explore, and integrate the views of those on the periphery or at the "fringe"— the poor, the weak, the isolated, the disinterested, and even the voices of other species with which we share the planet (through a human interpreter, of course). Accordingly, my colleague Sanjay Sharma and I have proposed the idea of *radical transactiveness* (RT), the ability to engage with fringe stakeholders possessing radically differing views, to build the competitive imagination necessary for future business success and the pursuit of a truly sustainable form of global development.[13]

Radical Transactiveness

The dominant development paradigm of the big agencies has been based on a planner's mentality: applying a simplistic external answer from the West without any real knowledge or understanding of the history, complexity, or resources that exist in the Third World. Moving beyond the planning mentality requires a new approach, one based upon indigenous knowledge and unique capabilities of local people, partners, and institutions. Radical transactiveness provides the basis for widening the corporate bandwidth that is crucial to the development of this more indigenous form of enterprise.

RT is "radical" because it focuses on gaining access to stakeholders previously considered extreme or fringe, for the express purpose of facilitating disruptive change and creating competitive imagination. RT is "transactive" because it seeks to engage the firm in a two-way dialogue with stakeholders so that each influences and is influenced by the other.[14] Interactions among diverse stakeholders extend the boundaries of the firm, offering the possibility for learning and growth not envisioned at the beginning of the process. RT thus allows a firm to understand the complex and evolving issues that may affect its future competitive position.

Exhibit 7.1 depicts the difference between core stakeholders—those visible and readily identifiable parties with a stake in the firm's existing operations—and fringe, or peripheral, stakeholders. Whereas core stakeholders gain a seat at the table by virtue of the power, legitimacy, or urgency of their claims, fringe stakeholders are typically disconnected from or invisible to the firm. They may be affected by the firm but have little, if any, direct connection to the firm's current activities. However, fringe stakeholders may hold knowledge and perspectives that are key both to anticipating potential problems and to identifying innovative opportunities and business models for the future. For example, under former CEO Carly Fiorini, Hewlett-Packard's "i-Community," in the village of Kuppam in India, was established to learn the possibilities for information technology and Internet use by the rural poor in developing countries. This was intended to help HP imagine and design the products and services that would respond to the real problems and needs of rural India.[15]

Exhibit 7.1
Engaging Fringe Stakeholders

Source: Hart, S. and Sharma, S. 2004. "Engaging fringe stakeholders for competitive imagination." *Academy of Management Executive*, 18(1): 7-18.

By opening communication channels to previously untapped sources of intelligence, RT helps the firm maintain a dynamic alignment of its strategy with the changing environment. Knowledge and learning from fringe stakeholders signal to the firm the investments it should make in appropriate resources and capabilities, allowing it to generate new value-creating strategies.[16] As noted previously, Hindustan Lever Limited (HLL) requires its managers to spend six weeks living in rural areas, to understand about the hygiene needs and practices of the rural poor. This knowledge has resulted in new product ideas (such as a combined soap and shampoo bar) and promotional programs (such as street theater) for rural markets. These innovations have also been adopted by Unilever subsidiaries in Brazil and other developing countries.

As Sanjay Sharma and I have suggested, RT consists of two subcapabilities: 1. The ability to extend the scope of the firm (fan out); and 2. The ability to integrate diverse and disconfirming knowledge (fan-in). These two phases are similar to the concepts of idea generation (divergence) and idea evaluation (convergence) described in the traditional creativity literature.[17]

Fanning Out: Extending the Scope of the Firm

Competitive imagination requires divergent thinking by managers to identify the unmet needs of new, yet-to-be served communities and markets. Divergent thinking is also necessary to envision new, disruptive technologies and business models that enable the firm to deliver functionality to customers faster, better, or cheaper than competitors. The knowledge needed to drive such innovation is usually widely dispersed outside the firm, within stakeholder groups that may be neither important nor salient, nor part of a firm's current network.

As the previous HP and HLL examples show, these stakeholders are often at the unseen periphery of the firm's stakeholder network, such as the urban homeless or the rural poor in developing countries, or are even nonhuman (for example, endangered species and nature).[18] In fact, Janine Benyus, author of the path-breaking book, *Biomimicry*, argues that by including biologists in the technology development process, it might be possible for companies to emulate (rather than dominate) nature in its designs. Spiders, for example, can manufacture a material (spider webs) at ambient temperature using no toxics that is stronger (pound for pound) than Kevlar. By treating nature as a mentor in product design, it may be possible to create a whole new generation of inherently clean and sustainable products. Distant voices from the fringe thus provide a panoramic view of a firm's changing circumstances and opportunities.

To be truly effective, fanning out requires the reversal of traditional stakeholder-management models, by "putting the last first."[19] This means making a conscious effort to completely reverse the rules of stakeholder saliency by identifying actors who have been completely invisible to the firm in the past. It is extremely difficult for managers in existing businesses to identify fringe stakeholders such as the rural poor, urban shantytown dwellers, or advocates for nature's rights. However, placing managers in situations that are the opposite of their current contexts opens them to hearing stakeholder voices from the periphery.

In the early 2000s, for example, in an effort to expand the scope of the firm, Grameen Bank founder Muhammad Yunus challenged his employees to embrace the poorest of the poor by focusing the bank's attention on beggars.[20] Beggars, he noted, had generally been excluded from the bank's portfolio because most current clients did not want to include them as part of their peer lending group, for fear that they would not pay back their loans. As a consequence, Yunus requested that every employee take the personal responsibility to recruit one beggar to become a client of the bank. This required each employee to directly confront the reality of the poorest of the poor. By 2005, over 23,000 beggars were recruited to the bank. In the process, bank employees have expanded their conception of what is possible by working directly with the beggars to get them on the path to microentrepreneurship. In one case, for example, a legless beggar who previously simply sat all day with a cup in hand, transformed his "strategic location" near the village center into a miniconvenience mart. With a $50 loan guarantee from the bank, the beggar now sells bananas, cookies, and beverages sourced from a local shop with a less desirable location.

Another example, this time in the context of an MNC, is the Biotechnology Advisory Panel set up by DuPont to consciously seek divergent views from the periphery to help it formulate a more robust strategy for biotechnology development. The company has purposefully sought to include a diversity of stakeholders from India, Africa, and Latin America in its deliberations. It has also invited environmental advocates, such as the former head of Greenpeace International, to provide divergent views on the issue. Exposing senior managers and business leaders to radically different perspectives has resulted in significant modifications and improvements to the company's approach to and strategy for biotechnology commercialization. New ideas have been generated for future business models in accordance with the company's push to move away from products based upon petrochemical feedstocks and into knowledge-intensive businesses with a biological base.

Exhibit 7.2 identifies the actions that firms can undertake to extend the scope of the firm. The costs in terms of managerial time and effort are likely to be a small fraction of what a large firm would normally spend on research and development to generate new ideas and innovations.

Managers should begin intense interactions with fringe stakeholders only after suitable cultural and ecosystem sensitivity training. They then can immerse themselves in radically different contexts to learn firsthand about the needs of those that they do not cater to with existing products. As a result, they come to understand the potential for and feasibility of applying innovative technologies to develop new business models and products. For example, Procter and Gamble has launched a pilot venture in rural Nicaragua to help its managers generate creative ideas by immersing themselves in a context where the company currently has no presence, infrastructure, or partners. By doing so, they avoid having the voices from the fringe contaminated by the dominant logic of the marketing model used to serve their existing markets.

Exhibit 7.2
Extending the Scope of the Firm

Objective: Identify and engage managers in business contexts that are the reverse of those which the business currently faces to generate imagination and ideas about potential new products, services, and business models.

Process

1. Conduct research around issues, such as climate change, biomimicry, social equity, poverty, human rights, etc., to identify stakeholders that are as different as possible from the current constituencies of the firm. The focus is on those regions and communities that have been heavily disrupted by globalization: communities with exploding population, environmental degradation and associated migration to urban areas, lack of education, mobility, communications, and basic hygiene and nutrition.

2. Create an inventory of potential sites and contexts where learning can take place for generating ideas for new business models that are sustainable in terms of economic potential, zero pollution, biodiversity, and ecosystem disruption, and enable capacity building in local communities.

3. Send managers to these jurisdictions to immerse themselves in the cultures, to understand the needs and functionalities required, and to explore the feasibility of new approaches for meeting customer needs in a radically different, innovative, and sustainable manner.

Costs: Training, managerial time, and travel

Benefits: Generating radical new ideas for products, services, and business models

Source: Adapted from Hart, S. and Sharma, S. 2004. "Engaging fringe stakeholders for competitive imagination." *Academy of Management Executive*, 18(1): 7-18.

Extending the scope of the firm by reaching out and seeking knowledge from fringe stakeholders enables managers to suspend disbelief, thereby broadening the corporate bandwidth. New knowledge is generated only when managers escape from the old ideas and mindsets that underpin the current business system. Effective fan-out thus focuses on engaging with unconventional and nontraditional stake-holders to understand dynamic and complex problems that might result in new, breakthrough products, technologies, or strategies.

Fanning In: Integrating Diverse and Disconfirming Information

Once the company's boundaries have been expanded and diver-gent thinking has opened up the firm to both new concerns and emerging opportunities for the future, the challenge is to integrate this new information into practical, useable strategies. Having initi-ated contact with these stakeholders, managers need to build bridges so that extended, informal conversations can take place. The transfer of tacit or unwritten knowledge residing in people and their traditions requires intense interaction; it cannot be exchanged in large group meetings or during formal negotiations. Practical strategies emerge only after the apparent contradictions between knowledge from fringe stakeholders and the current business model have been recon-ciled.

Just as living in a different country allows managers to better identify appropriate product/service modifications in developed mar-kets, spending time in homeless shelters, rural areas in developing countries, or areas where nature has been depleted or devastated provides a radically different physical and mental context to spark the imagination. To be able to absorb knowledge from fringe stakehold-ers, however, especially those that are adversarial or peripheral to the firm's current operations, managers need to empathize with differ-ences in perspectives. Empathy depends upon deep listening and speaking in depth with those who have different views.

As we have seen, HLL generates empathy by requiring all com-pany employees to spend six weeks living in rural villages and actively seeking local consumer insights and preferences as they develop new products.[21] The company has also created an R&D center in rural

India that focuses specifically on technology and product development to serve the needs of the poor and that sources raw materials almost exclusively from local producers. HLL uses a wide variety of local partners to distribute their products and also invests in developing the capabilities of those partners. Through local understanding and empathy, HLL has been able to generate substantial revenues and profits from operating in low-income markets.

By reconciling disconfirming information, Arvind Mills was able to create an entirely new value-delivery system for affordable blue jeans in India.[22] As the world's fifth-largest denim manufacturer, Arvind found Indian domestic denim sales limited because a $20–$40 pair of jeans is neither affordable to the masses nor widely distributed. In direct response, Arvind introduced Ruf and Tuf jeans, a ready-to-make kit of components (denim, zipper, rivets, patch) priced at about $6. A network of 4,000 tailors, many in small rural towns and villages, assemble the pants for customers, providing employment and building a motivated and decentralized distribution system for the kits. Ruf and Tuf jeans are now the largest-selling jeans in India, easily surpassing Levi's and other brand names from the United States and Europe.

In contrast, the failure of Nike's attempt in the late 1990s to produce an athletic footwear product for the booming low-income populations in China can be traced, at least in part, to a lack of empathy and inability to reconcile disconfirming information.[23] Based upon a relatively low price point ($10–$15 per pair), the "World Shoe" was designed (without extensive contact with potential customers) as a product that could appeal to the masses who could not afford Nike's top-of-the-line products. In China, Nike relied exclusively on its existing contract factory network to produce the product, utilized the firm's established in-country channels to distribute the World Shoe, and did not develop a context-specific marketing plan for the product. In fact, the World Shoe was displayed side by side with the $150 Air Maxx in upscale retail outlets in Beijing and Shanghai. Relying on familiar partners and the existing business model for high-end athletic footwear products left the World Shoe struggling to meet its sales goals. The initiative was terminated in 2002.

Designing and producing a lower-cost shoe using the existing business system meant, paradoxically, that Nike failed to reach its target customer. The company failed to develop an empathetic understanding of the context before designing the product. Nike was also singularly unsuccessful in resolving the contradictions that existed between its current business model and the one that would be required to appropriately serve the need for affordable athletic footwear. Thus, competitive imagination is sparked only when the company commits to integrating the disconfirming information introduced by fringe stakeholders.

As we saw in the last chapter, Mexico's largest cement company, Cemex, provides a more instructive example.[24] Cemex has achieved extraordinary success through a shrewd strategy of targeting developing countries such as Bangladesh, Egypt, Indonesia, Thailand, and others in Latin America. The poorest residents of these developing countries represent a special opportunity because they are currently served inadequately, if at all. Cemex learned how to tap the enormous market of low-income customers in developing countries by first studying how to do business with the poor in Mexico. By gaining an in-depth understanding of the constraints and conditions that existed in the shantytowns of Mexico, Cemex was able to forge a business model that reconciled the company's need for growth with the idiosyncratic needs of poor, do-it-yourself homebuilders.

Other examples reinforce the point. To help reconcile contradictions and leverage learning, GE now designates a senior executive to serve as point person for its new "Local Growth Teams," which are new initiatives in the company aimed at generating innovation from the bottom-up in emerging markets. In this way, not only are the individual initiatives protected, but efforts by the individual project teams can be better coordinated and learning more effectively communicated from one part of the company to another. Similarly, Unilever has created an international committee to transfer BoP-based innovations, such as HLL's products and promotion programs, to other countries and markets.

As Exhibit 7.3 shows, integrating diverse and disconfirming information means engaging, on an ongoing basis, with fringe stakeholders. This is how the radical new ideas and business models identified in the previous step are operationalized, tested, and leveraged. Such implementation takes into account the real needs of remote stakeholders and builds in the capacity to adjust and learn based upon actual experience. This step focuses on the implementation of practical solutions to the problems and opportunities identified in the fan-out stage. The final challenge is then to link both stages of the RT process into a coherent approach for new strategy formulation and implementation.

Exhibit 7.3
Integrating Diverse and Disconfirming Information

Objective: Incubate, implement, and leverage radical innovations and new business models.

Process

1. Organize and facilitate stakeholder dialogues involving line managers, product developers, and technologists in collaboration with fringe stakeholder representatives to develop specific new product and service concepts.
2. Incubate innovations and new business models by setting up taskforces consisting of operating managers, R&D engineers, and staff managers, some of whom have experienced the radically different stakeholder contexts.
3. Open continuing conversations with stakeholders in extreme contexts to test and refine ideas for products, services, and business models, ensuring that stakeholder needs are met and their concerns regarding negative social and environmental impacts are addressed.
4. Coordinate and exchange information in organizational committees that are horizontally diverse (SBUs, functional areas, geographic locations) and vertically diverse (across corporate hierarchies).

Costs: Coordination of taskforces and ongoing transactiveness with stakeholders.

Benefits: Generating disruptive innovations in products, services, and business models while addressing the economic, social, and environmental concerns of stakeholders at the fringe and preventing the creation of adversarial swarms.

Source: Adapted from Hart, S. and Sharma, S. 2004. "Engaging fringe stakeholders for competitive imagination." *Academy of Management Executive*, 18(1): 7-18.

Together, the capabilities of stakeholder fan-out and fan-in reinforce each other. By integrating knowledge from fringe stakeholders, radical transactiveness has the potential to challenge fundamental business models and frames of reference, leading to new bases of growth and competitive advantage. This capability also helps the firm engage stakeholders in an ongoing two-way dialogue that enables it to anticipate and respond to their concerns instead of facing unanticipated conflicts such as those faced by Monsanto.

RT thus means going far beyond the notion of radical transparency, which entails full and open disclosure of the firm's current activities, strategies, and impacts. Radical transparency, which has become increasingly common over the past decade, is targeted primarily at managing core stakeholders—those who can directly affect the current business by virtue of their power, urgency, or salience.[25] It seeks "permission" to operate from those interests and groups that might otherwise withhold resources, approval, or legitimacy.

In an interconnected world populated by tens of thousands of NGOs and activist groups, however, it is increasingly perilous to depend upon radical transparency alone. The experiences of organizations such as Monsanto, Nike, Shell, and the World Trade Organization demonstrate that fringe stakeholders with no direct connection to the organization's activity can have a significant impact on the company's ability to execute. RT thus helps the firm anticipate and even preempt such difficulties by identifying new strategies for a smarter, more inclusive form of globalization—strategies that seek, from the outset, to address social, cultural, and environmental issues. RT enables firms to cast a wider, more inclusive net to generate competitive imagination about possible future products, markets, and business models.

Expanding Our Concept of the Global Economy

To date, our tendency has been to take a very narrow view of what constitutes "the economy." We have framed the global economy, especially in the rich countries of the First World, as consisting exclusively of wage labor within firms that produce goods and services. We have focused almost exclusively on a narrow range of macroeconomic indicators, such as GDP per capita, thereby failing to take into account myriad other forms of economic activity that are critically important to people around the world. Not surprisingly, then, when we attempt to impose this model of global capitalism on the rest of the world, we encounter significant resistance precisely because we have failed to appreciate how the majority of people in the world currently live.

Scholars such as J.K. Gibson-Graham have pointed out, for example, that the formal money economy represents only the tip of the iceberg of economic activity in the world. Beneath the formal, private sector–based economy lies not only the public sector (schools, governments, agencies) and the informal economy (barter, self-provisioning, moonlighting, household production), as we have seen, but also myriad other arrangements and activities, such as producer cooperatives, communal enterprises, not-for-profit organizations, volunteering, gift giving, and what Hazel Henderson calls the love economy: work performed without pay by hundreds of millions of mothers, fathers, aunts, uncles, and grandparents in raising their families.[26]

When we add all of these activities together, they total many times what we record in our official GDP numbers in measuring the health of the economy. Our narrow measure is one reason, of course, why so-called developing countries look so anemic when it comes to economic growth and success: The majority of actual economic activity is taking place beneath the surface, in the public-sector, informal, and love economies. That is not to say that these economic activities are always efficiently accomplished, equitably distributed, or environmentally sustainable. Indeed, as we have seen, there are literally billions of people at the base of the economic pyramid whose needs are still being poorly met or who are actively exploited by extractive local producers, warlords, or despots.

The opportunity, therefore, is to expand our concept of both the economy and capitalism. Neither is a monolithic idea. Markets are ubiquitous throughout the world, from street vendors in the Third World to the New York Stock Exchange. A more inclusive form of capitalism can catalyze and spawn a range of economic activities and practices, even in those sectors that are currently considered noncapitalist (the informal sector, cooperatives, and family-based enterprise).

Capitalism, in other words, need not be hegemonic: Through the strategies they create, companies can expand the scope of the global economy beyond its current focus on the production of commodity goods for the wealthy in the formal economy. Similarly, the global financial system can expand its horizons beyond its current preoccupation with the free movement of capital, which has served primarily the interests of the wealthy while destabilizing foreign currencies and further impoverishing the poor, to become a truly effective tool in spreading opportunity and fighting poverty.

As businesspeople, we must now awaken to these possibilities. By creating a more inclusive form of enterprise, one that is based in the local context and built from the bottom up, we can combine the best of both worlds—the resources and technological capacity of the formal economy and the indigenous knowledge, human face, and cultural understanding of the informal sector and love economy. This is fundamentally different from the idea of corporate social responsibility, which relies on philanthropy to compensate for the damage done by conventional (alien) business strategies; instead, I am proposing that companies develop a new sense of intimacy with and embeddedness in the world so that they might better understand the real

problems that need to be solved for the majority of humanity.[27] The profit motive, seen through this lens, then serves to accelerate the pace of positive change by solving problems and creating new wealth, not by extracting resources from the many only to give them to the few.

From Alien to Native

As corporations have globalized their strategies over the past few decades, they have succeeded in developing worldwide supply chains capable of serving a customer base around the globe. However, these strategies—even ones focused on being locally responsive—still rely heavily on world-scale production and one-size-fits all solutions. These solutions may be appropriate for the wealthy at the top of the pyramid, but they hold little hope of being either appropriate to the real needs of the poor or within their means. To serve the poor effectively, companies need to hear the voices of those who historically have been excluded from capitalism's reach. Developing this skill will enable companies to make the transition from being alien forces in the world, with strategies that extract natural resources, plunder rural villages, and accelerate the rush to the city, to becoming native to the places in which they operate.

Unfortunately, most MNC strategies to date—even those developed with sustainability in mind—have remained alien. Monsanto's original attempt to commercialize genetically modified seeds and Nike's failed effort to develop an athletic shoe for low-income markets in China provide two instructive examples. Companies seeking to "deploy" clean technology and "target" the poor with affordable products while well intentioned, may inadvertently be engaged in the latest form of imperialism. Even the few MNC success stories described in this chapter and elsewhere—Hindustan Lever's BoP business development in rural India, Hewlett-Packard's i-Community in Kuppam, and Cemex's Patrimonio Hoy program—represent important first steps, but still have a ways to go before we can think of them as indigenous business models. Broadening the bandwidth is the first step in the development of native capability. The next chapter delves more deeply into what it means to become truly indigenous.

Notes

1. This insight is drawn from Wolfgang Sachs, *Planet Dialectics* (New York: Zed Books, 1999).

2. Some of Erik's most powerful ideas can be found in Erik Simanis, "Entrepreneurship and Global Development: An Antiessentialist Critique and Extension" (Chapel Hill: University of North Carolina, working paper, 2002).

3. My thanks again to Erik Simanis for this wonderful concept.

4. See, for example, Arturo Escobar, *Encountering Development* (Princeton, NJ: Princeton University Press, 1995).

5. My thanks to Erik Simanis and Gordon Enk for some of the language here; it is excerpted from our joint *Project Proposal for a Protocol for Strategic Initiatives at the Base of the Pyramid* (Ithaca, NY: Cornell University, 2004).

6. Helena Norberg-Hodge, *Ancient Futures: Learning from Ladakh* (Berkeley, CA: Sierra Club Books, 1991).

7. Polyandry refers to the practice of a woman having more than one husband. Such a practice limited the number of women having children and contributed to keeping the population in check.

8. See, for example, Wolfgang Sachs, *Planet Dialectics*; Gilbert Rist, *The History of Development* (New York: Zed Books, 1997).

9. Helena Norberg-Hodge, *Ancient Futures*.

10. For more information about this and the elements of true happiness, see Jonathan Haidt, *The Happiness Hypothesis* (New York: Basic Books, 2006).

11. See Wolfgang Sachs, *Planet Dialectics*; Arturo Escobar, *Encountering Development*; David Korten, *When Corporations Rule the World* (San Francisco, CA: Berrett-Kohler, 1995); Joseph Stiglitz, *Globalization and Its Discontents* (New York: W.W. Norton, 2002); George Soros, *On Globalization* (New York: Public Affairs, 2002); Jeffrey Sachs, *The End of Poverty* (New York: Penguin Books, 2005); and William Easterly, *The White Man's Burden* (New York: Penguin, 2006).

12. Daniel Pink, *A Whole New Mind* (New York: Riverhead Books, 2006).

13. Portions of the following section are excerpted from Stuart Hart and Sanjay Sharma, "Engaging Fringe Stakeholders for Competitive Imagination," *Academy of Management Executive* 18(1) (2004): 7–18.

14. The idea of a "transactive" approach to planning in the public domain was first articulated in John Friedmann, *Retracking America: A Theory of Transactive Planning* (New York: Anchor Press, 1973).

15. For a detailed description, see Deborah Dunn and Keith Yamashita, "Microcapitalism and the Megacorporation," *Harvard Business Review* (August 2003): 46–54.

16. Kathy Eisenhardt and Jeffrey Martin, "Dynamic Capabilities: What Are They?" *Strategic Management Journal* 21 (special issue) (2000): 1105–1121; and David Teece, Gary Pisano, and Art Shuen, "Dynamic Capabilities and Strategic Management," *Strategic Management Journal* 18 (1997): 509–533.

17. For an excellent summary of this literature, see Leigh Thompson, "Improving the Creativity of Organizational Work Groups," *Academy of Management Executive* 17(1) (2003): 96–111.

18. For examples of each of these, see David Collins, "Serving the Homeless and Low-Income Communities Through Business and Society/Business Ethics Class Projects: The University of Wisconsin-Madison Plan," *Journal of Business Ethics* 15(1) (1996): 67–85; C.K. Prahalad and Stuart Hart, "The Fortune at the Bottom of the Pyramid," *Strategy+Business* 26 (2002): 1–14; and Mark Starik, "Should Trees Have Managerial Standing? Toward Stakeholder Status for Non-human Nature," *Journal of Business Ethics* 14(3) (1995): 207–217.

19. For an in-depth discussion of this concept, see Robert Chambers, *Rural Development: Putting the Last First* (London: Longman, 1984).

20. Personal communication with Muhammad Yunus, April 2004.

21. See Miguel Angel Rodriguez, *Reinventing the Wheel: Hindustan Lever in India* (Barcelona, Spain: IESE, 2002).

22. M. Baghai, S. Coley, D. White, and C. Conn, "Staircases to Growth," *McKinsey Quarterly* 4 (1996): 39–61.

23. See Heather McDonald, Ted London, and Stuart Hart, *Expanding the Playing Field: Nike's World Shoe Project*, www.globalens.com, 2009.

24. See K. Herbst, "Enabling the Poor to Build Housing: Pursuing Profit and Social Development Together," *Changemakers.net Journal* September (2002).

25. R. Mitchell, B. Agle, and D. Wood, "Toward a Theory of Stakeholder Identification and Salience: Defining the Principle of Who and What Really Counts." *Academy of Management Review* 22 (1997): 853–886.

26. J.K. Gibson-Graham, *The End of Capitalism (As We Knew It)* (Oxford: Blackwell Publishers, 1996); J.K. Gibson-Graham, "A Diverse Economy: Rethinking Economy and Economic Representation," Working Paper; and Hazel Henderson, *Beyond Globalization* (West Hartford, CT: Kumarian Press, 1999).

27. My thanks to Ted London for letting me borrow the wonderful concept of "social embeddedness" from our joint work together. I should also acknowledge the work of Mark Granovetter who first articulated the phrase in the management context: "Economic Action and Social Structure: The Problem of Embeddedness." *American Journal of Sociology* 91(3) (1985): 481–510.

8

Developing Native Capability

Since C.K. Prahalad and I first introduced the idea of the "fortune at the bottom of the pyramid" in 1998, it has gathered considerable momentum. Over the past few years, the number of articles and
books, as well as conferences, programs, and corporate initiatives on
the BoP has mushroomed.[1] Indeed, some have even claimed that BoP
has now joined the ranks of business buzzwords! Many large corporations have transformed their business models to achieve the price
points and cost positions required to reach the poor: Single-serve
(sachet) packages, low-cost production, extended "mom and pop" distribution, microfinance, and NGO partnerships have become *de
rigeur*. Social entrepreneurship and microfinance have also come of
age. Yet in the rush to capture the "fortune" at the bottom (base) of
the pyramid, something may have been lost: the perspective of the
poor themselves.

A growing chorus of voices now raises the concern that corporate
BoP strategies represent nothing more than veiled attempts to "sell to
the poor," as though simply turning the poor into consumers will
address the fundamental problems of poverty and sustainable development. Recently, for example, SELCO's Managing Director, Dr.
Harish Hande, raised some serious red flags: "I am shocked, to say
the least, that people are looking at the BoP in a very unidirectional
way...Sell, sell, sell to the BoP, large markets, high potential
growth...As a friend of mine said, many people live in poverty while a
few live off poverty."[2] Professor Aneel Karnani at the University of

Michigan has perhaps captured the growing concern most provocatively in his paper, "Fortune at the Bottom of the Pyramid: A Mirage."[3] In this stinging critique, he argues that the BoP business proposition is at best a "harmless illusion" and at worst a "dangerous delusion." Rather than focus on the poor as consumers, he cautions, we need to view the poor as producers because the only way to alleviate poverty is to raise the real income of the poor.

I could not agree more! If corporations are to thrive in the twenty-first century, they must broaden their base and expand the pie for everyone, they must play a central role in narrowing the gap between rich and poor, and they must incubate and commercialize the disruptive technologies of tomorrow that leapfrog us toward a more sustainable world. They must come to understand and nurture local markets and cultures, leverage local solutions, and generate wealth at the lowest points on the pyramid. Producing in, rather than extracting wealth from, these communities will be the guiding principle: Indigenous enterprise, co-creating technologies, products, and services to meet local needs and building local businesses from the bottom up is the objective.

To do this, MNCs must combine their advanced technology and global reach with deep, local understanding of BoP communities. Although technology is important, strategies for the base of the pyramid cannot be realized without engaging local people. Indeed, efforts led by companies or development agencies trying to "solve" the problems of the poor or impose technological solutions have generally failed. For corporations, the best approach is to marry their global best practices with newfound local knowledge and understanding gleaned from widening the corporate bandwidth. Companies must come to view the poor more as *partners* and *colleagues* rather than merely *clients* or *consumers*. This mindset shift requires the development of a new, "native capability" to complement competencies in global efficiency, national responsiveness, and learning transfer that most MNCs already possess.

Next Generation Strategies and Skills

As we saw in the previous chapter, widening the corporate bandwidth through radical transactiveness is an important first step in the development of native capability, the skills and competencies needed for firms to become thoroughly embedded in the local context. Becoming indigenous requires firms to bridge the formal and informal economies because development at the base of the economic pyramid does not follow traditional patterns found in the developed world. As my colleague, Ted London, at the University of Michigan suggests, this means focusing on what is positive in the BoP, not just what is negative (corruption) or missing (Western-style institutions).

Unfortunately, most initial corporate forays into the BoP have been "alien" in nature. Most Western companies and large multinational corporations have simply adapted their current business models by repackaging existing products into smaller serving sizes (e.g., single serving sachets); outsourcing production to developing country partners; extending product distribution into shantytowns and rural areas; and working with NGOs to fill their skill gaps. While commendable as an initial step, such "first-generation" corporate BoP strategies have, in my view, failed to hit the mark.[4] These strategies represent arms-length attempts to quickly tap into a new market without understanding the real needs or aspirations of those living there.

Tragically, such "BoP 1.0" strategies, as I call them, have spawned a growing backlash among academics, civil society, and even local partners. If the enterprise-based approach to poverty alleviation is to flourish in the future, it is imperative that we move rapidly to a "second-generation" of corporate BoP strategies based on native capability (see Exhibit 8.1). As we will see, "BoP 2.0" requires more than merely deep listening: It calls for deep dialogue by engaging fringe stakeholders as colleagues and building trust through direct personal relationships; it means generating competitive imagination by combining the knowledge and skills of the company with those in the local community. Indeed, as my colleague Erik Simanis would say, becoming native requires business co-development and the creation of mutual value.

Exhibit 8.1
Second-Generation BoP Strategy

BoP 1.0	BoP 2.0
• BoP as producer/consumer	• BoP as business partner
• Deep listening	• Deep dialogue
• Reduce price points	• Expand imagination
• Extend distribution	• Marry capabilities
• Arm's length relationship via NGOs	• Direct, personal relationships

"Selling to the Poor"	"Creating Mutual Value"

Source: Adapted from Simanis, E. and Hart, S. 2008. *Base of the Pyramid Protocol*, 2nd Ed., Cornell University: Center for Sustainable Global Enterprise.

In short, effectively serving the base of the pyramid appears to require a completely different strategic approach. The successful BoP ventures discussed in previous chapters, for example, show that small-scale, locally-grown initiatives are well matched to the conditions in low-income communities. Indeed, they meet those markets' conditions better than the developed-world mantra of centralization of control and economies of scale, which require rule of law and well-functioning central institutions from the outset. In the sections that follow, I describe some of the critical new strategies and skills underpinning native capability that have emerged from our ongoing study of BoP business during the past decade.[5]

Engage First, Design Second

As we saw in Chapter 5, "Innovation from the Bottom-Up," when Cemex issued its "Declaration of Ignorance" regarding the use of its cement products by low-income customers in Mexico, it gave a group of managers the challenge of living in the shantytowns for six months to develop a better understanding of the constraints and problems faced by do-it-yourself homebuilders. There was one additional requirement: that they not think about cement at all during their time in the shantytowns. As one Cemex manager put it: "When we went into the community, we had to remove the cement chip from our brains."[6] This prohibition, as it turned out, was a critically important one. Freed of the burden of the short-term commercial agenda, the Cemex managers were able to win the trust of the local people, which ultimately led to new and unanticipated insights into how the company might better serve their needs. It also yielded a key insight about how to become indigenous: Local engagement should always precede product or service development. The Patrimonio Hoy program, with its remarkable embeddedness in the local shantytown environment, would never have happened if the project teams' primary objective had been to simply sell more cement.

When it comes to entering the BoP, then, large corporations must resist the temptation to behave like the proverbial child with a hammer, to whom everything begins to look like a nail. Pushing the company's existing products and solutions onto shantytown dwellers and rural villagers may indeed produce incremental sales in the near term, but will almost certainly fail in the long run because the solutions remain alien; witness Nike's failed attempt to introduce an athletic footwear product in the BoP.

A precommercial period of engagement is thus essential to develop empathetic understanding. Building trust also enables managers to engage in two-way learning with local people. The poor may, in fact, help them to see the shortcomings in their own companies—and perhaps even their way of life. As journalist Tom Friedman noted in his book *The Lexus and the Olive Tree*, people everywhere need the material wealth and sustenance supplied through work, trade, and the market as symbolized by the Lexus. However, people also need the olive tree—the sense of belonging, community, connection to nature, and larger purpose that comes from family, tribe, tradition, religion, and other nonmaterial sources.[7]

Today, the top of the pyramid, particularly in the U.S., has more than succeeded in supplying the Lexus for its people; in fact, obesity and overconsumption have become increasingly common, suggesting that as a culture we have overshot the mark on this dimension. However, the olive tree has, for some time, been in retreat at the top of the pyramid: Career mobility, urbanization, and the automobile culture have served to undermine family, erode communities, and dampen a sense of belonging to place. Religious fundamentalism may be seen, at least in part, as a compensatory response to the progressive loss of the olive tree in modern society.

The situation is exactly the opposite at the base of the pyramid: While lacking in the Lexus dimension, many Third World communities still earn their livelihoods in ways consistent with the preservation of their cultures and of their natural environments. The olive tree continues to thrive, despite threats from resource extraction, environmental degradation, and cultural disruption. It is here that those of us at the top of the pyramid can rediscover community and the wisdom of indigenous systems of agriculture, industry, shelter, water, and medicine if we allow ourselves to look.

In northern Nigeria, for example, a local teacher, Mohammed Bah Abba, was motivated by his interest in indigenous African technology to seek a practical, local solution to the problems of food spoilage, which causes disease and loss of income for thousands in the area.[8] Northern Nigeria is an impoverished region where people in rural communities eke out a living from subsistence farming. With no electricity and, therefore, no refrigeration, perishable foods spoil within days. Bah Abba's extremely simple and inexpensive earthenware pot-in-pot cooling device is starting to revolutionize lives in this semidesert area. This technology, which draws upon the ancient art of pottery and employs local pot makers, requires no external energy supply to preserve fruit, vegetables, and other perishables in hot, arid climates. The innovative cooling system consists of two earthenware pots of different diameters, one placed inside the other. The space between the two pots is filled with wet sand. The water contained in the sand between the two pots evaporates toward the outer surface of the larger pot, where drier outside air is circulating. The evaporation process causes a drop in temperature of several degrees, cooling the inner container, destroying harmful microorganisms, and preserving perishable foods. Bah Abba launched an enterprise using more than 500 local potters as producers to make them available to the rural poor. By the late 2000s, he was producing tens of thousands of pots annually with a retail price of about $1, and the enterprise had grown to encompass three additional countries in Africa, including Chad, Cameroon, and Niger.

Through engagement, then, we can awaken to new possibilities. In the process, we may discover the potential for new products and services—not to mention new ways of living—that could never have been envisioned before. For decades, Peace Corps volunteers have learned this lesson firsthand. When they first join, most young volunteers expect that they will be applying "advanced" knowledge from the rich countries to "help" the poor. Upon completion of their assignment, however, most freely admit that they learned more from the poor whom they were supposed to be helping, than the poor did from them.

For corporations, it may be difficult to truly engage because of the baggage associated with the existing commercial agenda—the tyranny of the current served market. For example, although focused on engagement, and not incremental cement sales, Cemex still sent its managers into Mexico's shantytowns to learn about poor homebuilders, even if they were also instructed to forget about cement sales, at least for a while. The mindset associated with the current business can still blind managers to new possibilities if not properly managed.

One way to overcome such biases is to put together consortia to do the engagement work. Including representatives from different industries might make it possible to cross-fertilize ideas and for each industry to stimulate the others. A consortium that included a wider diversity of industries might have been able to see that, despite their best intentions, Cemex's preoccupation with cement blinded it to the potential for leveraging more sustainable building methods as part of its offering. Furthermore, the presence of a microfinance expert might have been able to see that, in addition to creating a mechanism for paying for building materials, the Patrimonio Hoy program might incorporate a service to help shantytown dwellers gain legal title to the houses they build. Engagement thus opens up the possibility of identifying real needs from the point of view of the local people themselves. It also helps to focus and direct the technology and product development required to become truly native to a place.

Coinvent Custom Solutions

Companies interested in developing embedded businesses at the base of the pyramid can learn much from fields such as rural sociology, applied anthropology, and empathy-based design. Indeed, techniques such as participatory rural appraisal, rapid assessment processes, and quick ethnography open up valuable ways to hear the true voices of marginalized populations and begin the processes of understanding, mutual learning, and the creation of responsive strategies.[9] All these techniques stress the importance of codeveloping custom solutions to problems through two-way information flow. Rather than imposing pre-existing solutions from above, the emphasis is on working with local partners to codesign every aspect of the business.

In our study of BoP ventures, Ted London and I discovered that successful initiatives—those that became embedded in the local community—maximized the functionality of the product or service in terms that were important to local users. This often meant allowing the product and business model to coevolve. As one of our respondents indicated, successful initiatives require "everybody who touches it to make money."[10] Poorly performing ventures, on the other hand, tended to view the value proposition in terms of the product itself and often completed the development process at a geographically distant location, such as the corporate R&D center, before the business model was designed.

WorldSpace Corporation, for example, was created to provide direct satellite delivery of digital audio communications and multimedia services to the underserved emerging markets of the world, including Africa, the Middle East, Asia, and Latin America. The WorldSpace satellite network, which was launched in the late 1990s, consisted of three geostationary satellites capable of delivering more than 40 channels of crystal clear audio and multimedia programming directly to portable receivers, enabled with a proprietary chip. To recoup the cost of the satellite infrastructure, WorldSpace priced receivers in the $250–$500 range. Ultimately, it expected this unique global service to transmit quality information, education, and entertainment programming to a service area that included five billion people.[11]

Founder Noah Samara's original vision was to use direct audio broadcast via satellite to stop the spread of AIDS in Africa, but that horizon quickly expanded. In addition to spreading knowledge to make people healthier, better educated, and more aware of the precious environment in which they live, WorldSpace was also seen as a vehicle for bringing the poor the best music and literature of their native cultures, along with those from the great cultures of faraway lands.

Although the technology development associated with the WorldSpace venture was impressive, the company ultimately failed to secure a critical mass of users. Receiver price was clearly a roadblock to widespread adoption. However, even more significant was the company's inability to provide programming that users found useful or compelling. Because it relied on the central generation of content to be broadcast to large areas in the developing world, the company was unable to accommodate the varying tastes and priorities of local users. The centralized nature of the business model virtually prevented the kind of codevelopment and coevolution that is crucial to success. Despite its best intentions, WorldSpace was an alien technology, unable by its nature to develop a local face.

Contrast this with the approach taken by rural IT provider N-Logue.[12] Employing a specially designed wireless local loop (WLL) technology developed by the Indian Institute of Technology in Madras, N-Logue was able to offer village-based communication services through a coinvention strategy. The business model consists of three levels of interdependent networks. At the corporate level, N-Logue facilitates the relationships among the wide range of organizations (equipment vendors, NGOs, content providers, and government) that enable and support the entire system. At the next level, N-Logue maintains a regional network of franchised Local Service Partners (LSPs) who work in tandem with the corporation to set up Access Center nodes to which individual kiosk operators are connected. At the lowest level, local microentrepreneurs are recruited by the LSPs to establish village-level kiosk franchises that provide Internet and Voice over IP telephone access to the local population.

The kiosks essentially function as combination rural Internet cafes and pay phone booths. While N-Logue provides kiosk owners with training, support, and technical assistance, and LSPs provide some general content platforms that they might adopt, the local microfranchises themselves are responsible for deciding upon the actual product and service offerings and marketing strategies they will use. These have included not only access to specific content, based on the local needs of villagers, but also computer training classes, CD-ROM movie viewing, and other specially tailored services. Allowing kiosk operators to develop their own business strategies has resulted in locally appropriate solutions and new offerings that are difficult to develop within a centralized business structure.

As the N-Logue example makes clear, the context-specific nature of the base of the pyramid dictates that companies adopt a participatory approach to product and service development, in concert with local users. Coinventing custom solutions thus extends far beyond the idea of being locally responsive (adapting pre-existing solutions to local conditions), which pervades most of the thinking about global strategy in MNCs. To develop native capability, then, companies must learn how to coinvent and coevolve products and services so that they are appropriately embedded in the local ecosystem and culture from the start.

Fail Small, Learn Big

To facilitate the development of native capability, multiple low-cost probes appear vastly superior to a single, large-scale market test. Considering that any new initiative is bound to have unintended consequences, it is much better to "fail small, but learn big"—to fine-tune and perfect the business model on a small scale before seeking wider application. Indeed, small-scale experimentation offers the potential for rapid and continuous learning, as well as for modular scale-up if the experiment proves successful. Low-cost probes also make it easy to shut down failed projects before they become expensive burdens on the company or have large negative consequences on communities or the environment. Such initiatives must be evaluated for funding using a separate set of criteria and metrics, however, because they will almost never meet the short-term revenue and profitability targets associated with projects designed to expand existing businesses.

In this regard, it is beneficial to use a real-options approach rather than rely exclusively on the more conventional discounted cash flow logic to evaluate these projects.[13] Real-options analysis brings the logic of the private equity market into the firm, with an expected payoff in the time frame of five to seven years rather than the excessively short-term logic associated with conventional capital budgeting or excessively long-term logic associated with traditional R&D.[14] It effectively segments the project into several affordable chunks so that the decision to move forward can be made iteratively, after the completion of each stage, rather than through an "all-or-nothing" decision at the start of the project.

Without the flexibility afforded by real-options analysis, there will be the inevitable tendency to convert BoP experiments into philanthropy. This pitfall should be avoided at all cost because experience shows that giving away technology rarely succeeds in solving the problem.[15] The fact that it is often easier to convert BoP initiatives into corporate donations than it is to make the case for running them as viable business experiments shows how inflexible most corporations are when it comes to project evaluation and capital budgeting. The solution is to broaden the analytical lens for investment rather than taking the easy way out through the corporate foundation.

P&G, for example, has struggled to make the business case for its nutritional beverage drink, Nutristar, and its point-of-use water purification technology, PuR—both new products focused on the BoP. Both have gone through multiple rounds of small-scale market experimentation. Each stage has produced important information about how best to adapt the business model for successful commercialization. Unfortunately, multiple rounds of market probes do not stack up very well using discounted cash flow analysis as the measuring stick. The champions for each of these projects were ultimately pressured into turning them over, at least in part, to the philanthropic arm of the company. As George Carpenter, former Vice President for Sustainability at P&G, noted, however, philanthropy is a trap: Giving away such new technologies can never be financially sustainable because the scale of the problem far exceeds the corporate foundation's ability to address it.[16]

Creating a separate pool of investment capital to fund such low-cost probes, along with a separate organizational entity to house them, is one way to address this challenge. Without this early protection, the logic of short-term performance in today's business will almost certainly guarantee failure.[17] Nike's failed attempt to commercialize the World Shoe through its current production and marketing infrastructure makes this point only too clearly. Indeed, as Clay Christensen and Michael Raynor point out in their book, *The Innovator's Solution*, with disruptive new ventures, it is important to be impatient for profit, but patient for growth because it takes time for such ventures to reach the point of being scaleable.[18]

When it comes to the base of the pyramid, Christensen and Raynor's observation may be even more important because evidence suggests that when the point of scale-up is reached, growth can proceed at an explosive rate. For example, C.K. Prahalad shows that the time frame for new technology and product diffusion, which may take 10–15 years to play out in the developed market, is being collapsed into a period of perhaps 3–5 years in the BoP.[19] The implication for MNCs is clear: Don't give up on BoP ventures if they appear to be stalled after a few years; they may be just reaching the point that they are ready to take off—and when they do, be prepared for a rapid ascent!

Fly Under the Radar

World Water Corporation was founded in 1984 in response to a perceived vacuum in private business activity supplying water and power in developing countries.[20] With help from a team of Princeton University engineers, the company developed its first patented product in 1992, a solar thermal power system. Since then, it has added proprietary photovoltaic technology, most notably the AquaSafe solar-powered water pump. This technology can pump 10 times the volume of any other solar water pump in the world—more than 2,000 gallons of water per minute from rivers and other surface water. The technology can also be used to pump ground water up to 1,000 feet deep, to bring up clean water from wells. Given that water shortages are expected to be a major problem in the twenty-first century, the company was confident that its powerful solar water systems would find a big market worldwide. Based on this optimistic projection, the company went public in 1997.

By 2000, World Water Corporation had established operations in 17 developing countries. Typically, the company worked through the central government to sign long-term agreements to serve as consultant and contractor for water and energy programs, with a focus on rural areas. For example, World Water signed an agreement to become master consultant and contractor for all water and energy programs for the newly elected government in Somalia in 2000. The company had signed similar agreements in Pakistan and the Philippines, working with the leadership of both countries. The pilot phase of the Somalia project was worth $2.5 million and was planned to cover 25 communities.

To ensure that these very poor countries actually pay for their equipment and services, the company deals only in hard currency; it also seeks to collect down-payments of 10–15 percent at the start of each project. World Water also teams up with American banks and international financial institutions where possible to help the countries pay for the projects. Unfortunately, despite World Water's best efforts, the unstable and corrupt nature of its clients' governments has put the viability of the company at serious risk. The highly visible nature of the agreements makes the scale and scope of the agreement—and the potential profit for World Water—readily apparent to a broad range of bureaucrats, government officials, and others who might benefit from either derailing the project or currying favor before it is allowed to move forward.

As a result of these problems, the company's international business prospects have soured considerably. Over the past few years, in fact, it has sought to increase its presence in the U.S. market, particularly California, where a combination of water scarcity and electric power interruptions make World Water's product potentially attractive. World Water's stock price did not budge, despite the heady projections for growth in 2000: It was still trading at about 30 cents per share in late 2009.

Contrast this experience with the one described in Chapter 6, "Raising the Base of the Pyramid," for KickStart, the Kenya-based venture focused on technology and microenterprise development for the rural poor in East Africa. KickStart also focused on water pumping in the Third World but took a very different approach, both technologically and in terms of business model. As we have seen, KickStart's Moneymaker Micro-irrigation Pump is manually operated by small farmers and was codesigned with them to ensure product acceptance. At less than $100, the pump was directly affordable by the end consumer, meaning that KickStart could launch its business on a small-scale basis and allow it to grow organically over time. It bypassed the need to deal with the central governments of Kenya and Tanzania, thereby avoiding the complexity and corruption that World Water exposed itself to.

In short, KickStart, like most other successful ventures in the BoP that we have been able to identify, flew under the radar of corruption, thereby avoiding all the problems that go along with having to deal with difficult—and changeable—central regimes. By constructing a business model that went directly to the user and building it up from a local base of support, KickStart was able to engender trust and gain experience with the user community. This helps to avoid the corruption trap of bribes and "speed money" associated with weak central governments or failed states. Avoiding dependence on central institutions—national governments, corrupt regimes, and central infrastructure planning—thus appears to be a critical aspect of native capability. Let me be clear—I am not saying that BoP ventures should not seek or receive grants or assistance from developing country governments to further their business development, only that such ventures should not premise their entire competitive strategies on such relationships. In the final analysis, while both KickStart and World Water sought to help the rural poor gain better access to clean water, the former was able to become indigenous while the latter remained alien.

It is ironic that large corporations are willing to invest in massive—and often risky—projects while eschewing the smaller-scale, bottom-up approach described earlier. The belief that it is necessary to start big to get big is pervasive and may prove to be one of the most vexing challenges when it comes to serving the poor. Enron, for example, invested more than $2 billion in its Dabhol energy project in India, only to see the investment go up in smoke when corruption, changing political winds, and unacceptably high electricity prices turned stakeholders against the project. This aborted project also cost the American taxpayers more than $700 million in foregone loan guarantees by the Overseas Private Investment Corporation. What might have happened if even a fraction of this money had been invested in small-scale experiments in distributed energy generation?

Work with Nontraditional Partners

Ventures that face challenging new environments usually need to turn to partner organizations for missing resources and expertise. Indeed, governments often require MNCs to have a local corporate partner to ensure market access in emerging economies. Tarun Khanna and his associates, for example, have shown that partnering with the large business conglomerates in the developing world—the chaebols, grupos, and business houses—helps MNCs fill the institutional void by ensuring property rights, capital availability, and political support.[21]

When entering the base of the pyramid, however, firms may need to dramatically expand the potential field of alliance partners because the large national players familiar with the ways of global capitalism seldom serve the rural poor or shantytown dwellers in their own countries. Indeed, in our analysis of BoP ventures, we found that successful strategies (such as KickStart's) rely heavily on nontraditional partners, including local nonprofit organizations, community groups, and local (even village-level) governments. Unsuccessful strategies (such as World Water's), on the other hand, tend to rely heavily on traditional partners, such as national governments and large local companies. Not surprisingly, these traditional partners are as far removed from low-income markets in terms of knowledge and experience as the firms trying to launch the venture.

One BoP venture in Kenya, Honey Care Africa, created a particularly interesting three-way partnership with the private sector, the development sector, and the local community. Honey Care was established to make beekeeping accessible to poor farmers and to create a domestic source of high-quality honey for Kenya. The company has achieved success by doubling the income of many poor farmers, providing high-quality honey for the Kenyan market, and creating economic, social, and environmental value for local communities. Today, Honey Care is the largest producer of high-quality honey in East Africa.[22]

Traditionally, Kenyan communities used log hives, baskets, or clay pots for beekeeping. Unfortunately, although they were cheap to set up, these crude techniques produced small volumes of poor-quality honey. Honey Care thus based its business model on making advanced (yet context-appropriate) beekeeping equipment available to these small farmers. They procure this equipment from a third-party producer and sell it to a development-sector partner, which, in turn, works with local microcredit institutions to provide financing for small farmers to purchase the equipment. The company guarantees a steady income for the farmers by committing to purchase all their honey production, ensuring a loyal source of supply. Honey Care then sells the honey to distributors and retailers for sale to end consumers. The company has established a virtuous circle by creating a collaborative model that enables it to better understand and leverage the local social context. By working with non-traditional partners who were embedded in the local scene, it has been able to become indigenous while leveraging its core competencies in equipment procurement and marketing.

As another example, Bata, a leading retailer of shoes with operations throughout the developing world, has entered into an innovative partnership with the NGO Care in Bangladesh to gain access to rural areas in the country where their products have yet to penetrate.[23] Bata's products are well-suited to the BoP; indeed, they have developed a line of low-cost ($2–$5) yet high-quality shoes and sandals. Care, which has been in Bangladesh for more than 50 years, has invested extensively in entrepreneurial training for rural women and has trained in excess of 80,000 poor rural women throughout the country to run micro-enterprises, which include small grocery stores, handicraft production and retailing, commercial dairy operations, and bicycle rental businesses. By partnering with Care, Bata gains access to this network of rural microentrepreneurs interested in expanding their businesses to include shoe sales. In exchange, the rural women gain visibility and credibility as business people because few in the rural areas have any direct affiliation with a multinational brand. If the Bangladesh experiment is successful, the model could be spread to many other countries throughout the developing world.

Working with nontraditional partners thus means going far beyond the typical focus on customers and suppliers. By including civil society, community groups, and local players, firms are better able to understand and leverage existing strengths in the environment rather than trying to change that environment to resemble the Western way. Nontraditional partners provide intelligence on the local context, local legitimacy, and access to needed resources, none of which is available to MNCs attempting to go it alone.[24]

Build Social, Not Legal, Contracts

Despite the advantages of working with nontraditional partners, corporations have tended to ally themselves with the small number of entities in the developing world that understand the current global capitalist system, value their existing products, and respect intellectual property. Not surprisingly, local partners have most often been large domestic firms, central governments, or state-owned enterprises, whose primary business experience is centered on the urban elite in the developing world. As my colleague Ted London likes to point out, however, reaching the base of the pyramid requires entry strategies that move past preoccupation with Western-style rule of law and intellectual property protection because these do not exist in the base of the pyramid.[25]

As anyone who has traveled extensively in the developing world knows, counterfeit products and knock-offs abound, whether we are talking about Rolex watches, Nike running shoes, CDs and videos, computer software, or prescription drugs. Given the high cost structure and fat margins associated with most products for the top of the pyramid, companies depend on intellectual property protection—patents, trademarks, and copyrights—to guarantee their franchisees. Viewed from this perspective, the Third World appears hostile to MNCs, a place where value will be hijacked rather than added. However, when we look from the perspective of those at the base of the pyramid, we begin to see other commercial models.

In the informal sectors, relationships are primarily grounded in social, not legal, contracts, and the organizations with the most expertise in serving these populations—local government and civil society—have a strong social orientation. As the experience of the Grameen Bank clearly demonstrates, successfully operating in this space requires a capability to understand and appreciate the benefits of the existing social infrastructure, and not complain about its lack of Western-style institutions. Grameen's lending model, for example, entails no legally enforceable instruments whatsoever. Because there is no collateral, legal papers would be useless. If a borrower defaults, the bank staff works with her to restructure the debt or plan an alternative repayment schedule. The entire business model is based upon social capital and trust.

Although Nike's World Shoe venture was a commercial failure, it did, at the very least, demonstrate that the best way to deal with the counterfeit problem is not by using legal remedies against Third World countries, but rather by attempting to create products that poor people can actually afford. This requires a very different strategy, cost structure, and business model. Rather than cajoling its existing contract manufacturers in Asia to produce the low-end World Shoes (there was little incentive to do so because they were rewarded based on contribution margin), what if Nike had chosen to partner with the counterfeiters instead? Indeed, counterfeit producers possessed exactly what Nike lacked—production capacity—as well as distribution capabilities to reach precisely the low-income markets that Nike was trying to capture. Nike could have provided a dramatically improved shoe design (with the real Nike Swoosh) and also transferred its social and environmental practices to the counterfeit producers, a potential win-win for both parties, not to mention the workers, customers, and the environment. The result might have been a business model that competes based on social capital, quality, and value for money rather than trademark and legal protection.

Perhaps the pharmaceutical industry could also benefit by focusing on social rather than purely legal contracts. At present, the search for new drugs is focused almost entirely on the (often cosmetic) afflictions of the rich while overlooking the fatal illnesses of the poor. Indeed, medicines against tropical diseases like malaria, sleeping sickness, and tuberculosis make up a miniscule 1 percent of new drug patents. Lack of patent protection (and inability to pay) are usually cited as the reasons for this disproportionate figure. The reality, however, is that ignorance is to blame: Few people in pharmaceutical companies really know anything about either the challenges or the opportunities in the Third World.

Drug companies defend their current, lucrative markets in places such as the United States by agreeing—sometimes under duress—to run either tiered pricing programs (as with AIDS drugs) or drug-donation programs (as with Merck and river blindness treatment). Neither approach is financially sustainable: Any effort to seriously address the public health crisis that rages in the Third World through drug giveaways would bankrupt the industry. But what if the drug companies began with some real engagement, perhaps through low-cost probes, to develop commercial businesses in poor communities selling drugs that have already gone off patent (for example, pain relievers are sorely needed but are often unavailable). Such an initiative would work wonders for the industry's tarnished image around the world and would also build a direct relationship with the people most in need. Through this experience, the firms might also be able to identify some new and creative ways to address the public health problems of the world's poor—and make money doing it.

Recently, several companies in the pharmaceutical industry have ventured down this path. In 2008, for example, Pfizer launched a Global Access Initiative that included a cross-divisional task force focused on assessing barriers to the poor's access to medicine and possible new business models to overcome them. Pfizer also launched a partnership with Grameen to offer health insurance to the poor and to expand Grameen's network of rural clinics funded by prepaid insurance premiums and low fees. It is now becoming clear that Western drug companies ignore this space at their peril: The Indian pharmaceutical industry, for example, has already learned, out of necessity, how to deliver drugs coming off patent in the U.S. at a fraction of the cost charged by the established drug companies.[26]

Neville Williams, founder of SELCO, the largest supplier of solar electric home systems in India, argues that the key to success in the BoP is trust, not technology.[27] SELCO has built a reputation among the poor by making solar electricity affordable (through a network of participating banks) and reliable (through the creation of solar service centers). Because the poor are frequently exploited by predatory lenders and unscrupulous vendors, SELCO's reputation for fair dealing, dependability, and continuing care has become the key to its growth (about 30 percent per year). Indeed, Williams believes that trust and social capital form the real basis for sustainable competitive advantage at the base of the pyramid: Once poor customers come to trust you, they are disinclined to leave because most have experienced only poor service, unscrupulous vendors, or blatant exploitation. As BP and other corporations begin to enter the solar electric home system business, they are realizing that the business model is more important than the technology. There is a reason why many in India now refer to solar home electric systems generically as "SELCOs." The reason is trust—and trust cannot be copied.

Moving Beyond the Multinational Model

The current multinational model emphasizes global efficiency (world-scale production and global supply chains), national responsiveness (modifying products and operations to suit country differences), and worldwide learning (sharing experience across units within the firm) as the crucial capabilities for success.[28] Given the emerging challenges of poverty and population growth, economic slow-down in the developed markets, and global-scale environmental change, however, these conventional capabilities are now clearly inadequate. In fact, at times, reliance on these in the context of the BoP can actually be damaging.[29]

As noted in Chapter 5, "Innovation from the Bottom-Up," GE CEO Jeff Immelt publicly recognized in 2009 the insufficiency of conventional "glocalization" strategies for the challenges that lie ahead: For decades, GE has sold modified versions of Western products to emerging markets. Now, however, to avoid pre-emption from the emerging giants of the developing world, it will be crucial for the company to become adept at "reverse innovation," driving innovation from the base of the pyramid and moving it up-market where appropriate. Immelt's clarion call makes clear that for MNCs to flourish in the twenty-first century, they must acquire a new capability—a native capability—to complement their existing skills.

Native capability requires that MNCs expand their conception of the global economy to include the varied economic activities that occur outside of the formal, wage-based economy. They must embrace the informal economy, and tailor their business models to enhance the way people currently live. Creating sustainable livelihoods means strengthening local communities and restoring the environment, not extracting resources and forcing people to move in the pursuit of factory jobs. Spanning these worlds provides the basis for developing the climate needed for business to thrive by building respect for agreements, transaction transparency, and mutual trust. Indeed, MNCs, in partnership with local entrepreneurs, NGOs, and local governments, can help build a system of governance from the ground up rather than waiting for corrupt central governments to reform.[30]

Native capability means learning to engage extensively with the local people on their terms in a true spirit of mutuality. It means working on bottom-up coinvention of more sustainable ways of living. It means experimenting with small-scale, low-cost probes and flying under the radar to work directly with local communities, rather than seeking to cut deals with corrupt central regimes or national champion firms. It means working with nontraditional partners—local NGOs, communities, and town and village governments—where the real knowledge about local conditions resides. And it means building the business model around social rather than legal contracts because trust and social capital are the *lingua franca* in the BoP.

Unlike the conventional multinational model, which focuses on transferring proprietary resources from within the firm, native capability assumes that the critical knowledge for success lies beyond the firm's boundaries. MNCs, not their local partners, are the ones that must do the unlearning. Given that, competitive advantage is premised less on protecting existing proprietary technology or intellectual property and more on developing trust and social capital. Generic principles and learning from specific settings, however, can and must be transferred and applied in other BoP contexts and "trickled up" to the top of the pyramid where appropriate; that is how capability is fostered and spread. The time has come for MNCs to move beyond the traditional conception of multinational success. What is needed now is a systematic approach for corporations to become truly embedded—part of the local landscape rather than alien forces that impose their will from the outside.

Notes

1. Portions of this section are extracted from: Erik Simanis and Stuart Hart (with Patrick Donohue, Duncan Duke, Gordon Enk, Michael Gordon, and Tatiana Thieme), *The Base of the Pyramid Protocol: Toward Next Generation BoP Strategy*, (Cornell University, Center for Sustainable Global Enterprise, 2008).

2. Email from Neville Williams, Founder of SELCO, December 14, 2006.

3. Aneel Karnani, "The Mirage of Marketing to the Bottom of the Pyramid," *California Management Review* 49 (2007): 90–111.

4. Erik Simanis and Stuart Hart, *The Base of the Pyramid Protocol: Toward Next Generation BoP Strategy*.

5. This ongoing exploratory study, which has been conducted through the Base of the Pyramid Learning Laboratory over the past decade, involves on-going interviews with dozens of MNC managers, 24 original BoP venture case studies, and analysis of archival materials. For preliminary results, see Ted London and Stuart Hart, "Reinventing Strategies for Emerging Markets: Beyond the Transnational Model," *Journal of International Business Studies*, 35 (2004): 350–370. This section is also informed by our ongoing work on the BoP Protocol. Special thanks to Erik Simanis and Ted London for their contributions and insight on this work.

6. My thanks to Richard Wells for this wonderful quote.

7. Thomas Friedman, *The Lexus and the Olive Tree* (New York: Anchor Books, 2000).

8. See "Nigerian Wins Prize for Developing Clay Pot Cooler," www.mclglobal.com/History/Sep2000/29i2000/29i0t.html. I thank Erik Simanis for drawing it to my attention.

9. Robert Chambers, *Whose Reality Counts: Putting the First Last* (London: ITDG Publishing, 1997); James Beebe, *Rapid Assessment Process: An Introduction* (New York: Altamira Press, 2001); and W. Penn Handwerker, *Quick Ethnography* (New York: Altamira Press, 2001).

10. Ted London and Stuart Hart, "Reinventing Strategies."

11. See World Space Corporation Frequently Asked Questions, www.worldspace. com.

12. For a more complete description of N-Logue, see Joy Howard, Charis Simms, and Erik Simanis, *Sustainable Deployment for Rural Connectivity: The N-Logue Model* (Washington, D.C.: World Resources Institute, 2001).

13. See M. Amran and N. Kulatilaka, *Real Options* (Boston: Harvard Business School Press, 1999); and M. Milstein and T. Alessandri, "New Tools for New Times: Using Real Options to Identify Value in Strategies for Sustainable Development" (paper presented at the Academy of Management Annual Meeting, Toronto, Ontario, 2000).

14. Richard Foster and Sarah Kaplan, *Creative Destruction* (New York: Doubleday, 2001).

15. The experience with the appropriate technology movement and foreign aid programs over the past 40 years leaves little doubt that giving technologies to the poor fosters neither the pride of ownership nor the personal stake needed to ensure continued utilization.

16. George Carpenter, presentation at the Sustainable Enterprise Academy, York University, Toronto, Canada, April 2004.

17. See Clayton Christensen, *The Innovator's Dilemma* (Boston: Harvard Business School Press, 1998).

18. Clayton Christenson and Michael Raynor, *The Innovator's Solution* (Cambridge, MA: Harvard Business School Press, 2003).

19. C.K. Prahalad, *The Fortune at the Bottom of the Pyramid* (Upper Saddle River, NJ: Wharton School Publishing, 2005).

20. See www.worldwatersolar.com/2-Background.html.

21. See, for example, Tarun Khanna and Krisna Palepu, "Why Focused Strategies May Be Wrong for Emerging Markets," *Harvard Business Review* July–August (1997): 41–51.

22. See "IFC-Backed Kenyan SME Project Wins Sustainable Development Prize," 7 January (2003), http://web.worldbank.org.

23. My thanks to Jesse Moore of Care Canada for this example, which he presented at the Base of the Pyramid Learning Laboratory in September 2004.

24. Dennis Rondinelli and Ted London, "How Corporations and Environmental Groups Cooperate: Assessing Cross-Sector Alliances and Collaborations," *Academy of Management Executive* 17(1) (2003): 61–76.

25. See Ted London and Stuart Hart, "Reinventing Strategies."

26. C.K. Prahalad, *The Fortune at the Bottom of the Pyramid*.

27. Neville Williams, personal communication, April 2004.

28. See, for example, Chris Bartlett and Sumatra Ghoshal, *Managing Across Borders* (Boston: Harvard Business School Press, 1989); and C.K. Prahalad and Yves Doz, *The Multinational Mission* (New York: Free Press, 1987).

29. Ted London makes this case most persuasively in his Ph.D. dissertation: *How Capabilities Are Created: A Process Study of New Market Entry* (Chapel Hill, NC: University of North Carolina, 2004).

30. See C.K. Prahalad, *The Fortune at the Bottom of the Pyramid*.

9

Re-Embedding Innovation Strategy

In 1944, economic historian Karl Polanyi observed in his land-mark book, *The Great Transformation*, that the birth of industrial capitalism was premised on a radical shift in how people perceived the relationship between the economy and society.[1] Prior to the 1850s, markets were seen as an important but small part of a diverse economic system that was embedded in the social fabric of communities. Beginning in the 1860s, after the American Civil War, Polanyi observed that the new concept of "market economy" began to change this long-standing relationship: Economic life became *disembedded* from society and viewed as a self-contained system whose greatest potential could be released through the unimpeded operation of impersonal, efficient markets.[2]

In fact, it was during the second half of the nineteenth century that "the economy" was conceptualized as a separate entity that could be managed in its own right, and the modern discipline of Economics was born. According to this new way of thinking, every person was either a buyer or seller; every relationship a transaction. Everything, including people and the environment, was a potential production input subject to the laws of supply and demand. Social welfare, in this new context, was maximized by getting more goods into the hands of more people. The idea of the mass market was born, and with it, the modern industrial corporation.

Today, corporate innovation strategies still reflect this production-driven, "disembedded" quality. Communities are seen as "target markets." Ecological systems are treated as "natural resources" that supply "raw materials" and provide "waste sinks." People's aspirations for a better life register as "potential market demand." Selling more products to more people is an internal, technical challenge tackled through data-driven methods of marketing research and new product development. Despite constant advances in innovation practice, this core strategic logic has remained unchanged since its inception nearly 200 years ago. And for better or worse, most recent corporate efforts to reach today's emerging mass market—the four billion people at the BoP—have continued to rely on the same disembedded way of thinking.

Comparing Apples and Oranges

On the surface, Grameen's Village Phone (discussed in Chapter 5, "Innovation from the Bottom-Up") and Hindustan Lever's Project Shakti (discussed in Chapter 6, "Raising the Base of the Pyramid") appear to be quite similar in character. In fact, HLL was heavily influenced by the Grameen experience in putting together its Shakti Entrepreneur (SE) strategy in the early 2000s. Indeed, both BoP initiatives were constructed around local village women serving as "microentrepreneurs"—in Grameen Phone's case to sell phone service and in HLL's case to sell a variety of personal care products such as soaps, lotions, and detergent, in affordable single-serve packaging. The women in both models relied on the use of microcredit to purchase the necessary equipment/inventory, and in both cases, they also received training prior to getting started. HLL partnered with local nonprofits for training and relied heavily on pre-existing women's self-help groups to provide the financing. Grameen, in contrast, drew upon its large stable of women borrower's from the Bank and provided training and financing accordingly. Because both of these initiatives have now expanded to include tens of thousands of women entrepreneurs, they are often offered as two successful examples of how innovative business models and strategies can open up vast new markets among the underserved at the BoP.

To appreciate the full story, however, it is necessary to peel back the onion another layer. In thinking about innovation, we tend to focus our attention on the structural similarities of business models like HLL's Shakti and Grameen's Village Phone. In so doing, we ignore a crucial dimension on which they often differ significantly—what my colleague Erik Simanis has called *business model intimacy*.[3] Indeed, given its long-standing presence in the villages where it launched the Village Phone, Grameen Bank had already made itself a trusted partner and knew personally the women selected to become the "Phone Ladies," most of whom were former borrowers. Lacking this degree of "embeddedness," HLL's Shakti Project had to rely on pre-existing self-help groups to recruit the women entrepreneurs and provide the financing. This more impersonal approach resulted in turnover rates approaching 50 percent in the early going—and a growing sense of discontent from the self-help groups that provided the financing to the failed SEs.

Grameen created a groundswell of demand by empowering the phone ladies to use their best judgment in how to market phone services, literally pulling the new business into villages and allowing Grameen to scale rapidly while growing revenues and profits. The Shakti Entrepreneurs, however, had comparatively little discretion in how best to go about their business: They were assigned a predetermined set of inventory with fixed prices. And because their relationship was a contractual one with the company, failure to sell the goods put them at personal financial risk. Because of high turnover and less-than-stellar sales results, HLL has followed a resource-intensive push strategy that, despite creating a distribution presence across thousands of villages, hangs its profitability hopes on a long-term, general upward trend in rural consumption.

Henry Ford was famously quoted as having once said: "Why is it every time I ask for a pair of hands, they come with a brain attached?" It almost seems as though HLL was looking for little more than pairs of hands to serve as distribution channels, whereas Grameen engaged the full person in its approach. In fact, Grameen Bank has been able to use these embedded and intimate relationships to cocreate a variety of new services and industries over the past decade, ranging from energy and telecommunications to health care and fisheries. HLL's disembedded Shakti Project, on the other hand, is unlikely to grow into anything more than a new distribution channel for their existing products, few of which offer a compelling value proposition for rural families. In short, while structurally similar, when examined more closely at the level of human and business process, comparing Grameen Phone to the Shakti Program is like comparing apples and oranges.

What lessons should we take away from this comparison? To unleash the wellspring of growth at the BoP, companies must step beyond the structural features of their business models and re-embed innovation strategy back into society and the community. To do so requires the development of a new capability, one that has much more to do with developing bigger managerial mindsets than it does smaller sachet packages. It means suspending traditional assumptions regarding new business development. It requires corporations to place the corporate "hammer" on the shelf and live alongside those in the community in a spirit of humility and mutual learning. It requires developing a personal relationship of trust, understanding, and respect through which new possibilities for locally-embedded businesses can emerge.

Re-embedding innovation strategy takes the company "back to the future." Just as in the days prior to the modern industrial corporate model, business model intimacy means building the kind of relationship where the identity of the company is fused with that of the community. Embeddedness thus means cocreating a new business from the ground up, with the company as a key part of its foundation. Achieving this level of integration and trust requires an entirely new business process—one based on dialogue and joint action, not just market research data and sales targets.

Toward a Base of the Pyramid Protocol

Beginning in 2002, several corporate members of our BoP Learning Lab (described in Chapter 5) began to articulate the need for a new, more embedded business process for the BoP. They voiced concern that their firms' current set of capabilities and routines—for market research and new product development—were inadequate to the task of effectively serving the needs of BoP communities. Foreshadowing what was to come, some even feared that widespread use of existing corporate routines in the BoP could "do damage" and even "produce a backlash" because of their potentially invasive, insensitive, or extractive nature. This sense of growing unease with the current corporate approach provided the impetus for the development of the Base of the Pyramid Protocol (or, simply, the Protocol), which sought to translate the idea of native capability and embedded innovation into a systematic new business process. The effort was launched in 2003 as a partnership among Cornell University, University of Michigan, William Davidson Institute, World Resources Institute, and The Johnson Foundation with corporate partners DuPont, SC Johnson, Hewlett-Packard, and Tetra Pak.[4]

With my colleagues Erik Simanis, Gordon Enk, and the Core Project Team,[5] we began by exploring relevant work in related fields (including anthropology, social work, human geography, development studies, and design) and methodologies (including participatory rural appraisal, quick ethnography, rapid assessment process, asset-based community development, and empathy-based design). Following this research, a four and a half-day Protocol Design Workshop was convened in October 2004 at the Wingspread Conference Center in Racine, Wisconsin. The workshop convened a diverse group of academics, international development professionals, NGO representatives, social entrepreneurs, market researchers, and corporate executives to craft this radically new business process. Results of the design workshop, which included a code of conduct as well as the Protocol itself, were placed in the public domain in March 2005.[6]

As an embedded innovation process, the Protocol brings together a company and a community to conceive, launch, and coevolve a new business and a new market. Six companies have now launched BoP Protocol initiatives (see Exhibit 9.1). The first (pilot) project was initiated in 2005 in Nairobi, Kenya by S. C. Johnson & Sons, Inc. In 2006, Solae LLC, a DuPont subsidiary in the food and nutrition industry, launched initiatives in a village and an urban slum in India. These two initiatives provided important early experience and are discussed further in this section.

Exhibit 9.1
Current BoP Protocol Projects

- **SC Johnson (Kenya)—2005**
  - Latrine cleaning business that integrates SCJ cleaning products
  - Serving six slums across Nairobi
- **DuPont/Solae (India)—2006**
  - Food and cooking business that integrates Solae's soy protein
  - Approaching financial sustainability in one village cluster and two slums
- **Ascension Health (USA)—2008**
  - Neighborhood-based "health" and community revitalization
  - Phase II activities underway

- **The Water Initiative (Mexico)—2008**
  - Community health business concept that integrates TWI's water technology
  - Beginning scale-out in first community and transplantation to second
- **Baxter Healthcare (Ecuador)—2009**
  - Cocreate new enterprises using small-scale health technology
  - Completing pre-field phase
- **Gates Foundation (Africa)—2009**
  - Cocreate new enterprises to address the malaria epidemic in Africa
  - Completing pre-field phase

Source: Adapted from Simanis, E. and Hart, S. 2009. "Innovation from the inside out," *Sloan Management Review*, Summer: 77-86.

Beginning in 2008, the Protocol was applied for the first time as the basis for launching a start-up company—The Water Initiative (TWI). TWI, which is also described in more detail later in this chapter, is a new venture that started in Mexico, focused on cocreating a commercial approach to provide clean drinking water for the poor and underserved. In addition, two new Protocol projects were launched in the past year: an initiative by Baxter Healthcare focusing on the cocreation of new BoP enterprises around emerging health care technology, and a new project with SC Johnson funded in part by the Bill and Melinda Gates Foundation to codevelop enterprise-based models for addressing malaria in Africa.

The Protocol process has also been adapted to the developed world and is currently being used in the United States by Ascension Health, a $9-billion health care company. Ascension's goal is to cocreate a commercially viable approach to achieving better health outcomes among the uninsured, beginning in Flint, Michigan, where nearly 40 percent of the population is without health insurance.

The BoP Protocol process commences with a "pre-field" phase that involves the following:

- Convening the company Leadership Team
- Forming the field Immersion Team
- Training the team in core BoP business concepts
- Selecting the project site(s)
- Identifying local partners

The company Leadership Team is composed of 6–8 key executives from the different functional areas (e.g., technology, marketing, production, HR, finance, communications, sustainability) and 1–2 key corporate or business executives. Their role is to create the "white space" for the Protocol initiative, protect it from the corporate "antibodies," and ensure that adequate resources are made available to sustain the effort. An Immersion Team of 4–6 people is ideally composed of 2–3 people from the corporation with knowledge of the technology portfolio and demonstrated entrepreneurial ability, as well as 1–2 people with prior knowledge and experience in community engagement and the BoP Protocol. This team is trained in core BoP business concepts, participatory methodologies, including the Protocol, as well as team building and consensus decision-making. Once trained and on the ground, 1–2 additional people are recruited from the local community as Immersion Team members. Either an urban (shantytown) and/or rural site (village) are selected by the company in a region of strategic interest. Once the project site(s) has been selected, the Immersion Team can begin the process of identifying local partners to work with on the ground. In all, the "pre-field" phase typically takes 6–9 months and is crucial to the success of the effort in the field.

Reflecting the "next generation strategies and skills" discussed in the previous chapter, the "in-field" portion of the Protocol process is divided into three interdependent and overlapping phases of activity, each with a specific business outcome (see Exhibit 9.2):

- **Phase I: Opening Up**—Phase I begins with a company immersion in the community using home stays to build personal rapport and trust. It culminates with the cocreation of a business concept together with a core team of community partners. The business concept creatively marries the company's and the community's resources, capabilities, and energies and serves as the jumping off point for the next phase. This phase typically requires 3–4 months of intensive time on the ground in the community.

- **Phase II: Building the Ecosystem**—Phase II focuses on engaging a group of early adopters in the community in action learning and small-scale tests to evolve a working business model. A new business organization is also formalized with the core community partners. The result is a community-tested business prototype ready for launch on a wider scale. This phase typically requires a full year, especially in rural areas, where seasonality can be a critical factor in business success.

- **Phase III: Enterprise Creation**—In Phase III, the company and core partners reach out to an even broader community segment to create an initial brand and product/service offering. Action learning is used to evolve the business model and build local management capacity sufficient to manage and grow the business. The result is a locally-embedded business and a committed "seed" market. This phase typically requires another 6–9 months.

The outputs of this process include a proven business model that integrates the company's and the community's capabilities, a fledgling business, and an initial "seed" market. Together, these elements form the platform for taking the venture to scale. Indeed, for the sponsoring company to generate a level of value that justifies the time and commitment of an initial BoP Protocol initiative, the business model needs to be efficiently expanded, transferred, and re-embedded in hundreds, if not thousands, of other communities in new geographies. To reinforce, rather than erode, the personal connections and shared commitment established by the initial business, however, the scaling-out process must follow a path different from typical scaling strategies. Two complementary approaches are recommended: organic propagation and business transplantation.[7]

Exhibit 9.2
The BoP Protocol Process

Source: Adapted from Erik Simanis, 2006. Presentation of BoP Protocol.

The first step in scaling the BoP business is *organic propagation*—expanding the fledgling business from its point of origin throughout the entire host or "parent" community. Through word-of-mouth and the recruitment of additional community members as business partners, the business is effectively "pulled" into and spread through the original host community. Next, a strategy of *business transplantation* is used to spread the business to new communities and geographies without repeating the entire cocreation process used to generate the business in the first place. The company reaches out to new communities using business "ambassadors" from the original team to plant the "seed" business concept in the new location. Through this process, representatives from the original parent business communicate the core idea to a new community while simultaneously engaging the new partners in "making it their own." Rapid market appraisals can be utilized ahead of the visit to identify the geographies and communities where some version of the business is most likely to succeed.

Learning by Doing

The BoP Protocol was first pilot tested with SC Johnson in Kenya beginning in 2005. As a result of the company's close involvement in the development of the Protocol process, the head of corporate sustainability and the Chairman and CEO, Fisk Johnson, provided enthusiastic support and funding for the effort, which was led out of the corporate sustainability organization.

A six-person Protocol Team[8] was formed that worked in partnership with SC Johnson's Kenya subsidiary in two communities: Nyota Township, a subsistence-based smallholder farming community in the Nakuru District, and Kibera (Nairobi), the largest slum in East Africa with an estimated population of 700,000. For 11 weeks, the team lived and worked alongside their hosts in Nakuru and Kibera, experiencing their daily lives as part of the immersion phase of the process. They also brought together business and local community groups for intensive needs assessment, resource sharing, and new business idea generation sessions. The aim was to mutually explore how the company and the communities could leverage each other's capabilities to generate business concepts that create value for all and that neither could have achieved by itself.

For a variety of reasons, the efforts to apply the Protocol process in Nakuru proved unsuccessful:[9] The rural team's partner, Egerton University, was a hub for training in and application of Participatory Rural Appraisal (PRA) methodology. And while the Protocol drew on PRA methods in its development, the two approaches have distinctly different purposes—community empowerment versus new enterprise development. This misalignment in purpose ultimately resulted in the rural application of the pilot losing traction.

The story was different, however, in the slum community. As a result of Phase I, "Opening Up," the Kibera community and SC Johnson Kenya coidentified a new business opportunity with sufficient potential to merit the launching of Phase II, "Building the Ecosystem."[10] By becoming part of the local community, the team forged valuable relationships with the residents and a critical partnership with Carolina for Kibera (CFK), a local NGO, and several entrepreneurial youth groups generating income through the Taka Ni Pato ("Trash for Cash") garbage collection, recycling, and composting program. In collaboration with CFK, SC Johnson worked with several of these youth groups to form a "Coalition of Youth Entrepreneurs" across three slums in Nairobi: Kibera, Mathare, and Mitumba. These communities are some of the poorest in Kenya, comprising 1.2 to 1.5 million people.

Phase II of the Protocol effort culminated in the pilot launch of a new business—"Community Cleaning Services (CCS)"—in July 2006. CCS was a partnership among SC Johnson, CFK, and nine youth groups across the three slum communities. CCS married SC Johnson's expertise in cleaning, sanitation, and insect control with a household-scale service model offered on a commercial basis through the youth groups. Initial service offerings included garbage collection, sanitation, carpet cleaning, furniture care, insect control, window screening, and wall repair and patching. The youth groups incorporated SC Johnson products, such as Baygon, Raid, Pledge, and Windex as part of their portfolio of services and acquired important business skills in marketing, customer service, and bookkeeping. In turn, SC Johnson learned a great deal about the shantytown environment and how their technologies, products, and services could be adapted and improved to better serve the needs of this exploding market; this included opportunities to "bulk sell" many of their formulations through a service model, virtually eliminating the need for packaging.

A one-year pilot period to refine the core business model yielded a number of important learnings that have since been used to refocus and refine the business concept. As the first organization to provide services directly to homes in the Nairobi slums, SC Johnson and CCS found that residents were understandably hesitant to let the youth entrepreneurs into their homes to provide the range of services being contemplated. Building an organization composed of young entrepreneurs also presented challenges, with turnover and skill development being key concerns. As a result, the commercial model has been reinvented to focus on public latrine cleaning rather than providing service to private residences.[11]

The latrine cleaning business is now being launched using a microentrepreneur model rather than the CCS organizational structure. And while it is too early to call this business a success, it appears to have potential, despite the limited staff support for the effort. Indeed, the company is sufficiently encouraged by the experience in Kenya that it has expanded its BoP efforts into Rwanda (smallshareholder pyrethrum growers) and Ghana (a Gates Foundation-sponsored effort focused on malaria). SC Johnson is committed to continuing to experiment at the BoP because creating triple bottom line benefits for developing market consumers is a key part of its overall sustainability strategy.

Building on the SC Johnson pilot effort, DuPont's Solae (Soy Protein) joint venture decided to apply the BoP Protocol in India. The project was championed by the CEO of the company and was led by a senior executive from the sales and marketing division. There was also strong support from DuPont's corporate sustainability team and Chad Holliday, the CEO of DuPont.

Beginning in April of 2006, three returning members of the Kenya project guided a Solae immersion team in India through the "Opening Up" phase.[12] The Solae team consisted of two MBAs from the Indian School of Business, four senior-level development professionals of a local NGO, and one Solae employee who was involved periodically. Again, both an urban shantytown and a rural village site were selected, this time in and around Hyderabad, India. At the rural site, the Solae team partnered with Modern Architects for Rural India (MARI), which works intensively in the area to promote strong community-based organization for the poor. In the slum, the primary partner was the Society for the Integrated Development of Urban and Rural Areas (SIDUR). Both sites were successful in applying the Phase I Protocol methodology to generate a cocreated business concept.

In the slum community, for example, the Solae team and its local partners (mostly women from local self-help groups) cocreated an imaginative business concept—the Solae Culinary Rooftop Garden. One of the underutilized resources identified during Phase I of the Protocol were the rooftops of substantially built structures like schools and commercial buildings. Because there was virtually no green space in the slum, the women felt that making use of the rooftops as "parks" would provide a quiet space for them to bring their children and families. At the same time, since soy protein—Solae's core product—was not really part of Indian cooking, it was proposed that a cooking facility with a "chef" be placed on the rooftop to enable women to experiment with the incorporation of soy into recipes that might then spread throughout the community. Soy would, of course, be for sale as well on the rooftop. A similar business concept was cocreated in the rural area—A Solae Cooking

Well Center—that would enable similar experimentation in soy cooking but also provide a place for people from the community to host major events like weddings. Both business concepts embedded Solae's core product (soy) as the "Intel Inside" of a much broader, community-based business model that would serve to "pull" it into the communities.

In 2007, these two business ideas, along with a third that was cocreated with a team in Mumbai, moved into Phase II of the Protocol. Throughout the year, various elements of the cocreated business models were tested, and the entrepreneurial teams were developed. A new platform was created with the company—Nutrition for Sustainable Development (NFSD), headed by a senior executive with extensive developing country experience. And a person from Solae India's organization was assigned to make the growth of these new businesses his priority. Indeed, both businesses seemed poised to move toward commercial launch, but internal organizational change within DuPont and Solae served to derail the effort. First, the CEO of Solae was replaced, effectively eliminating the protected "white space" that the project had enjoyed within the company.

An effort was made to reposition the initiative as a DuPont corporate effort because the experience could potentially benefit other DuPont businesses. Unfortunately, the nearly simultaneous retirement of the VP for Sustainability at DuPont along with CEO Chad Holliday effectively removed the coalition of support for this effort within the corporation at-large. Tragically then, during 2008, despite the best efforts of project lead Erik Simanis and others, the fledgling businesses were spun off from DuPont: during the first quarter of 2009, Solae provided one last quarter of working capital to enable them to exit gracefully from the businesses.[13] The SC Johnson and DuPont/Solae Protocol initiatives provided critical early learning about the process. Together, they formed the basis for an updated and revised version of the Protocol model, which was published in 2008.[14]

Taking the Initiative on Water

In 2006, while recovering from surgery, serial entrepreneur Kevin McGovern decided that he wanted to devote the rest of his professional life to the development of a company that addressed directly the growing world water crisis, specifically the lack of affordable clean drinking water for the underserved. McGovern had been a principal in several other successful water-related ventures such as KX Industries, the water filter producer, and Sobe Water, the nutritional water company that was sold to Pepsi in the early 2000s. But this new venture would be different: It would focus on developing a commercially and environmentally sustainable way to serve the drinking water needs of those at the base of the pyramid.

As noted in Chapter 2, "Worlds in Collision," fully two billion people lack dependable access to clean drinking water. Pathogen contamination causes billions of cases of diarrheal disease and millions of deaths each year. In addition, water contaminated with arsenic, fluoride, pesticides, and heavy metals is a major cause of morbidity, cancer, and premature death throughout the world. Rapid urbanization is increasing demand for water faster than piped infrastructure can expand. Undependable (and sometimes unscrupulous) water vendors or expensive bottled water are often the only options in peri-urban communities. Rural communities are also chronically underserved and often depend on tube wells with falling water tables or contaminated surface water sources.

To make matters worse, centralized water treatment plants are inherently inefficient and environmentally unsustainable: It takes tremendous amounts of energy, chemicals, and money to purify water to drinking water standards even though less than 2 percent of this water is actually used for drinking and cooking (most is used for less demanding applications like washing, bathing, and irrigating). In addition, nearly half of the purified water from treatment plants leaks out of antiquated pipes before it reaches its final destination. Leaky pipes also provide plenty of openings for recontamination. Given the reality of the world water situation, it became clear to McGovern that point-of-use systems, offered through enterprise-based models, showed the greatest promise to make clean, convenient, and affordable drinking water available to underserved households and communities.

As a Cornell Trustee and member of the Center for Sustainable Global Enterprise's Advisory Council, McGovern had become increasingly interested in the BoP Protocol approach and was intent on building his new enterprise—The Water Initiative (TWI)— around it. He observed that most water ventures focused almost exclusively on marketing specific technologies (like filters) to the world's poor and under-served, usually without great success. TWI therefore began with a different premise; it was founded on two principles that represented departures from conventional wisdom.[15] First, there is no single solution or "magic bullet" to the clean water crisis. Water problems and challenges vary multilocally, from one region to the next, and any successful company would have to take this reality into account. Second, rather than seeking merely to sell existing products through social marketing and other "push" strategies, TWI would engage people from local communities in the cocreation of its business concept. Using the BoP Protocol as the foundation for this approach, TWI would aim to develop a business that combined the knowledge and resources of the company with those of the local community. In so doing, TWI would focus on building "community pull," rather than "product push," as its basis for penetrating underserved communities—a strategy that would set it apart from other water ventures.

Latin America (specifically Mexico) was chosen as the initial location for incubating the new business, in part because of its geographic proximity to the U.S., facilitating travel and time onsite by company principals. I became involved in this new venture early on and worked with McGovern to assemble the management team, with a special focus on Mexico. Richard Wells, a specialist in sustainable business in Mexico, joined the team shortly thereafter, as did Gene Fitzgerald, an

MIT Professor with extensive technical expertise in water technology and purification. In 2007, my doctoral student, Duncan Duke, was recruited to serve as the initial Immersion Team leader for the TWI BoP Protocol process of business cocreation in Mexico.[16]

With a first round of financing in place from McGovern and angel investors, additional management team members were assembled, including technologists from leading institutions such as Cornell, MIT, UCLA, Harvard, Yale, Nanyang Technological University in Singapore, and Monterrey Institute of Technology in Mexico. Experienced entrepreneurs and business executives were also engaged to play leading roles from such businesses and institutions as The Coca-Cola Company and PepsiCo, Pall Corporation, Filtertek, Bell Labs, GE, SoBe Beverages, KX Industries, Amberwave, Pfizer, IDB, and USAID.

In 2008, TWI USA formalized its Mexican entity by incorporating The Water Initiative of Mexico. Rick Renjilian later joined the company as Chief Operating Officer and became closely involved in the development of the Mexican business. TWI Mexico launched the Protocol process in Chapala, a poor community in North Central Mexico near the city of Torreon, where arsenic contamination was the most pressing drinking water problem. Government-supplied water also contained excessive amounts of chlorine (used to kill pathogens), so local people preferred to buy expensive bottled or *garrafon* (jug) water because it tasted better. However, neither of these water sources were necessarily free of arsenic or pathogens. TWI's R&D team thus set out to develop an affordable, point-of-use technology to remove arsenic and excess chlorine, while providing protection against pathogen contamination when needed.

During Phase I of the Protocol process, the Immersion team partnered initially with the Catholic Church in the community, given the dearth of potential NGO partners. With the support and legitimacy provided by the Church, the TWI team attracted a number of interested partners or "socios" from the immediate community. A Mexican entrepreneur with relevant technical experience, Luis Siliceo, joined the on-the-ground team at this stage; he became well-versed in BoP Protocol methodology and eventually assumed the leadership of the cocreation process. Homestays and trust-building exercises produced a committed group of local partners intent on building a successful business together. Ultimately, a business concept was developed that embedded TWI's platform technology in a wider community-based process of Healthy Dialogue Groups (HDGs), which engaged mothers and families to encourage healthier lifestyles.

In addition, ideas for complementary products using TWI's healthy water were developed by the socios. One of the early complementary products developed was "FruTWI"—a line-up of healthy fruit drinks made with purified TWI water and various fresh fruit concentrates. Socios were able start their own microbusinesses selling FruTWI, offering a good-tasting and healthy alternative to Coke and other soft drinks, and providing welcome opportunities for income generation. The business model also included a set of activities focused on community greening, including TWI involvement in school events and neighborhood clean-up projects (see Exhibit 9.3).

Exhibit 9.3
The TWI Business Concept

Source: Duncan Duke, 2008. Presentation of the TWI Business Concept.

Thus, the cocreation process produced a business concept that created value at several levels, providing essential "community pull."

The Protocol process was also key to the development of TWI's platform water treatment technology itself. Initially, the TWI team had assumed that any in-home water purification device would have to be as "bare-bones" as possible to make it affordable for the poor. By engaging the community in the cocreation process, TWI quickly learned that local residents did not want a cheap device on the roof to remove arsenic from the water. In fact, most people were not particularly concerned about arsenic contamination since they could not taste or smell it in the water. Instead, people aspired to have something in their homes that they could be proud of. They wanted "healthy" water, but they also wanted water that was cold and tasted good. It was through this process that the design of the "WATERCURA" purification product came about (see Exhibit 9.4). Even with these added functionalities, however, the WATERCURA can still be operated without any external energy source, reducing both its cost and environmental footprint. The device also permits disassembly and remanufacture, which also holds down cost and reduces waste.

Exhibit 9.4
The Watercura

During 2008–2009, a second site was launched as the first step in "transplanting" the Chapala-based business concept to a new community, San Luis Potosí (SLP), Mexico. SLP has many of the same characteristics as Chapala but differed on one dimension: Instead of arsenic, fluoride contamination was the major problem. This challenged TWI's R&D team to develop an appropriate technology for fluoride removal to embed in the transplanted business in SLP. Business "ambassadors" from Chapala visited SLP, and within a short time, a new group of socios had formed with a commitment to building a similar business in SLP.

By early 2010, the business had taken root in Chapala with over 100 socios and hundreds of WATERCURA units in place. Many challenges remain, but by "failing small and learning big," TWI is poised to take the business to the next level in the coming year, pending second-round financing. SLP is also moving forward, with FruTWI and other similar complementary products (such as salsa and soup concentrates), providing the early revenue for socios until the fluoride removal technology is perfected. The results of these two "pilots" demonstrate that TWI's co-creation approach can effectively address water issues at the local level by embedding an affordable, profitable platform technology into a business model developed through interaction between community teams and TWI's technologists. In such a way, it is possible to solve the uniquely difficult and previously unaddressed water problems of each community served, while still creating a scalable business model.

At the heart of the business model, socios sell the WATERCURA units while overseeing their installation and service. Customers pay for this service in weekly installments that are much less than the cost of bottled water and directly competitive with garrafon (jug) water. At a fundamental level, WATERCURA meets the community's drinking water needs; but coupled with its social support network, it enables people to use their water consumption as a lever for creating and establishing the healthy lifestyle habits they aspire to. With the Chapala and SLP launches underway, TWI will expand to other appropriate communities in Mexico and seek to develop a purification technology that addresses pathogen contamination as the primary problem. While what was learned from Chapala will be leveraged in scale-out, the businesses that result will be modified to meet each new community's specific needs. Eventually, the company aspires to expand throughout Latin America and ultimately, the world. Like water poured in a glass, TWI's business takes the shape of the communities in which it does business.

The Three Big Challenges

Many things have been learned and insights generated from the six BoP Protocol initiatives undertaken to date. In addition, a number of specific on-the-ground techniques developed by the immersion teams have also been developed and will be documented in a *BoP Protocol Field Guide.*[17] The pioneering efforts by SC Johnson, DuPont/Solae, Ascension Health, Baxter, Gates Foundation, and the Water Initiative have generated a tidal wave of interest in the BoP Protocol, not only within MNCs, but also among entrepreneurs, governments, and civil society organizations. The transition to BoP 2.0, it would seem, is now underway.

Based upon experience to date, I see three main challenges for leaders and change agents in moving embedded innovation forward, particularly within existing companies. The first challenge is fundamentally *psychological*. Most business people simply have no knowledge of or experience in impoverished communities—be they rural villages and urban shantytowns in the developing world or deindustrialized inner cities in developed countries. What is unfamiliar often appears risky—better to go with the "devil you know" than take what appears to be a "flyer" on something completely foreign. Many managers carry around biases and assumptions that stand in the way of taking the Great Leap to the BoP. As my colleague Ted London suggests, a good test of this is to ask your company colleagues to say the first three things that come to mind when they think of the "base of the pyramid." A few might say something rash along the lines of "the poor are lazy or else they would not be poor." More commonly, however, their descriptions will focus on what is lacking in the BoP—education, resources, rule of law, physical connectivity, and so on.[18]

Unleashing the potential of embedded innovation thus requires a shift in mentality among a coalition of key actors within the firm—those that can make or break the initiative. And as we have seen, the best way to change people's minds is for them to have first-hand experience on the ground. This is where some of the tools of Radical Transactiveness can be especially useful: Organize a "trek" to a developing country, for example, so that key executives can see that the poor, in fact, can be resourceful and entrepreneurial and hungry for new opportunities to improve their own lives. Convincing your colleagues and superiors to devote the time to such an undertaking, however, requires persuasive power. Indeed, as Daniel Pink suggests in his wonderful book, *A Whole New Mind*, the art of storytelling and persuasion may hold the key to innovation in the twenty-first century.[19] Although businesspeople are often suspicious of stories, they also know that statistics can be used to tell lies and are often needed to show why one project is marginally superior to other comparable options. When pitching a "blue ocean" innovation, however, a powerful and convincing narrative can carry the day, overriding the need for "data" to prove the case. Bottom line: Practice your storytelling skills or find a good consultant with the skill. This was essential in all six BoP Protocol initiatives to date.

The second big challenge for embedded innovation is *organizational*. As we have seen, BoP initiatives (like the Nike World Shoe) that are placed within existing businesses are almost certain to fail because they are inevitably held accountable to the same system of metrics and incentives as conventional new products or line extensions. The corporate immune system is very strong—any project that deviates too far from the norm is quickly surrounded by "antibodies" and rendered harmless! It is essential, then, to construct an appropriately protected "white space" that enables this new form of innovation to grow at its own pace; this also means establishing a timeline, set of deliverables, and metrics that are specifically developed for the BoP initiative. A completely separate "skunkworks," however, is undesirable because the initiative needs to link to corporate-level resources and capabilities while at the same time maintain sufficient independence from the routines that govern the core business.

Depending solely on the goodwill and support of the CEO or any other single senior executive can also be risky. In our experience, the "white space" can come crashing down if this person changes positions, leaves the company, or is replaced—witness what happened with the DuPont/Solae initiative. It is for this reason that we recommend the creation of a BoP Protocol Leadership Team consisting of 8–10 key executives that span the company, as discussed earlier. A senior corporate executive's support is also critical, however, because the Protocol initiative should be seen as a companywide innovation, and such a person can effectively connect the dots across the company and act as a catalyst. The Leadership Team must also ensure that the initiative has the appropriate degree of autonomy and that funding is in place. Experience suggests that corporate BoP Protocol initiatives are best funded through the R&D budget, as the entire process can be appropriately framed as "business model R&D."[20] This eliminates the expectation for quick returns, rapid scale-up, and other expectations typically associated with conventional new business development projects.

This leads us to the third and final big challenge for embedded innovation, which is *strategic*. Think of BoP Protocol initiatives as incubators for new businesses that require protection and nurturing before they can be fully launched. Framed in this way, the on-the-ground immersion team will require protection but must also have the necessary authority to develop the strategy and business model in ways that they deem most appropriate, including which external groups and partners make the most sense. Given the challenge and complexity of the cocreation process, as described in this chapter, the immersion team must have the autonomy to act without excessive interference from the company. In fact, as Jeff Immelt at GE suggests, a "Local Growth Team" (their term for a protected BoP initiative) should be viewed as a separate unit with the power to develop its own strategy, organization, and products, and ultimately, its own P&L responsibility. The leadership team should hold the immersion team accountable for the timelines and deliverables that are mutually agreed to but should not inject themselves into the process on the ground. Our experience with the Ascension Health project has shown us that having "too many cooks in the kitchen" can seriously compromise immersion teams' ability to build the trust and social capital necessary in the community to enable the initiative to take root. Suspending disbelief and trust in the process is therefore essential to enable the work on the ground to proceed effectively.

Leading the Next Great Transformation

Commercial strategies for serving the base of the pyramid have mushroomed over the past few years: Unilever, Philips, DuPont, SC Johnson, P&G, Pfizer, BP, Intel, AMD, Microsoft, Dow, Nike, Rio Tinto, ABN AMRO, DSM, Friesland Food, SABMiller, Tata Group, Eskom, Cemex, Natura, and Holcim represent only the "short list" of major global corporations that have initiated or deepened commercial efforts in the BoP since 2005. Yet, paradoxically, the original vision of the BoP, which held out the promise of combining business growth with a sustainable development agenda, today is in danger of imploding. Most corporate BoP initiatives have relied on BoP 1.0 strategies, and as a consequence, have not realized the "fortune" that they thought awaited them in the rural villages and slums of the world. As a consequence, some companies have scaled back their investments in this space or limited their BoP strategies to value-engineered versions of their current products for sale in lower income target markets. Indeed, the few 1.0 "success" stories may lead some companies to believe that the only fortunes to be made at the BoP will come packaged in billions of single-serving sachets.

There is, however, a way forward that does not throw the proverbial baby out with the bathwater. Sustainably addressing global poverty requires a new practice of development that enables jointly-defined agendas of change through partnership, not "magic bullet" solutions airdropped into communities.[21] Providing for the needs of an additional four billion people without overwhelming the earth's ecological systems will require an order-of-magnitude reduction in environmental impact, a challenge best met by harnessing the most advanced clean technologies from across the globe. Indeed, new technologies and Western knowledge are not inherently foreign— they only become foreign when they are parachuted into communities and run roughshod over existing socio-cultural institutions.

The issue, therefore, is not whether corporations can play a role in a more sustainable form of development, but how. The answer, my colleagues and I suggest, is through embedded innovation. Embedded innovation helps ensure that corporations' clean technologies, valuable organizational competencies, and imagination build onto, not over, existing community assets and ecological webs. Embedded innovation ensures that jointly created solutions have the commitment of the wider community behind them, providing the necessary "pull" for the enterprise to succeed. And perhaps most importantly, embedded innovation develops a deep base of entrepreneurial capacity in the community, a capacity that enables an ongoing stream of local innovation and positive change.

It required a great transformation in thinking and behavior to realize the industrial revolution—the period of capitalism that made possible an unprecedented level of prosperity and material comfort within the mass markets of the West. It will require an equally great transformation in corporate growth and innovation strategies to bring forth a new, more inclusive form of capitalism— one that extends the benefits of enterprise to the entire planet, while at the same time preserving the ecological foundation on which we all depend. But with every fundamental change comes tremendous opportunity. Seizing this opportunity will require a new corporate competence based on dialogue and intimacy, on open- ness to learning and experimentation, and on a constant exercise of humility.

Notes

1. Karl Polanyi, *The Great Transformation: The Political and Economic Origins of Our Time* (New York: Farrar & Rhinehart, New York and Toronto, 1944).

2. This opening section is adapted from: Erik Simanis and Stuart Hart, "Innovation from the Inside Out," *Sloan Management Review* Summer, 2009: 77–86.

3. The remainder of this section is drawn from our coauthored article on the topic: Erik Simanis and Stuart Hart, "Innovation from the Inside Out."

4. Parts of this section are abstracted from: Erik Simanis and Stuart Hart, "License to Imagine: Business Co-Creation at the Base of the Pyramid."

5. In addition to Erik Simanis, Gordon Enk, and myself, the colleagues on the BoP Protocol Core Team include: Duncan Duke (Cornell University) and Michael Gordon (University of Michigan).

6. For more details, see www.bop-protocol.org.

7. Erik Simanis and Stuart Hart, *The Base of the Pyramid Protocol: Toward Next Generation BoP Strategy* (Cornell University: Center for Sustainable Global Enterprise, 2008). This document can be downloaded at www.bop-protocol.org.

8. Erik Simanis, Patrick Donohue, Justin DeKoszmovsky, Tatiana Thieme, Cather- ine Burnett, and Nyokabi Kiarie.

9. For an in-depth analysis of both the SC Johnson and Solae protocol experiences, see Erik Simanis, *The Anatomy of Market Creation: Insights from the Base of the Pyramid* (Cornell University, Doctoral Dissertation, 2010).

10. Portions of the Kenya project description are drawn from: Scott Johnson, "Dia- logue on Sustainability," S. C. Johnson & Son, Inc., January 15, 2007.

11. Justin DeKoszmovszky, a member of the original Immersion Team, is now the SC Johnson lead for this BoP business initiative within the company.

12. The three returning immersion team members were Erik Simanis, Patrick Donohue, and Tatiana Thieme.

13. For further details, see Erik Simanis, *The Anatomy of Market Creation: Insights from the Base of the Pyramid.*

14. For detail, see Erik Simanis and Stuart Hart, *The Base of the Pyramid Protocol: Toward Next Generation BoP Strategy.*

15. Portions of this section are adapted from TWI's "2008 Business Plan," available upon request from www.thewaterinitaitive.com.

16. Duncan is currently completing his doctoral dissertation based largely on this experience.

17. The Field Guide is currently being developed.

18. Ted London, "Building Better Ventures for the Base of the Pyramid," William Davidson Institute, Working Paper, 2010.

19. Daniel Pink, *A Whole New Mind* (New York: Riverhead Books, 2006).

20. See Ted London, "Business Model R&D for New Market Entry," William Davidson Institute, Working Paper, 2010.

21. This section is adapted from: Erik Simanis and Stuart Hart, "Beyond Selling to the Poor," Cornell University: Center for Sustainable Global Enterprise, Working Paper, 2008.

10

Building the Sustainable Global Enterprise

The chapters that came before charted the course to a more inclusive and sustainable form of commerce. Exhibit 10.1 summarizes the journey that we have taken in this book. As we have seen, greening has been an important first step because it eliminated the myth that a trade-off exists between a firm's financial and societal performance. Driven by the realization that pollution is waste and dialogue with stakeholders is superior to court battles, greening opened the door for companies to take a proactive stance toward social and environmental issues. Indeed, pollution prevention and product stewardship have succeeded in reducing waste, emissions, and impact, while simultaneously reducing cost, risk, and stakeholder resistance. The incremental gains associated with greening, however, have been clearly inadequate: They only slow the rate of destruction rather than fundamentally changing course.

Moving beyond greening, therefore, is critical both to a sustainable world and to a sustainable enterprise. Driven by an accelerating rate of technological change and the growing realization that something fundamental must change if we are to accommodate a population of 8 billion to 10 billion human beings on the planet, beyond greening provides the motivation for companies to think in terms of reorientation rather than just adjustment. Leapfrogging to inherently clean technologies through disruptive business models that start from the base of the pyramid enables companies to confront directly the two biggest problems facing humanity: poverty and global-scale environmental degradation. These also provide the basis for the repositioning and growth that will be needed for companies—and society—to thrive in the future.

Exhibit 10.1
The Path to Inclusive Commerce

As we have seen, however, strategies for the base of the pyramid and clean technology, if narrowly construed, still position companies as outsiders, alien to both the cultures and the ecosystems within which they do business. By seeking only to "deploy" clean technology or "target" the poor with inexpensive products, some companies have inadvertently sewn the seeds for a growing backlash against the global capitalist agenda. The next sustainability challenge, therefore, is to become indigenous. By incorporating the true voices of those who have previously been bypassed by globalization and by learning to codevelop technologies, products, and business models with nature and local people, companies can become native to the places where they operate. This requires a healthy dose of humility and respect, as well as a greater appreciation for the many and varied ways that people choose to live. Through bottom-up innovation on a human scale, corporations effectively become embedded—part of the local landscape. In so doing, the corporate sector becomes a primary driving force for global sustainability. And in the process, visionary companies realize opportunities of untold proportion.

Like the nineteenth century industrialists who transformed the market economy by creating the modern institutions of capitalism (namely the great industrial corporate model that continues to this day), we too are living during a time of significant transition. As noted in the Prologue, we are now experiencing "The Great Disruption"—when both Mother Nature and Father Greed have hit the wall at the same time. Our challenge—and opportunity—is nothing short of reinventing capitalism once again into a sustainable form of commerce that includes all of humanity in its bounty and sustains the underlying natural capital upon which we all depend.

Enabling existing companies to first recognize and then pursue these opportunities is no small challenge. As we have seen, shattering the trade-off myth associated with pollution and prosperity was a crucial first step in realizing the full potential of greening. Moving beyond greening and becoming indigenous will require that we break free from the tyranny of another set of implicit trade-offs and assumptions. Indeed, the air is filled today with rejoinders such as "We can't serve the poor profitably," "Business should not be expected to solve the world's problems," and, most recently, "You are either with us, or you are with the terrorists." These are all false dichotomies that oversimplify and therefore obscure the possibilities for more nuanced and inclusive solutions. Focusing creative energy on dissolving these trade-offs—and the orthodox thinking that supports them—can provide an avenue for companies to identify the breakthrough business strategies of the future.

Making It Happen in the Real World

In this book, I have tried to suggest what companies might do to pursue the path of a sustainable form of global enterprise—the strategies, practices, and capabilities that are required. What is less clear is how to pursue this path, particularly within the context of large, incumbent, multinational corporations. Indeed, as Raghuram Rajan and Luigi Zingales point out in their book *Saving Capitalism from the Capitalists*, it is precisely the large incumbent corporations that most often stand in the way of fundamental change.[1] I close the book, therefore, with some thoughts on what it will take to make sustainability happen in the real world of budgets, bosses, quarterly earnings reports, discounted cash-flow analysis, and the discipline of the investor community.[2] Leaders and change agents in companies will need to delight all the stakeholders, avoid the top-down bias, think as a disrupter, reinvent cost structures, transform the meaning of scale, and align the organization. Most important, to enable employees to build the "sustainability cathedral," senior managers will have to step up to the challenge with visible and tangible commitments that far surpass what they have been willing to do to date.

Delight All the Stakeholders

It has been said that capitalism is like a knife: It can be used to cut off your brother's arm, or it can be used to butter bread and feed the hungry—the same knife. The problem with capitalism is thus not the profit motive; the problem is how the profit motive is conceptualized. As John Mackey, Founder and CEO of Whole Foods, points out, there is a persistent myth that the ultimate purpose of business is to maximize profit for the investors. However, the maximization of profit is not a purpose; instead, it is an outcome. The best way to maximize profits over the long term is to *not* make them the primary goal. Indeed, as Mackey makes clear, profits are like happiness: They are a by-product of other things like having a strong sense of purpose, meaningful work, good friends, and deep relationships. Those who focus obsessively on their own happiness are usually narcissists—and end up miserable. Leaders of great companies have always understood that you make money by doing good things rather than the other way around.[3]

At the World Economic Forum in January 2009, in the depths of the global financial meltdown, speaker after speaker emphasized that we were in the midst of a transformation. Both Klaus Schwab and Tony Blair emphatically stated that the days of "mercenary capitalism" were over; that we have now embarked on the age of "stakeholder capitalism." This met with resounding applause. The problem is, very few entrepreneurs or business people really know what this means, let alone how to do it. As Ed Freeman pointed out in his classic book over 25 years ago, the key is learning how to jointly optimize the well-being of *all* stakeholders and constituency groups associated with the business, rather than elevating one stakeholder above all others.[4] In fact, if we are true adherents to financial theory, then investors should be considered the "residual claimants"—they receive what is left after all other stakeholders have been appropriately served.

Paradoxically, then, companies that focus on "shattering the trade-offs" among seemingly competing stakeholder interests (like investors, communities, and the environment) can evolve competitively superior strategies that produce superior returns—the definition of a truly sustainable enterprise. In fact, in the recent book, *Firms of Endearment: The Pursuit of Purpose and Profit*, the authors identify 30 companies that are managed to optimize total stakeholder value instead of focusing strictly on profits. They tracked the long-term stock performance of these companies compared to the S&P 500 and found that they had extraordinarily high stock market returns both over the short term and the long term.[5]

Mackey's own firm, Whole Foods, is a case in point. The core values of the company are to sell the highest quality natural and organic foods available; satisfy and delight the customers; support team members' happiness and excellence; care about their communities and the environment; and create wealth, profits, and growth. While striving to optimize the value of its entire set of interdependent stakeholders, Whole Foods is also the fastest growing and most profitable public food retailer percentage-wise in the United States: Whole Food's stock price has increased almost 2,500 percent since its IPO in 1992. The lesson: "hit and run" players like predatory lenders and Ponzi scheme artists can make lots of money in the short term by ignoring or even damaging some of their stakeholders. But eventually the negative feedback loops catch up to them. Sustainable enterprises—those interested in flourishing for the long term—learn to delight all their stakeholders.

The emerging crisis for Toyota provides another example. As of early 2010, what appeared to be a minor technical problem with floor mats sticking to accelerator peddles has mushroomed into a public relations disaster and perhaps a serious blow to the company. Indeed, it now appears that Toyota knew about technical problems that caused their vehicles to uncontrollably accelerate years (and many deaths) before, but saved hundreds of millions of dollars by convincing customers and regulators that it was only a minor issue. Only now, under the threat of legal action is the full story coming to light. By placing the bottom line above the interests of other key stakeholders, Toyota might have made more money in the short term, but in the long run might lose its preeminent reputation and perhaps the value of its brand.

Avoid the Top-Down Bias

Large corporations have great difficulty fomenting innovation from the bottom up. When firms are left to their own devices, new programs and strategies are usually decreed by senior managers and then sent down the reporting chain for implementation. Unfortunately, when it comes to sustainability, a top-down approach to implementation can seriously limit and even damage the company's hopes of realizing the opportunity. In fact, a strong market presence at the top of the pyramid can actually blind managers to the possibilities elsewhere.

P&G, for example, has had great difficulty shaking off the influence of its renowned brand-management system when entering low-income markets or looking to commercialize leapfrog technology. When the firm was test-marketing its new nutritional beverage product, Nutristar, for example, initial efforts were negatively affected by the company's traditional approach to product launch at the top of the pyramid. The local subsidiary in the Philippines was not familiar with the low-income segment of the population, and the company's standard approach failed to hear the true voice of the new customer. Ultimately, the team had to abandon this test market. They later decided to launch a pilot project in a country where the company did not currently have a local subsidiary. This enabled them to construct a true "learning" market by working with local communities and NGOs to do the pilot testing. Ironically, then, the corporation's strong presence around the world became a liability when it came to incubating new businesses at the base of the pyramid.[6]

DuPont has also struggled to devise ways to make the Great Leap to the BoP. Senior management has made reaching the base of the pyramid a strategic priority for the company; business leaders have been charged with initiating efforts in this regard. Indeed, a process has been put in place to identify, evaluate, and invest in new business opportunities in emerging markets. Yet despite this commitment, the company has backed away from efforts to cocreate new markets at the BoP through embedded innovation. Instead, DuPont's remaining BoP initiative works through the company's existing business units and seeks primarily to extend existing technologies and products into underserved markets. In this sense, it is fundamentally an incremental initiative. Although there is nothing wrong with such a process (looking for product-line extension opportunities is a good way to generate near-term growth), it underscores the difficulty that MNCs have when it comes to breaking the hold of the current business system.[7]

Even the vaunted Hindustan Lever's initial attempts to reach the base of the pyramid were incremental in character: minor formulation changes for soaps and shampoos and single-use sachet packaging so that poor people could afford to buy it. Getting to bottom-up innovation through true engagement requires a fundamentally new and different approach. As we have seen, the BoP Protocol represents one such strategy for codevelopment and mutual value creation. To enable this, senior managers need to create the structural conditions that enable internal entrepreneurs to break free of the current system. At a minimum, this calls for a separate investment fund and a protected organizational "white space" where these ventures can germinate without the same hurdle rates, corporate overhead burdens, and growth expectations carried by the existing business divisions.[8] It does not require a massive investment of resources. As we have seen, even a few million dollars committed in this manner has the potential to buy important options for the future—and create a growth engine that can help the company avoid saturation and stagnation in the current businesses. As noted economist E. F. Schumacher would say, "Man is small, and therefore, beautiful. To go for giantism is to go for self-destruction."[9]

Think as a Disrupter

As the experience of the Grameen Bank shows, it is critical to think in terms of creative destruction rather than continuous improvement when it comes to the pursuit of sustainability. Often this means turning the existing technology and business model on their heads. That, in turn, means getting outside the current corporate straightjacket of central research and development. Such a system is particularly well suited to the current top of the pyramid model, with its emphasis on world scale, global supply chains, and one-size-fits-all products. It is singularly inappropriate, however, when it comes to bringing forward the sustainable technologies and business models of tomorrow.

To think as a disrupter, it is necessary to conduct R&D and market research focused on the unique situations and requirements of the poor, by region and by country. As a first step, such research can seek to adapt current technology to local needs. In fact, disruptive thinking can sometimes help to turn current shelf technology (technology that has yet to find a commercial application) into gold. Think about it: Many technologies are on the shelf because they are disruptive to the current business system. Empowering a team to look at these technologies through a new lens—clean technology and the base of the pyramid—can open up new horizons of possibility.

Many companies have resorted to donating patents to universities as a form of philanthropy and good will. Perhaps it would be wise instead to take a fresh look at these technologies, with the perspective of a disrupter. A few years back, for example, we started a project at Cornell to re-evaluate the shelf technology in the university's intellectual property office.[10] Literally hundreds of patents were sitting dormant, mostly because no large corporation could be found with an interest in licensing them. In the space of a couple of weeks, a few MBA volunteers versed in sustainability and BoP business logic were able to identify more than a dozen patents that could provide the basis for start-up ventures focused on clean technology disruption from the base of the pyramid.

Perhaps even more important, however, research should seek to identify useful principles and potential applications from local practices. In BoP communities, significant knowledge is transmitted orally from one generation to the next. Being respectful of traditions but willing to analyze them scientifically can lead us to new knowledge. Acupuncture was laughed at 30 years ago. Meditation was dismissed as a fad. Body Shop's creative CEO, Anita Roddick, built a business based on understanding the basis for local rituals and practices. For example, she observed that some African women use slices of pineapple to cleanse their skin. On the surface, this practice appears to be a meaningless ritual. However, research shows that the active ingredients in pineapple clear away dead skin cells better than chemical formulations.

To think disruptively, MNCs must develop major research facilities in developing regions such as China, India, Latin America, and Africa. The focus of these facilities, however, should not be conventional R&D. Instead, they can and must serve as jumping-off points for radical trans- activeness and the development of native capability. Few MNCs have made much of an effort in this direction. Unilever is an exception: It has highly regarded research centers in India, employing more than 400 researchers dedicated to the problems of India's urban slums and rural villages. Clearly, GE has also planted a stake in the ground in this regard by committing itself to a strategy of "reverse innovation." Indeed, in May 2009, GE announced that over the next six years, it would spend $3 billion to create at least 100 health care innovations that would sub- stantially lower costs, increase access, and improve quality.

Reinvent Cost Structures

Managers must dramatically reduce cost levels relative to those at the top of the pyramid. To create products and services the poor can afford, companies must reduce their costs by orders of magnitude to say, 10 percent of what they are today. This cannot be achieved by fine-tuning the current approaches to product development, produc- tion, and logistics. The entire business process must be rethought with a focus on functionality, not on the product itself.

As suggested earlier, focused R&D and technology development will be critical to reducing costs. Companies such as N-Logue in India, as we have seen, are focusing their R&D energies on afford- ability by creating Wireless Local Loop technology that dramatically lowers connectivity costs in rural area. Galanz has also used the unique expectations of low-income Chinese as a driver in developing highly affordable and energy-efficient microwave ovens. Thus, view- ing the constraints imposed by the BoP as innovation drivers provides one important avenue for driving down costs.

The distributed and localized nature of most clean technology and BoP opportunities also offers opportunities for lowering costs through business model innovation. MNCs typically think in terms of capital intensity and labor productivity, based upon their experience at the top of the pyramid. Exactly the opposite logic applies in the BoP. Given the vast number of underemployed people at the base of the pyramid and the fragmented nature of the distribution system, the business model must provide jobs for many, as did Ruf and Tuf jeans from Arvind Mills: The company employed an army of local tailors as stockers, promoters, distributors, and service providers all rolled in one, even though the cost of the jeans was 80 percent below that of Levis. Thus, designing people-intensive rather than capital-intensive businesses provides another important vehicle for reinventing cost structures.

ITC, the Indian company that created the e-choupal initiative, has also done pioneering work in business model innovation in its paper business. Recognizing that India suffers from extensive soil loss and degradation, ITC launched a wastelands reforestation initiative in collaboration with rural villages throughout India. The company works with villagers as "foresters" to plant trees on wastelands, effectively reforesting lands that had been lost to erosion and overuse and providing local livelihood opportunities. By reforesting wastelands, water retention also increases, addressing another pressing problem throughout the country: falling water tables and water scarcity. Finally, local community partners sustainably harvest these trees to provide ITC with a low-cost, high-quality source of pulp for its paper-making operations. As of early 2010, ITC's wasteland reforestation initiative covered 100,000 hectares of land and provided 46 million person-days of employment.

Lowering cost structures also forces a debate on ways to reduce investment intensity. This will inevitably lead to greater use of information technology to develop production and distribution systems. As noted, village-based phones are already transforming the pattern of communications throughout the developing world. Add to this the Internet, and we have a whole new way of communicating and creating economic development in poor, rural areas. As we have seen, creative use of IT is emerging in these markets as a means to dramatically lower the costs associated with access to products and services, distribution, and credit management.

Transform the Meaning of Scale

The dominant logic for most MNCs today is that scale literally means "big"—world-scale factories, global supply chains, and international markets. Achieving scale means making big investments and spreading the costs over even bigger markets. Today's large corporations do not think twice about investing billions of dollars in one new project, whether it's a new car platform, a chip fab, a pulp mill, or an energy infrastructure project. Placing such big bets often produces spectacular success—but sometimes means horrific failure. Executives' careers are made and broken based upon how well they manage these investments. New businesses must start big to cover the corporate overhead, clear the hurdle rate, and generate the growth needed to feed the corporate monkey in the near term. Indeed, project-evaluation and capital-budgeting tools are carefully tuned to identify the best of the big ones. Projects that do not fit this description, either because they are initially too small or because they have a delayed payback, are shunted to the side, regardless of their potential. Only square pegs can fit in square holes.

Building a sustainable global enterprise, however, demands that MNCs transform (or, at least, broaden) the meaning of scale. As we have seen, most clean technologies are disruptive; disruptive technologies are typically smaller in scale and more distributed in character. Indeed, many of the most exciting emerging technologies, such as distributed generation of renewable energy, point-of-use water treatment, and microfinance, completely reverse the logic of "bigger is better." Indeed, with nanotechnology, production takes place at the molecular scale. Furthermore, effectively reaching the base of the pyramid requires a revolution in business models. Local engagement, codevelopment, and low-cost probes are the *modus operandi*. Therefore, achieving scale in this new arena means marrying distributed capability and learning with world-class technology and global reach. Growth is modular, not monolithic; it occurs from the bottom up through an organic process of coevolution rather than top down, through massive investment in world-scale facilities. It requires native capability, not global scale or local responsiveness.

The industrial age mantra of "economies of scale" may be coming to an end. Managers should therefore centralize only where there are clear and demonstrable advantages. Begin with the assumption that decentralization is the right choice until someone can prove to you otherwise. Question more intently the logic behind economies of scale implicit in world-scale proposals. Are they really a good use of scarce capital resources? Do they foreclose other pathways prematurely? Should some of the company's investment capital be spread over a wider range of smaller, more distributed experiments? Do some projects that appear too small initially have the potential to scale rapidly through modular, organic growth and become very large businesses? Questions like these can help managers to broaden and ultimately transform the meaning of scale.

Aligning the Organization

Pursuit of a sustainable form of global enterprise is often thwarted by inconsistent or even conflicting elements in organizational infrastructure. Strategies cannot be realized unless the organizational structure and formal systems enable them. Goals cannot be reached without the right people with the right skills using the right processes. Visions can never become real without a serious intent to actually reduce them to practice.[11]

Exhibit 10.2 lists the elements of organizational infrastructure that are critical to align. There is no question that setting a compelling and challenging vision and mission for corporate sustainability is a key to success. Indeed, it has become increasingly clear that great companies have great purposes that were created by their original founders and still remain at the core of their businesses. A compelling corporate vision and mission enables senior leadership to challenge its people to do something great, to establish a "big, hairy, audacious" goal (BHAG), in the words of Jim Collins and Jerry Porras, a goal that is worthy of their highest aspirations, hopes, and dreams.[12] Ray Anderson, CEO of the Atlanta-based carpet manufacturer, Interface, has established a very hairy sustainability goal indeed for the company: to never take another drop of oil from the Earth. This is clearly audacious because the company's current core product—commercial carpet made from PVC and nylon—is based entirely on petrochemicals.

Exhibit 10.2
Aligning the Organization
for Sustainability

- **Vision/Mission**: Setting the sustainability "BHAG"
- **Goals**: Establishing measurable targets
- **Strategy**: Identifying the sustainable value portfolio
- **Structure**: Creating separate experiments, white spaces, and funding
- **Systems**: Designing new measurement, rewards, and project evaluation tools
- **Processes**: Enabling new technology, product, and market development approaches
- **People**: Integrating sustainability into recruiting, leadership development, and performance evaluation

As we have seen, Walmart's highly aspirational sustainability goals have also served to catalyze widespread innovation both within the company and, even more importantly, throughout its entire supply chain. ITC in India has also set—and achieved—some very audacious goals: Over the past decade, the corporation has actually become carbon and water *positive* across its entire operation. This means that through their business activities, they sequester more carbon than they emit, and they regenerate more water than they use. Clearly, the company is on the road to becoming "more good" rather than "less bad."

Although sustainability-based BHAGs are important, they cannot stand on their own because they define a future state that is well beyond the current grasp of most people in the company. It is necessary to articulate some tangible steps that allow people to make progress toward the vision. That is the purpose of clearly stated and measurable goals. DuPont, for example, has committed to a set of sustainability goals that move the company toward its vision of creating sustainable solutions essential to a better, safer, healthier life for people everywhere. One corporate goal, for example, is to reduce greenhouse gas emissions by at least 15 percent (from a base year of 2004) by 2015. This is an aggressive goal, to be sure, but it directs the attention of employees to the next steps they must take and clarifies appropriate strategies to pursue.

Too often, companies set lofty visions and goals for sustainability, only to have them fall apart at the level of strategy. When this happens, external stakeholders—particularly NGOs and civil society groups—conclude that the company is engaged in little more than public relations and "greenwashing." It is important, therefore, for companies to be clear on what their actual portfolio of strategies will be. The sustainable value portfolio developed in Chapter 3, "The Sustainable Value Portfolio" (and elaborated further in Exhibit 10.1), is a useful tool for planning the right mix of greening, beyond greening, and even indigenous programs and initiatives. Baxter Healthcare and Dow Corning, for example, have both used this tool to help ensure that they have the mix of strategic activities needed to drive their companies forward toward their goals, particularly in moving beyond greening.

Even where there is clarity with regard to strategy, however, companies can and often do run aground when it comes to implementation. Compelling vision, lofty goals, and aggressive strategies never make it out of the starting gate if the organizational structure and formal systems conspire to kill the projects and punish the people responsible for them. As we have seen, such "corporate antibodies" often treat anything new as an alien invader. In fact, this misalignment may be one of the most significant problems facing large corporations today.

Nike's failed World Shoe initiative can be attributed, at least in part, to misalignment of strategy, structure, and measurement systems. The first mistake was to locate the venture within the athletic footwear business group; this forced the World Shoe group to make use of the manufacturing and distribution systems used for Nike's high-end products. Indeed, because existing contract manufacturers were rewarded based upon contribution margin, there was a built-in disincentive for them to even produce the low-priced World Shoes in the first place. Similarly, the company's pricing formula forced the fledgling venture to price the product beyond what its managers knew was acceptable to their target market, dooming it from the start. Finally, by forcing the venture to market its products through the company's existing distribution channels—primarily high-end retailers in China's large cities—Nike virtually guaranteed that it would never be able to reach its target customer base.

Establishing a separate venture or "white space" for the World Shoe, one that had the freedom to design its own production, marketing, and distribution strategy apart from the established Nike pricing formula, might have given the venture a fair chance to realize its full potential, a market of potentially vast proportion. Instead, it was shut down after failing to make even the modest sales targets that had been set, defeated by the inflexibility of the corporate structure and formal systems.

It is thus of critical importance that large corporations make the organizational space necessary for innovative new ventures based on disruptive clean technologies and BoP markets to flourish. As we saw in Chapter 9, "Re-Embedding Innovation Strategy," creating a separate organization and funding mechanism is an important starting point. That is not to say that such ventures should be allowed to lose money for an extended period of time. On the contrary, there is no reason such ventures cannot be profitable from the very start. As Clay Christensen and Michael Raynor suggest, when it comes to disruptive new ventures, senior management should be patient for growth and impatient for profit; expecting such ventures to become very big very fast fails to appreciate the organic and modular nature of their growth.[13]

Furthermore, the people who have the courage to undertake these experiments and ventures should not be punished if they fail. Even if successful, some roles in BoP initiatives are temporary; if such roles are perceived as carrying a career stigma, then the best people will not step up to the challenge. BoP pioneers thus need paths for "soft landings" and re-entry should the initiative prove unsuccessful or take a different course. New and innovative measurement and reward systems are therefore crucial in moving us toward a sustainable form of global enterprise.

The critical need for alignment of formal systems, particularly measurement systems, can be seen through Monsanto's experience in establishing a separate Sustainable Development Sector within the company in the mid-1990s.[14] CEO Bob Shapiro's instinct was exactly on target in establishing this sector. The company needed a place where innovative new ideas could be identified and pilot-tested if the businesses of the future were to come forward. During the mid- to late-1990s, the sector was working with a range of new technologies, as well as new partnerships in developing countries focused on the needs of poor, small shareholder farmers. Unfortunately, the pressures of the company's measurement system rendered most of these projects stillborn. By imposing the same growth and profitability targets on the fledging new sustainability ventures as were used on investment proposals within the established business units (such as agricultural chemicals), the company effectively foreclosed its option on the future.

In addition to organizational structure and formal systems, it is important to align the informal (cultural) processes that exist within companies: the technology, product, and market-development processes, in particular. In fact, these processes may hold the key. It is relatively easy to change boxes on the organizational chart and alter the discount rate used to evaluate investment decisions; it is a bit more difficult—but perhaps more powerful—to change the way people behave in the company through the processes they follow. We have learned this lesson over the past two decades with such process-oriented programs as quality management, Six Sigma, and business process re-engineering, to name a few. For companies like SC Johnson, DuPont, Ascension Health, and Baxter, the BoP Protocol represents an important first step in developing such new process capabilities.

Designing processes that focus on the commercialization of sustainable technologies and businesses is a surprisingly underutilized tool in large corporations. It is a potentially very important way to guarantee some real action, unlike the rhetoric often associated with vision, goals, or even strategic plans. Philips, for example, has developed a very simple but elegant process for new sustainable business and market development. Philips businesses (and employees, in general) are invited to submit their ideas for projects that focus more effectively on the unmet needs of people worldwide. Project proposals need to outline the economic, environmental, social, and personal aspects of the solution that they intend to deliver. A separate pool of money has been created to fund the best of these new business experiments. In addition, the senior management of the company now requires each of Philips's businesses to move forward with at least one venture focused on the base of the pyramid each year.[15]

This brings us to the final element in organizational alignment: people. This element has been virtually ignored by most corporations, but it could turn out to be the most significant of all. Much could be accomplished if the message contained in the corporate sustainability vision statement were actually integrated into corporate recruiting, leadership development, and performance evaluation. I can speak from firsthand experience when I say that, despite the best of intentions, few companies ensure that the recruiters they send to business schools are knowledgeable about sustainability issues. Even fewer firms include some understanding of or experience in sustainable enterprise as part of their hiring criteria for MBAs.

Research by my Cornell colleague Bob Frank suggests that ignoring students' commitment to social responsibility, ethics, and sustainability in the recruiting process may be a missed opportunity for firms committed to such aims.[16] Frank and his colleagues have found that there are significant salary differentials for "morally satisfying" jobs compared to those jobs seen as less socially motivated. In fact, research evidence clearly shows that students require large premiums before they are willing to work for less socially responsible employers. Thus for companies, commitment to sustainability can serve as a magnet for recruiting the best people at a salary level below that of competitors lacking similar commitment.

When it comes to training and development, few MNCs have yet reached the point that they consider global sustainability a significant enough issue to make it an integral part of the leadership development process. Fewer still have made sustainability performance an integral part of the performance evaluation and promotion process. The Tata Group in India is a notable exception to this statement. Indeed, over the past decade, they have developed an integrated approach to embedding a sustainability mindset into their systems, processes, and people. The time is now for corporations to close the loop on their own rhetoric by recruiting, developing, and rewarding people who display capability and imagination in moving the company and the world toward sustainability.

The importance of aligning these elements of organizational infrastructure should not be underestimated. Employees will quickly become cynical and even alienated if they run too frequently into roadblocks or have to take undue career risks to move the sustainability agenda forward. By pointing all the organizational arrows in the same direction, corporate leaders can send a strong signal that encourages employees to step forward and invest their creative energies in the enterprise. Ultimately, that is the only way to ensure success.

Building the Cathedral

In his book *Reinventing the Bazaar*, John McMillan argues persuasively that large firms can never mimic the creative and innovative behavior of small firms, for one simple reason: ownership.[17] The owner of an asset has the right to any residual returns that it generates. If returns are unexpectedly high, the owner gets the windfall. Large firms can divide themselves into smaller units responsible for their own costs and revenues, thereby heightening incentives. Divisional managers can be paid according to their division's performance. But large firms can never precisely duplicate ownership. A divisional manager does not have residual control, so decisions can be overridden from above. If the division turns out to be wildly more successful than anyone foresaw when the manager's contract was written, the parent firm will probably find a way to harvest the profits. In short, not being an owner—lacking the rights to residual returns—puts a damper on the motivation to invest creatively and to take risks.

So how can corporations possibly unleash the creative power of their people, a virtual prerequisite to realizing the full potential of sustainability? The answer is ownership! Not ownership of residual returns, but rather ownership of ideas and the ability to champion their development. MNCs must bestow on their people what my colleague Erik Simanis has described as the "license to imagine." Companies must enable their employees to pitch and run with new ideas—ideas that help to move us toward a sustainable world—in ways that would never be possible on their own or in small start-up enterprises. Corporations must, in short, make meaning for their employees and allow them the chance to align their personal values with what they do on the job everyday.

I am reminded of the parable of three people at work on a construction site. All were doing the same job, but when each was asked what his job was, the answers varied. "Breaking rocks," replied the first. "Earning a living," answered the second. "Helping build a cathedral," said the third. Too many people in large corporations still view their work as either breaking rocks or, at best, earning a living. Sustainability is the cathedral building of the twenty-first century. There can be no more important goal, no nobler aspiration, and no greater business opportunity. What we lack in our companies is not resources, but rather imagination. We must turn people lose to build the cathedral of sustainability.

Senior executives must develop the courage to speak out publicly regarding the importance of sustainable development and the role that they can play in its realization. Corporate governmental affairs must come to mean more than lobbying to maintain the status quo or bending the political process to serve the company's short-term interests. Instead, business must champion the needed global framework conditions—international protocols and agreements—that governments, civil society, and multilateral agencies have been unable to deliver on their own. For example, the recent launch of the United States Climate Action Partnership (USCAP), an initiative uniting several leading U.S. corporations in a call for swift policy action on global climate change, shows that companies can take a proactive stance in leading us toward a sustainable world in the years ahead.

Building the cathedral of sustainability also requires senior executives to create the structural space for disruptive new technologies and business experiments to flourish. This includes allocating the necessary investment capital to fund their development, protecting the ventures—and their entrepreneurs—from "corporate antibodies" and the tyranny of the current incumbent business, and recognizing and rewarding those who succeed in nurturing the businesses of the future.

While senior executive leadership is crucial, it is also important for each individual and employee to take the bull by the horns. The best place to start is by charting your own personal vision and action plan for sustainability. What can you do, within the realm of your current role, to move the company—and the world—toward sustainability? Write it down. Commit to it. When you have created a practical vision of what you want to achieve, take note of the current reality. As Bryan Smith, my colleague in the Sustainable Enterprise Academy, points out, current reality is not the problem—it simply defines the set of resources, people, and opportunities that you have to work with. Note your current reality and then assess the gap between it and your vision.[18]

The wider the gap is between vision and the current reality, the more "creative tension" there is. Your challenge is to put together a coalition of people and resources and then build the momentum within the organization to close the gap. That is how you realize the vision. When the first one is realized, move on to the second. Enroll others within the organization to make a similar commitment. Creating a sustainable form of global enterprise is not about waiting for the magic bullet to be handed down from senior management. Instead, it is about hundreds or even thousands of people in the organization deciding to commit to the pursuit of their personal visions and action plans, with global sustainability as the driving force.

Postscript

As we embark upon the second decade of the new century, business has emerged as the most powerful institution on the planet. Seven hundred years ago, it was religion; the world's cathedrals, mosques, and temples stand as testimony to the primacy of organized religion in the world at that time. Two hundred years ago, it was the state; no tour would be complete without visits to the impressive palaces, capitol buildings, and governmental complexes of the world that remind us of how centrally important government was in the age of enlightenment. Today the most powerful institution in the world is business: Witness the office towers, banks, and commercial centers that dominate today's largest cities. Although no one denies the continuing and crucial importance of government, religion, and civil society, there can be little doubt that commerce has become the dominant institution.

But as we have seen, there are storm clouds on the horizon: Starting in 2008, a series of crises gripped the planet—the oil price spike, the world food shortage, the subprime lending debacle, the global financial crisis, and finally, the Great Recession. Add to these crises the already long list of ongoing mega-problems—climate change, loss of biodiversity, poverty, inequity, hopelessness, terrorism—and it becomes clear that we have reached a fulcrum point in history. Unless global capitalism can extend its bounty to the entire human community in a way that respects cultural diversity and husbands the natural capital upon which it depends, we may well witness the marginalization of this great institution in our lifetime. Unfortunately, there is no candidate institution waiting to step into the breach to assume leadership: Global governance is in its infancy; nation states are consumed by their own narrow self-interests; religious fundamentalism has become a divisive rather than constructive force, and civil society lacks the resources and technology to make a large enough impact on its own. Today, multinational corporations are the only truly global institutions that exist.

It now seems clear that environmental collapse, global terrorism, and geopolitical meltdown all wait in the wings if business fails to step up to the challenge. After five decades and over $2 trillion in foreign aid, the top-down prescriptions of the development regime have largely failed. The United States, the lone military superpower in the world today, is mired in a parochial and counterproductive struggle between two outmoded ideologies: liberal versus conservative. Tragically, neither is appropriate for the challenges that lie ahead. We desperately need a third way, one premised on a combination of global interdependence, sustainability, local self-reliance, and bottom-up entrepreneurship. Commerce may be the only institution with the resources, capabilities, and global reach to make it happen. Today, capitalism truly does stand at a crossroads: My hope is that this book has shed some light on how best to negotiate the perilous intersection ahead.

Notes

1. Rajan Raghuram and Luigi Zingales, *Saving Capitalism from the Capitalists* (New York: Crown Business, 2003).

2. Portions of the following sections have drawn from C.K. Prahalad and Stuart Hart, "The Fortune at the Bottom of the Pyramid," *Strategy+Business*, January (2002): 2–14.

3. See Chapter 4 by John Mackey in Michael Strong (ed.), *Be the Solution: How Entrepreneurs and Conscious Capitalists Can Solve All the World's Problems* (Hoboken, NJ: John Wiley & Sons, 2009).

4. Ed Freeman, *Strategic Management: A Stakeholder Approach* (Marchfield, MA: Pittman Publishing, 1984).

5. David Wolfe, Rajendra Sisodia, and Jagdish Sheth, *Firms of Endearment: The Pursuit of Purpose and Profit* (Upper Saddle River, NJ: Wharton School Publishing, 2007).

6. George Carpenter (P&G), presentation at the Sustainable Enterprise Academy, April 2004.

7. Eduardo Wanick (DuPont), presentation at the Base of the Learning Laboratory meeting, Monterrey, Mexico, February 2004.

8. Clay Christensen and Michael Raynor draw a similar conclusion regarding the incubation of disruptive innovations in large incumbent firms in their book *The Innovator's Solution* (Boston: Harvard Business School Press, 2003).

9. E. F. Schumacher, *Small Is Beautiful: Economics as if People Mattered* (New York: Harper Torchbooks, 1973) 150.

10. My thanks to Dick Cahoon, Director of Cornell's Center for Technology, Entrepreneurship, and Commercialization, for this opportunity.

11. Among the few efforts to explore the leadership and organizational challenges associated with sustainability are Bob Doppelt, *Leading Change Toward Sustainability* (Sheffield, UK: Greenleaf Publishing, 2003) and Dexter Dunphy, Andrew Griffiths, and Suzanne Benn, *Organizational Change for Corporate Sustainability* (London: Routledge, 2003).

12. Jim Collins and Gary Porras, *Built to Last* (New York: HarperCollins, 1994).

13. Clayton Christensen and Michael Raynor, *The Innovator's Solution*.

14. My thanks to Kate Fish and others at Monsanto for giving me the opportunity to work with the fledging Sustainable Development Sector.

15. Personal communication, Jan Oosterveld, Group Management Committee, Royal Philips Electronics, July 2004.

16. Robert Frank, *What Price the Moral High Ground?* (Princeton, NJ: Princeton University Press, 2004).

17. John McMillan, *Reinventing the Bazaar: A Natural History of Markets* (New York: W.W. Norton, 2002).

18. I am indebted to Bryan Smith for this approach to personal action planning, which draws from his work with Peter Senge and the Society of Organizational Learning.

Epilogue: Looking Forward

When the hijacked planes flew into the World Trade Center towers and the Pentagon on September 11, 2001, many believed that the world had changed fundamentally. They were wrong. The world was exactly the same as it had been the day before. The horrific events of 9/11 simply focused our attention in a new way: It was now clear that the world was inextricably interconnected and that unrest in one part of the globe would not remain geographically isolated.

Many in the wealthy nations of the West—particularly the United States—became aware, perhaps for the first time, of what others in developing countries had known for a long time: When people are desperate, disenfranchised, or humiliated, they will resort to just about anything to relieve that condition. Most will seek resolution through modest means, such as working harder, migrating to find new opportunities, or perhaps even resorting to petty crime. Others will turn to organized protest or seek political solutions. A few will resort to the ultimate expression of alienation and repudiation: terrorism.

There is little doubt that the leaders of terrorist organizations are, more often than not, driven by extremist ideologies. Militant Islam, for example, weaves together fundamentalist religious beliefs, moral values, and a radical political agenda to create a particularly virulent form of such extremism. As the leaders of such groups know, however, special circumstances are required to attract the large numbers of people needed to effectively advance and support the cause. Most people are not born to be suicide bombers or militia members. It takes a lifetime of neglect, despair, dashed hopes, thwarted opportunities, or worse—intimidation, exploitation, and humiliation—to drive most people to such extremes.

The point is that it truly "takes a village" to support an organized terrorist movement. Only by reversing the conditions that breed acceptance and support of such behavior—poverty, inequity, hopelessness, loss of dignity—will we deal with the root causes of the problem. Yet while thousands of lives were lost or altered forever by the events of 9/11, and hundreds of known terrorist leaders have since been killed or captured, these underlying conditions remain largely unchanged—or have perhaps even worsened. Terrorism, in short, is a symptom; the underlying problem is unsustainable development.

Draining the Swamp

The Middle East in the early twenty-first century provides perhaps the starkest example of unsustainable development in modern history.[1] Oil has made a few elites enormously wealthy and powerful, while the masses have seen little of the benefit. Western dependence on oil has allowed dictators and despots to reign supreme, as long as they ensure that the oil keeps flowing. Indeed, Washington and the West have supported the very Muslim tyrannies that al Qaeda and other extremist groups seek to destroy.[2] Tragically, then, the developed world's growing dependence on oil from the Middle East virtually ensures that this vicious cycle will continue. And to make matters worse, the massive consumption of fossil fuels with its attendant carbon emissions endangers the very climate system upon which we all depend.

A proud culture boasting scientific and artistic achievement second to none, the Arab world today is a shadow of its former self, rife with hopelessness, despair, and a profound sense of humiliation. Journalist Tom Friedman describes the problem in the Middle East as not so much a poverty of money, but rather a poverty of dignity.[3] Western popular culture, often a direct affront to Islamic values, has permeated every corner of the region. Indeed, Islam's traditional emphasis on charity, social security for all, and the integration of the sacred into everyday life seems, to many Muslims, to be at odds with the Western conception of development and modernization.[4]

Tens of millions of young Muslims in the Middle East are coming of age at a time of record unemployment and lack of opportunity. Doctors, lawyers, and other professionals are churned out of universities only to work as day laborers and waiters. Religious extremism and nihilism provide potentially attractive escapes from the grinding sense of frustration and humiliation. Should we be surprised that growing numbers of young Muslims are attracted to a cause that takes away their pain by providing a sense of purpose, however misguided, as well as affiliation and economic security? Could it be that the metaphor of "war" as the frame for addressing the terrorism problem has served more to alienate and spread fear than to expand our vision of what is possible? In our efforts to "drain the swamp," have we inadvertently ended up creating a quagmire?

It seems that what is needed is a compelling and persuasive alternative to extremist ideologies and terrorism—a vision of hope, mutual respect, and opportunity—that can offer the prospect of a better life to the masses in the Middle East and the Muslim World. Witness, for example, the U.S. military's recent initiative seeking to address the root causes of terrorism through the use of an "indirect approach" focused on capacity-building, economic development, and opportunity creation.[5] What if we spent a small fraction of the money committed to military effort to empower and support small-scale enterprise development throughout the region? What if we flooded the region with teachers, health care providers, social workers, small business developers, and microfinanciers rather than merely more uniformed soldiers and Western contractors? Could sustainable enterprise and BoP venturing become the new *raison d'etre* for the "special forces" of the twenty-first century?

Indeed, what if we saw the Muslim World as the ultimate challenge in the creation of a sustainable form of enterprise? Some elements of this are already present in Abu Dhabi's Masdar Initiative, which seeks to foment the clean-tech revolution by building a sustainable, carbon-neutral city. But couldn't all the strategies discussed in this book—clean technology, the Great Leap Downward, creative destruction, radical transactiveness, native capability, embedded innovation—serve as potential antidotes to the current vicious cycle of violence throughout the region? Imagine, for example, incubating the renewable, distributed energy system of the future in the very belly of the petroleum beast itself. Could there not be a more delicious irony? But more important, could there not be a more pressing need?

The Next Tsunami

On the day after Christmas in 2004, a great tidal wave washed over most of the coastal communities of South Asia, leaving death and destruction on an unprecedented scale in its wake. With over 150,000 dead and tens of billions of dollars in damage, the world rallied to the aid of the millions of victims: Governments rose to the challenge by contributing hundreds of millions of dollars in disaster relief; charitable contributions from private citizens from across the world reached record levels in an outpouring of support and sympathy. Companies ramped up production to supply the needed goods and services from water purification equipment to emergency shelter to medical supplies. NGOs, disaster relief agencies, and even the military mobilized on a massive scale to airlift and distribute emergency aid to the hundreds of remote communities that had been devastated by the disaster.

In Indonesia, Thailand, and Sri Lanka, extremist movements, terrorist groups, and warring factions set aside their differences, at least for the short term, to address the human suffering and devastation that lay in the great Tsunami's wake. Indeed, the possibility for unity—between rich and poor; Christian, Buddhist, Hindu, and

Muslim; corporate, government and civil society; developed and developing—was palpable. The flood had created the pretext for collaboration and common cause, at least for a while. But what happens now that the immediate tragedy has passed and world attention is drawn away to other issues? Hurricane Katrina, the New Orleans Debacle, a growing crisis in Afghanistan, and now, the Haiti disaster have all served to distract Americans from the continuing tragedy in Asia. Predictably, with the passage of time, the aid has dried up, leaving these communities destitute and impoverished. Will the region now become an even greater hotbed for extremist movements and terrorist activity? Or can we envision another wave after the Great Tsunami—one based upon the principles developed in this book?

Indeed, with the South Asia coastline still in ruins, there is an opportunity to drive the reconstruction process through an enterprise-based model organized around a vision of sustainable development. For visionary companies, this offers the chance to leapfrog directly to clean technology, wireless telecommunications, distributed generation of renewable energy, point-of-use water purification, sustainable agriculture, and environmentally sound building techniques. For the financial sector, the opportunity exists to help local people pull themselves back up by the bootstraps through microfinance and microentrepreneurship, rather than perpetuating a deepening cycle of aid-based dependence.

In short, the next wave could be an orchestrated effort to bring inclusive capitalism to the region, with the potential to diffuse forever the insurgency movements that result from inequity, poverty, isolation, and hopelessness. Imagine the possibility of creating common cause with Indonesia—the largest Muslim nation in the World—to create a sustainable future for the country's devastated west coast. It might be possible to transform an entire generation's view of the United States and western capitalism. The time is now for the major corporations of the world to step up to this challenge—to forge the partnerships with the multilaterals, governments, NGOs, and local players necessary to make it happen. In fact, the same logic applies to the sustainable redevelopment of New Orleans, Afghanistan, Haiti, and other distressed or deindustrialized regions around the world, such as Detroit, Michigan.

Tragically, political solutions to the world's social and environmental problems have not been forthcoming—witness the impasse in Copenhagen and the steady slide back to "business-as-usual" in the wake of the global financial crisis. Indeed, the framework conditions needed for global governance have remained elusive, aid and philanthropy have not been adequate to the challenge, and the use of force appears to create more problems than it solves. Economic globalization has shown promise, but thus far, it has not managed to reach the majority of humanity. Increasingly, people around the world are asking the question, must capitalism's thirst for growth and profits serve only to exacerbate poverty and environmental deterioration? If the answer to this question is yes, as a growing chorus of antiglobalization activists believe, then there is little hope.

As I propose in this book, however, the answer to this question must be an emphatic "No." The major challenge—and opportunity—of our time is to create a form of commerce that uplifts the entire human community of 6.7 billion and does so in a way that respects both natural and cultural diversity. Indeed, that is the only realistic and viable pathway to a sustainable world. And business can—and must—lead the way.

Who Will Be the Twenty-First Century Watchdog?

While business can play a catalytic role in moving us toward a sustainable world, it has also become increasingly clear that the institutions of global capitalism alone cannot be the answer. With the implosion of the global financial system in 2009, many began to question once again whether greed and the profit motive could ever be reconciled. The anger spilled over from "Wall Street" to "Main Street" with government bailouts of failing automobile companies and continuing massive subsidies to incumbent players in the energy, food, health insurance, and pharmaceutical sectors, to name only a few—all of this at a time when individuals, families, and small businesses around the world were left to sink or swim in one of the worst economic slowdowns since the Great Depression.

To be sure, global companies are large, complex—and paradoxical. For every far-sighted corporate sustainability initiative, there are also legacy investments and unsustainable practices that must be countered. DuPont, for example, is committed to reinventing itself around renewable energy and bio-based materials yet continues to be one of the major toxic emitters in the United States; BP proclaims that it is moving "Beyond Petroleum" yet continues to be a major advocate of oil and gas exploration in the Arctic National Wildlife Refuge in Alaska; Interface, the world's largest commercial carpet producer, has vowed that ultimately, it will not take "another drop of oil from the earth," yet it sources virgin PVC made from petrochemical feedstock for its booming carpet business in Asia. Remember too that Monsanto championed the cause of "Food, Health, and Hope" yet produced seeds exclusively for first-world crops genetically modified to resist pests and withstand herbicide treatment. In the end, only a "stakeholder swarm" of NGOs and activists from around the world held them accountable. Why should Citibank, Goldman Sachs, Aetna, or WellPoint be any different?

So while global corporations have the capacity to lead us toward a sustainable world in the years ahead, it is also apparent that an empowered and connected civil society is essential in the role of watchdog and endorser. In fact, it is precisely MNCs' size and visibility that make them susceptible to this form of "bottom-up" discipline (compared to smaller, less visible local companies). This new reality should also serve as a wake-up call for governments: Learn how to design more effective systems of corporate monitoring and regulation

---

by modeling the emergent properties of the Internet-connected stakeholder swarm! We need it now more than ever.

Given the velocity of change in the world, I have tried to do much more than simply update the material contained in the 2007 second edition. Indeed, I have endeavored wherever possible to incorporate recent trends and new initiatives in this third edition of the book. In fact, the developments over these past three years have been significant enough that we felt it appropriate to change the subtitle of the book: What was previously "Aligning Business, Earth, and Humanity" has now become: "Next-Generation Business Strategies for a Post-Crisis World." This change reflects the belief that we have reached the tipping point for the change and transformation required to move us toward a more sustainable world. For all of our sakes, I sincerely hope that this belief proves to be correct.

Notes

1. For in-depth treatments of the causes and consequences of the radical Islamic movement, see Benjamin Barber, *Jihad Versus McWorld* (New York: Ballantine Books, 1996); and Fear's Empire (New York: W.W. Norton, 2003).

2. An anonymous intelligence veteran makes a compelling argument that it is not opposition to the West's secular, democratic way of life that is behind the global Islamic insurgency, but rather the West's unsustainable policies toward and practices in the Middle East itself. See *Imperial Hubris* (anonymous) (Washington, D.C.: Brassey's Inc., 2004).

3. Tom Friedman (*New York Times*), presentation at Kenan-Flagler Business School, University of North Carolina, April 2003.

4. For an insightful discussion of the "hideous schizophrenia" implicit in Western conceptions of liberalism, see Paul Berman, *Terror and Liberalism* (New York: W.W. Norton, 2003).

5. For a summary of some of the creative thinking on this topic, see: Kent Butts and Jeffrey Reynolds, *The Struggle Against Extremist Ideology: Addressing the Conditions that Foster Terrorism* (Carlisle Barracks, PA: U.S. Army War College Center for Strategic Leadership, 2005). See also: Miemi Winn Byrd, "Combating Terrorism: A Socio-Economic Strategy," *JFQ Forum* 41 (2006): 15–19; David Fridovich and Fred Krawchuk, "The Special Operations Forces Indirect Approach," *JFQ Forum* 44 (2007): 24–27.

Index

Symbols

2x2 matrix, 81
    buzzwords, 85-87
    innovation, 83
    sustainability, performance drivers, 82
3P (Pollution Prevention Pays), 89

A

acid rain, 55
affluence (A), 51
agricultural biotechnology, 34-35
agriculture
    disruptive innovation, GM crops, 155-157
    mandis system, 188
Ancient Futures, *Learning from Ladakh*,
    204-206
Anderson, Ray, 294
antiglobalization, 139
antiglobalization demonstrators, 38
Aracruz Celulose, 70
ArcelorMittal, 91
Arvind Mills, 218, 291
Ascension Health, 259
Asian tsunami, economic effect of, 310-312
assessing sustainability impact, 189-192
Asset Recycle Management, 28
auto industry, sustainability, 99
    clean technology initiatives, 101-103

AUTOnomy project, 129-131
avoiding top-down bias, 286-288

B

Bah Abba, Mohammed, 232
banking, multicredit loans, 95
Base of the Pyramid Impact Assessment
    Framework, 190
Base of the Pyramid Learning Laboratory, 31
Base of the Pyramid Protocol, 40, 257-262,
    265-266
Base of the Pyramid. *See* BoP (Base of the
    Pyramid)
Bata, 244
Baxter Healthcare, 258
becoming indigenous, 282-284
benefits of greening initiatives, 30
Benyus, Janine, 214
beyond greening, 30-33
BHAG (big, hairy, audacious goals), 294
biomimicry, 52
birth rates, 51
BoP (base of pyramid), 31, 139-141
    business creation, 182-184
    business model innovation, evaluating
        sustainability impact, 191-192
    consumer surplus, providing through
        business model innovation,
        182-184

▥ Wharton School Publishing

In the face of accelerating turbulence and change, business leaders and policy makers need new ways of thinking to sustain performance and growth.

Wharton School Publishing offers a trusted source for stimulating ideas from thought leaders who provide new mental models to address changes in strategy, management, and finance. We seek out authors from diverse disciplines with a profound understanding of change and its implications. We offer books and tools that help executives respond to the challenge of change.

Every book and management tool we publish meets quality standards set by The Wharton School of the University of Pennsylvania. Each title is reviewed by the Wharton School Publishing Editorial Board before being given Wharton's seal of approval. This ensures that Wharton publications are timely, relevant, important, conceptually sound or empirically based, and implementable.

To fit our readers' learning preferences, Wharton publications are available in multiple formats, including books, audio, and electronic.

To find out more about our books and management tools, visit us at whartonsp.com and Wharton's executive education site, exceed.wharton.upenn.edu.